AD MMXXIV Ma
St. Diego, Cal.

Discipline Yourself for Godliness

Beau,
   I hope this book serves you well on your journey to serve Him well!
   By His grace! For His glory!
With grit, gratitude and reckless generosity!
Burn the ships Beau!
   Don't look back!
Te amo con todo mi corazón!
     Uncle   Psalm 19

Discipline Yourself for Godliness

DR. JOHN S. BARNETT

TULSA

To order a copy of this book write us at:
DTBM
5200 S. Yale suite 300
Tulsa, OK 74135
or simply email us at:
books@dtbm.org

Discipline Yourself For Godliness | © 2007 by John S. Barnett

Published by Müllerhaus Publishing
5200 South Yale Ave. | Suite 501| Tulsa, OK 74135

All right reserved. No part of this publication may be reproduced, stored in a retrieval system or transmitted in any form by any means, electronic, mechanical, photocopy, recording or otherwise, without the prior permission of the publisher, except as provided by USA copyright law.

Cover and Interior Design by
Müllerhaus Publishing Group | **mullerhaus.net**
ISBN 13: 978-0-9798345-0-9
ISBN 10: 0-9798345-0-3

First printing, 2007 | Printed In the United States of America
Library of Congress 2007938427
All Scripture quotations in this book, except those noted otherwise, are from the New King James Version of the Bible.

The Bible version used in this publication is THE NEW KING JAMES VERSION. Copyright 1979, 1980, 1982, Thomas Nelson, Inc., Publishers.

References marked NASB are from The New American Standard Bible, copyright 1960, 1962, 1963, 1968, 1971, 1972, 1973, 1975, and 1977 by the Lockman Foundation and are used by permission.

References marked NIV are from The Holy Bible: New International Version, copyright 1973, 1978, 1984 by the International Bible Society. All rights reserved. Used by permission of Zondervan Publishing House. The "NIV" and "New International Version" trademarks are registered in the United States Patent and Trademark Office by International Bible Society. Use of either trademark requires the permission of International Bible Society.

9 8 7 6 5 4 3 2 1

DEDICATION

THIS BOOK IS DEDICATED TO the precious saints of Tulsa Bible Church who have loved, supported, and prayed me through: Twelve wonderful years of shepherding them (I Peter 5:2), Eighteen thousand glorious hours of studying God's Word to 'show myself approved unto God' (II Tim. 2:15), and over 1100-plus messages that God has led me step-by-step to prepare and present to them in the Power of His Spirit, for the Glory of Him alone Who is Lord of the Church—Jesus Christ the Chief Shepherd. It has been the joy and passion of my life to serve you by serving Christ.

SPECIAL THANKS

MY THANKS TO GOD FOR the magnificent team assembled and led by Doreen Claggett who has personally put together this series of 37 messages I preached at the Tulsa Bible Church from December 29th 2002 through January 4th 2004 into chapters. My thanks are also to God for Jim Kelley who has expertly and diligently captured and typed every spoken word of every message for this book and my first two books also, and made them into treasured manuscripts for my use in further ministry. And then my thanks to Doug Miller and Müllerhaus for all the magic they put into the art and layout from front cover to back—and everything in between. And then many thanks go to the team that edits these pages over and over to try to lessen all my mistakes. Here are the three teams: Verse Proofers--Dan Belcher, Mark Turrell, Lori Hagen, Karen Webb, Phil Miller; English Editors: Rachael Branch & Rebecca Hattaway; Content Editors: Marcia Reeves, Becky Bonham, Jack Babbitt, Marlene Bolton, Liz Garrison, Phil Smith, Jama Raubach, and Renee Gilligan. Praise God for your faithfulness, investment, and gracious labors of love!

CONTENTS

INTRODUCTION . . . . *IX*
APPENDIX A *345*
BIBLIOGRAPHY *347*

Disciplining Yourself for Godliness—1 Timothy 4:7

CHAPTER 1: THE ONLY WAY TO NOT WASTE YOUR LIFE 01

CHAPTER 2: PSALM 119: THE FOUNDATION OF A WORD FILLED LIFE 17

CHAPTER 3: A WORD FILLED LIFE OFFERS TRUE SECURITY 35

CHAPTER 4: DISCIPLINE ONE—THE SCRIPTURES: GOD'S PERFECT PATH FOR US 49

CHAPTER 5: DISCIPLINE TWO—SPIRIT-FILLED LIVING: AN OVERFLOWING LIFE 69

CHAPTER 6: DISCIPLINE THREE—MEDITATION: FINDING QUIETNESS IN ULTRA BUSY TIMES . 83

CHAPTER 7: MEDITATION: FINDING HOPE IN FEARFUL TIMES 103

CHAPTER 8: MEDITATION: FINDING COMFORT IN PAINFUL TIMES 119

CHAPTER 9: DISCIPLINE FOUR—STEWARDSHIP: LIVING TOTALLY FOR JESUS 133

CHAPTER 10: STEWARDSHIP: GIVING FREELY TO JESUS 151

CHAPTER 11: STEWARDSHIP: GIVING WORSHIPFULLY FOR ETERNITY 169

CHAPTER 12: DISCIPLINE FIVE—SIMPLICITY: REORDERING TO GOD'S PRIORITIES . . . 183

CHAPTER 13: DISCIPLINE SIX—SUPPLICATION: PRAYER IS THE POWER OF A WORD FILLED LIFE . 201

CHAPTER 14: SUPPLICATION: WITH JESUS IN THE SCHOOL OF PRAYER 215

CHAPTER 15: SUPPLICATION: HOW TO UNLEASH THE POWER OF PRAYER 231

CHAPTER 16: DISCIPLINE SEVEN—SUFFERING AFFLICTION: BUILDING THE BEST LIFE POSSIBLE . 253

CHAPTER 17: SUFFERING AFFLICTION: TESTING GOD'S PROMISES 271

CHAPTER 18: SUFFERING AFFLICTION: FOCUSING ON OUR MASTER TEACHER 285

CHAPTER 19: SUFFERING AFFLICTION: CONQUERING OUR UNSEEN BUT DANGEROUS ENEMY . 307

CHAPTER 20: A VICTORIOUS LIFE FULL OF NEW BEGINNINGS 331

DISCIPLINE YOURSELF FOR GODLINESS

Introduction

Everything seems so fragile these days. News gets old in seconds, emails in hours, movies in days, electronic gadgets in weeks, cars in months, and buildings in years. Nothing seems enduring in our world. We live more and more in a world that is temporary. From the delete button on the email screen to the trash can on our digital cameras—everything seems to be short lived. All around us we see decay, even on the cosmic level everything is headed toward what physicists call 'heat death'.

WHAT LASTS FOREVER?

When we get to the end of everything--what is left? In other words, what will last forever? The Bible ends with the book called Revelation. The last chapter is Revelation 22, and that last chapter ends with only three things left in eternity that really matter: God, Heaven and one more element—servants serving God.

Have you paused to notice who are those surrounding God's Throne? Revelation 22:3 And there shall be no more curse, but the Throne of God and of the Lamb shall be in it, and His servants shall serve Him. NKJV Servants are those who choose to discipline themselves to serve God. All that lasts are God and those who serve Him; that is what God's Word is all about. If we are to someday spend eternity serving God, how are we doing at disciplining ourselves to be His good, faithful, and godly servants? That is the question answered in these pages. May we all seek and receive His "well done" when Christ examines and measures our lives.

John Barnett

Tulsa, Oklahoma

September 15th 2007

1

> Each one's work will become clear; for the Day will declare it, because it will be revealed by fire; and the fire will test each one's work, of what sort it is
> —*1 Corinthians 3:13*

A Word Filled Life Is the Only Way to Not Waste Your Life

WE ARE NOT OUR OWN.[1] As a redeemed child of God we have a life to live that ends with a personal examination by the One we love, the One who bought us, and the only One who really matters—Jesus Christ our Lord. How we've used our time on Earth will one day be tested by fire—the fire of Christ's presence that will burn away everything we did which wasn't pleasing to Him.

How can we live in a way that truly pleases the Lord? Is it something we have to guess about or wonder whether we are doing what He desires?

The description of what lasts and pleases Him is in God's Word. To glorify Christ to the maximum by how we live takes choosing to stay in step with His plan. That plan, His Word, is intended by God to fill our lives. Hence, a Word filled life won't be burned up, which is the only way to not waste the life He has given each of us to use for His glory. If I could describe the best life possible—a life of peace, serenity, security, and joy—it would be the Word filled life!

[1] MP3 CD Audio DYG-37:040104AM, MP3 CD Audio DYG 20:030622AM Each of the 37 messages used to write these chapters is also available in both audio and/or text format from the original sermon at www.DTBM.org.

God's Word contains clear guidelines for how to have an exciting lifetime filled with confidence, purpose, direction, and hope. The Scriptures instruct us on how to have a joyous Word filled marriage and the most harmonious and loving family possible—a Word filled family![2] And a Word filled work life can be the most satisfying, purposeful, and rewarding employment for an entire lifetime!

God wants to greatly bless us through the Word filled life and into senior citizenship! Then, as we face that appointment with Christ to show what we have done with our lives (2 Corinthians 5:10), we can enter His presence with joy—thrilled to be with the One who loved us, and whom we love supremely.

No matter who you are or where you are in life, your age or what your past might be, God has described His perfect plan for you in the Scriptures. The Lord of heaven and earth has much to say about the optimal operating range we should live within, and has instilled in each of us every needed option to operate and fulfill His plans.

We find the details on how to do all those things in God's Word. If you want to live life the way God says it should be—the best life possible—live a Word filled life!

> 2 For more on marriage and the family, see my book, The Joy of a Word Filled Family. Available at www.discoverthebook.org

What Were Christ's First Words in Ministry?

In the New Testament, Christ's recorded words during His ministry on earth are highlighted in what we call a "red letter edition" Bible. To me, it is astounding to read these first words Jesus said after He was introduced publicly at His baptism:

> … "It is written, 'Man shall not live [exist, continue, go on] by bread alone [eating our physical food], but by every word that proceeds from the mouth of God' " (Matthew 4:4).

In other words, Jesus was saying, "It is not enough just to eat and exist and have physical life. If you want to have a full and abundant life in your youth, marriage, family, work, and senior years, as I designed it to be, you must allow My every Word to fill your life!"

The only way for us to have the mind of Christ is to invite His leadership into our lives by becoming filled with His Word so His Spirit can use those words to sanctify (John 17:17), guide (Psalm 119:105), defend (Ephesians 6:17), encourage (Romans 15:4), and feed our spiritual lives (Matthew 4:4). In Colossians 3:16-17, Paul equates the necessity for filling our lives with God's Word with the filling of the Spirit. Compare Ephesians 5:18-20 with the Colossians 3 passage, the lists are identical, and lead to the conclusion that the fullness of the Spirit is equal to His Word filling our lives!

What Is a Word Filled Life?

A Word filled life is
God's way of communicating with us.
Teach me, O LORD, the way of Your statutes,
and I shall keep it to the end (Psalm 119:33).

You can't be sustained, nurtured, and have life the way God intended unless it is a Word filled life. Every time you open God's Word, prayerfully ask Him: Open my eyes, that I may see wondrous things from Your law (Psalm 119:18). This is like going online and downloading fresh, new, personal e-mail from God Himself. Have you heard from Him lately? You can, as often as you want. Just prayerfully open your heart before the Word of God and, like a wireless device, your soul will start getting both encouraging and challenging "download messages" from heaven.

A Word filled life is
God's way of recharging our batteries.
"It is the Spirit who gives life; the flesh profits nothing. The words that I speak to you are spirit, and they are life" (John 6:63).

We expend strength daily in the battle of "plain old life." We need spiritual power to go on—to receive direction, comfort, and all God wants for us in our spiritual lives. When we stop our busy lives to get in the Word, it quickens[3] us, giving life and power through the Spirit of God.

3 Note: "Quicken us" is an old-fashioned way of saying "Fill us with life!" I will be using the biblical term "quicken" again as I discuss Psalm 119 in upcoming chapters.

Look at the beginning of John 6:63: "It is the Spirit who gives life ...." Perhaps you have been going through life in your own strength and failed to realize whatever you do in the flesh "profits nothing"—even if you are teaching a Sunday school class, or performing other ministries in the church. You may even be doing a personal Bible study without first connecting with God by praying, "I want Your Spirit to speak to me. Teach and lead me through this Book." If you don't connect with Him, however, and get charged spiritually, it all amounts to nothing because verse 63 says, "… The words that I speak to you are spirit, and they are life." Why go through life with a dead spiritual battery and miss the vital calls from the Lord? Read the Word daily because it is an essential, life-giving battery charger.

A Word filled life is
God's way of giving us hope.
… Everything that was written in the past was written to teach us, so that through endurance and the encouragement of the Scriptures we might have hope (Romans 15:4 NIV).

When Paul wrote Romans (A.D. 55-58), only a handful of New Testament books had been written (perhaps James, 1 and 2 Thessalonians, and one of the Gospels). So "everything that was written in the past" primarily referred to the Old Testament. Have you ever read through the Old Testament? Did you pay attention to the type of people God used? Many had messed-up personal lives, family lives, public lives, spiritual lives, and everything-else lives. But the Lord changed all that.

The Word of God is the key that unlocks a Word filled life, a constantly hope-filled life, no matter what your situation. In one of my counseling sessions, after the person tearfully finished pouring out the tragic details of a sinful life, I said, "You know what? The Christian life is a series of new beginnings. Right now, you can start over—all fresh, cleansed, and brand new with the Christ who gives you hope!"

A Word filled life is

God's way of cleansing us.
... He [will] sanctify and cleanse ... with the
washing of water by the word (Ephesians 5:26).

Although the context of that verse is speaking of the various roles of the Spirit-filled life, and it is a husband sanctifying and cleansing his wife with the Word, the ultimate lesson is this: as you allow the Word to fill your life, it will constantly sanctify, bathe, and cleanse you. God wants this for every one of His children.

I used to work at a custom pool company where I ran a jackhammer. If you run one of those things very long, you shake and sweat, and get covered in crushed debris and dust. By the end of the day, the first thing I wanted to do was take a hot shower to get clean again. So it is spiritually. When Jesus washed His disciples' feet, He reminded them we all get our feet dirty as we walk through life.

As the day starts and after it ends are two great times to take showers and physically stay fresh and clean. So it also is with staying spiritually clean. Through the washing of water by God's Word, He thoroughly cleans us so we may freely come into His presence for joy-filled fellowship.

A Word filled life is

God's way of giving us weapons for victory.
... [Take] the shield of faith with which you will be able to quench all the fiery darts of the wicked one. And take the helmet of salvation, and the sword of the Spirit, which is the word of God (Ephesians 6:16-17).

The only offensive weapon we have in our spiritual life—the Sword of the Spirit—is the Word of God. Is there something troubling you? Some old habit, old fear, or old insecurity making you spiritually falter, that keeps you wanting to go on the offensive? A Word filled life provides you with the weapons for victory so you can ... Resist the devil and he will flee from you (James 4:7).

When you feel spiritually cold, you will know to Draw near to God ... (James 4:8). And when old shackles enslave you, you can remember since "... the Son makes you free, you shall be free indeed" (John

8:36). Should you start feeling hopeless, you can recall Romans 15:4. God expects you to use His Word as an offensive weapon to fight the world, the flesh, and the devil as he attacks.

A Word filled life is
God's way of teaching us discernment.
… Solid food belongs to those who are of full age, … those who … have their senses exercised to discern both good and evil (Hebrews 5:14).

You exercise spiritually by daily being in the Word of God. Your soul needs constant exercise to grow strong enough to discern between good and evil, what is pleasing to God and what is not, the fruitful and what will be consumed at the judgment seat of Christ.

When I was a boy, my mother, an antiques buff, used to take me to garage sales to help her discern between the real and the fake. She especially liked Sterling silver and pearls, but because her eyes were not good, and her teeth not her own, she needed my assistance. She taught me the markings (British, European, and American), so by reading the backs of the silverware I could easily spot Sterling. As for pearls, Mom taught me to scrape them on my teeth to find the rough ones—the genuine pearls. Perhaps you can spot real silver and pearls because your senses have also been exercised, but have you exercised your soul yet? Can you discern immediately if the direction a conversation, relationship, or business deal is heading is not good? A Word filled life is one in which your spiritual muscles get strengthened as your soul receives daily exercise in the Word.

A Word filled life is
God's way of helping us feel secure in Christ.
… Lay aside all filthiness and … wickedness, and receive with meekness the implanted word, which is able to save your souls (James 1:21).

To "lay aside" is similar in meaning to the putting aside of our soiled clothes at the end of a hard, dirty day. Prior to receiving the Word, you should put aside any sin that will hamper your humbly coming to feast at the Lord's table of fellowship. He promises: If we confess our sins, He is faithful and just to forgive us our sins and to cleanse us from all unrighteousness (1 John 1:9). Just as clean garments at the end of a filthy day feel so very refreshing, so does keeping clean accounts with God. Regular confession and cleansing through the Word keeps our consciences clear so we can feel secure in our fellowship and peace with Christ.

The opposite is also true, however. Sins that are not forsaken grieve God's Spirit and make you feel distant, then detached, and finally feel insecure about salvation. Believers who sin act like unbelievers; unbelievers who act like unbelievers soon feel lost and insecure.

A Word filled life is
God's way of growing us so that we can taste God's goodness.
As newborn babes, desire the pure milk of the word, that you may grow thereby, if indeed you have tasted that the Lord is gracious
(1 Peter 2:2-3).

A craving for God's Word with the same intensity a baby craves milk is characteristic of a Word filled life. Without that craving, discernible spiritual growth is unlikely. If you do not have such a desire for the Scriptures, pray 1 Peter 2:2 back to the Lord and ask for a passion for His Word as you commit to the daily reading habit. Then rejoice as you taste of His goodness by getting to know Him intimately through His precious Word.

So, why live a Word filled life? It is God's perfect way of communicating, recharging your battery, giving hope, cleansing you, providing weapons of victory, teaching discernment, helping you feel secure in Christ so you can taste of God's goodness. All those benefits of a Word filled life can be distilled down into one verse: You will show me the path of life; in Your presence is fullness of joy; at Your right hand are pleasures forevermore (Psalm 16:11).

The Lord God of the Universe wants to lead you in His perfect path, to fill you with joyful fellowship, and to keep you secure in His sovereign hand at work in your life. He also wants you to rejoice in the knowledge that He created you to accomplish some specific works for His glory. Look at Ephesians 2:10: … [You] are His workmanship, created in Christ Jesus for good works, which God prepared beforehand that [you] should walk in them. Are you delighting in the fact you are Christ's workmanship—a beautiful work of art—designed for good works? And that He has placed you here on earth to accomplish something in particular for Him—something unique and wonderful? Such truth is at the heart of why you should long to live a Word filled life!

God wants to do something in you that only you and He together can accomplish. He wants to write Himself across all the pages of your life, which happens when you allow His Word to take control of your heart, mind, and life. Ezra experienced this when he … prepared his heart to seek the Law of the LORD, and to do it, and to teach statutes and ordinances in Israel (Ezra 7:10). As he zealously studied God's Word, and faithfully practiced it, Ezra then led others to do the same. Ezra was a testimony of how to faithfully live a Word filled life.

Until I began studying Ezra's life in depth, I never knew much about him. I always thought: Ezra? That is one of the more boring books of the Old Testament. What's the deal with Ezra? As a result of my studies, however, he has become a monumental person in my mind. Finally, I understand why, to the Jews, only Moses eclipses Ezra in Jewish history.

Ezra: A Wonderful Model of Living a Word Filled Life

Ezra's life has touched each Jew and every Christian to this day. The Jewish people revere him as the one who launched the Jewish synagogues and perpetuated the study of the Word of God. In fact, synagogues still follow the reading schedule Ezra devised 2,500 years ago. They read in a certain spot every time they gather in an ongoing through-the-Scripture study. And it is Ezra who copied all the Scriptures into the Hebrew form we have today. The entire Old Testament is the product of his careful work.

Under the inspiration of God, Moses began recording the Bible 3,500 years ago. Since Moses was from Egypt, he wrote from his basic understanding of language learned in the Egyptian schools. After Moses, 500 years later, David wrote another large portion of the Bible under the influence of the Phoenicians in whose realm he lived. The Mosaic writing in that Egyptian and the Phoenician-style

Hebrew all came to be the collection of books we now know as the Old Testament.

As time progressed, except for the scholars, the old forms of written Hebrew became unreadable to later generations. At that moment in Jewish history one man stepped forward to remedy this problem—Ezra. He copied every word of the Old Testament canon into what we now call Biblical Hebrew. God used him to pull together the group we know as the scribes, men who faithfully and tirelessly copied the Word. Ezra captured the Biblical Hebrew, codified it, made it consistent, and brought it forth to be copied, and recopied, again and again, until the time of the Dead Sea Scrolls and modern manuscripts from which we get our present-day Bible.

It is interesting that Ezra wasn't in school when he did this. God told him, "Leave what you are doing and travel up through the Fertile Crescent, and then down to the heart of the land of My people, Israel. I want you to minister to the remnant of people who are there." Ezra was in Persia (modern-day Iran) when he walked 975 miles to get to Jerusalem. There, he worked with about 50,000 people, a worldly congregation saturated in the ways of Babylon and Persia.

Some of them, abandoned by the Babylonians, left to till the land; others were returnees with Zerubbabel; and about 5,000 of them (1,500 of them men) came with Ezra. But a very worldly Babylonian group of people, some of which had basically lost their faith, had been so deeply affected by the Babylonian and Persian influence they barely knew or believed in God.

What if you and I had to go face 50,000 or more people like that? What would we do? Ezra 7:10 reveals the proper answer, and not just for Ezra 2,500 years ago, but for all who desire to do what God has planned only for them.

I have a simple philosophy of life: planned neglect. I purposefully plan to neglect everything except what God wants me to do. Why? I can only achieve well what God wants me in particular to accomplish. Ezra also had a very simple philosophy of life: "If I am going to bring lasting change to those I am called to serve, I will have to start with my own life." He lived out that philosophy by learning to point his heart frequently toward doing God's will.

Ezra 7:10 defines the secret of his towering success:

... **Ezra had prepared** ... [to establish, set up, accomplish, make firm; to direct toward (moral sense); to arrange, order]: Ezra just packed up and got ready to go. He prepared by meditating on God's Word so everything was put in order in his heart, to make him receptive to what God wanted.

... **his heart to seek** ... [to resort to, frequent (a place); to consult, investigate, to ask for, require; to practice, study, follow]: Ezra learned from the Lord, and readied his heart to follow God. That is a great way to look at what God wants from us.

... **the Law of the LORD, and to do it** ... [to observe, celebrate, to acquire]: "Do" is an interesting word. Ezra wanted to observe and celebrate the Lord, acquire Truth from Him, and then live it so he would be prepared to teach others.

... **and to teach statutes and ordinances in Israel.** After learning the Word, and living by it, he wanted to fulfill God's calling by leading others to follow what he had learned.

What was the result of Ezra's deep commitment to the Word of the Lord? I personally believe the longest chapter in the Bible, Psalm 119, is Ezra's testimony of the effects in his life from meditating on God and His Word. I have read every available commentator and commentary on this subject, and opinions vary. Mostly, they say Psalm 119 could have been written by David, Hezekiah, Nehemiah, or perhaps Daniel. But, after much research, and forty years of reading this psalm, I am persuaded the one man who copied every single character of the text of every single book of that Old Testament, and brought it into uniform ancient Biblical Hebrew, was Ezra, chief of the scribes, who started the synagogues and the reading of the Word of God. Hence, references to Ezra throughout this book will be from this frame of reference.

Not only am I persuaded Psalm 119 is Ezra's testimony, but I believe it is also the probable content of his teaching and preaching to the exiles who came home to Jerusalem to seek the Lord.

Psalm 119 beautifully reveals Ezra's Word filled life and, by both example and instruction, he exhorted others to do the same. That worshipful love for God and His Word led to radical changes not only in Ezra's life but also in countless other lives for the past 2,500 years. Just these verses alone should be enough to convince anyone of Ezra's deep devotion and commitment to the Lord: (Emphasis added to the verses below.)

- **I will praise You with uprightness of heart,** when I learn Your righteous judgments (v. 7).
- **I will keep Your statutes**; oh, do not forsake me utterly! (v. 8).
- **I will meditate on Your precepts**, and contemplate Your ways (v. 15).
- **I will delight myself in Your statutes**; I will not forget Your word (v. 16).
- **I will run the course of Your commandments**, for You shall enlarge my heart (v. 32).
- **I will walk at liberty**, for I seek Your precepts (v. 45).
- **I will speak of Your testimonies also before kings,** and will not be ashamed (v. 46).
- **I will delight myself in Your commandments**, which I love (v. 47).
- **My hands also I will lift up to** [in my hands I will carry] **Your commandments**, which I love, and I will meditate on Your statutes (v. 48). Literally, God's Word was close at hand!

One holy habit in particular empowered Ezra to keep his commitment to the Lord on a consistent basis—meditation. What is meditation? In essence, it is the spiritual discipline of practicing Christ's words in Matthew 4:4: "Man shall … live by … every word that proceeds from the mouth of God." That is the secret of every one of God's great warriors—those who have a heart like Ezra's.

Ezra's Secrets of Meditation

Seven times Ezra confessed a secret of his meditation. Here is his Psalm 119 pathway: (Emphasis added to the verses below.)

First Secret—Purifying Meditation:
How can a young man cleanse his way? By taking heed

*according to Your word. ... I will meditate on **Your precepts**, and contemplate **Your ways** (vv. 9, 15).*

Note that these verses reveal two ways to describe the Word of God: "precepts" and "Your ways." The Bible contains God's precepts, the individual elements which make up life; "Your ways" represents the big picture of the direction of God. Ezra was basically saying, "Meditation purifies my life. As I look at the individual requirements of what to expect from Your precepts, and the way (direction) this whole thing is going, as You have revealed, I more clearly realize what You want and do not want. And following the Truth sanctifies me."

Second Secret—Illuminating Meditation:
*Open my eyes, that I may see wondrous things from Your law. ... Princes also sit and speak against me, but Your servant meditates on **Your statutes** (vv. 18, 23).*

This talks about the Word of God being opened and clearly seen, or illuminated. As Ezra was meditating on God's statutes (another description for God's Word), he received the insight needed to respond to affliction the way God intended. Each time Ezra described God's Word he was saying, "I look on the Bible in every different way. I look at it as statutes, or codes: it is God's code, the standard by which I want to live. Therefore, it is what I meditate on, what I can use to make sure my life is up to God's standard."

Third Secret—Refreshing Meditation:
*My soul clings to the dust; revive me according to Your word. ... Make me understand the way of **Your precepts**; so shall I meditate on **Your wonderful works** (vv. 25, 27).*

The whole stanza (verses 25-32) talks about a life refreshed through the Word. "Works," another name for the Bible, drew Ezra to meditate. He was saying, "I meditate on Your hand in the past, and what You are doing, and the wonderful works You have promised." As he meditated on the Word, Ezra was refreshed by clinging to God, having his heart enlarged by Him, and thus becoming stronger in the Lord.

Fourth Secret—Testifying Meditation:

*I will speak of Your testimonies also before kings, and will not be ashamed. ... My hands also I will lift up to **Your commandments**, which I love, and I will meditate on **Your statutes** (vv. 46, 48).*

Verse 46 speaks of the testifying power of God's Word. Ezra was saying, "When I lift up my hands to Your commandments, and meditate on Your statutes, I can testify to what You are doing in my life—not in days gone by, but today." What does the lifting up of hands in verse 48 mean? He was saying, "What I do is bound by Your Word, clean hands, and a pure heart. Therefore, I am going to completely do as You say; I am going to obey You—to gladly meditate on Your statutes—Your precious Word, which I love!"

Fifth Secret—Refining Meditation:

*I know, O LORD, that Your judgments are right,
and that in faithfulness You have afflicted me. ... Let the proud
be ashamed, for they treated me wrongfully with falsehood;
but I will meditate on **Your precepts** (vv. 75, 78).*

Ezra was expressing, "Your Word trains me precept upon precept, line upon line, here a little, there a little (Isaiah 28:10) so meditation is my highest priority in life. For only through Your precepts can I be refined to serve You better!"

Sixth Secret—Focusing Meditation:

*I have restrained my feet from every evil way, that I may
keep Your word. I have more understanding than all my teachers,
for **Your testimonies** are my meditation (vv. 101, 99).*

The entire Bible is a testimony. It testifies you can operate when there are only eight people in the whole world who believe in God. "You can make it!" was thus Noah's testimony. Job's testimony claimed: "You can still operate when you lose family, friends, fortune—and everything else you once held dear!" "When you are all alone and discouraged, and haven't got a friend in the world," said Elijah, "you can still keep on keeping on!" David testified: "Even if you are on the run for your life, and your own family hates and pursues you, and is trying to kill you, you can go on through God's strength." Daniel's life told us: "You can still operate in a foreign country in which you are surrounded by a pagan, wicked culture threatening you!" The Bible recorded the lives of these people as a testimony of God's great and wonderful works. Thus, Ezra loved to meditate on His Word!

Seventh Secret—Interceding Meditation:
*I rise before the dawning of the morning, and cry for help; I hope in **Your word**. … My eyes are awake through the night watches, that I may meditate on **Your word*** (vv. 147–148).

This is interceding meditation. I can easily imagine Ezra praying for those people—praying God would be at work in their lives, praying they would turn back to the God of their fathers, and praying they would honor His Word.

Do you remember what happened when Ezra led in prayer before the people (Nehemiah 8:1-12)? They stood all day long and listened as he explained the Word of God. At the end, they were weeping and wailing. I believe his prayers were answered. Why? Because Ezra chose to ask the Lord for every character quality necessary to fruitfully live. He had a worldly congregation, but he started with his own life. He learned to point his heart frequently toward doing God's will. Thus, God radically changed him. Through Ezra, He changed a whole generation. And Ezra's life testimony is still changing lives today.

Do you also want to be great for God? Then learn what He has to say; live what He has to say; and lead others to follow God's way. That is the best life possible—a Word filled life!

My Prayer for You:
Father in Heaven, I pray the readers of this book will choose to prepare their hearts like Ezra did. May they seek to live according to Your every Word, and to lead others in their lives toward You. There is no limit to what can be accomplished because You have prepared some good works for each of us to do. I thank You that everything we need in this life, that will last forever, is tied to Your Word though the power of Your Spirit and for Your glory. Oh God, we discern where You want to lead us when we are full of Your Word. We feel the fullness of Your presence when we are full of Your Word.

that place of powerful usefulness when we are filled with Your Word. But we can only get full when we let Your Word in little by little, day by day. And Lord, for those who haven't even begun because they have never started in Jesus by faith, or received Him whom to know is life eternal, having never said, "Yes, Lord," never said, "God be merciful to me a sinner"—I pray at this very moment they might begin the greatest journey of all, the journey of faith and learning of their great salvation in You, oh Christ, in whose name I pray. Amen.

2

Blessed are the undefiled in the way, who walk in the law of the LORD!
—*Psalm 119:1*

Psalm 119: The Foundation of a Word Filled Life

MY LAST YEAR IN SEMINARY was a final push to learn all I could about God's Word.[4] The summer before graduation, I had an incredible opportunity to spend three months in Los Angeles. For a seminary student, this was like being invited regularly to a free all-you-can-eat smorgasbord of the tastiest foods possible. There was so much to learn in Southern California during the early 1980s.

Each Saturday I would go to a convenience store, buy a newspaper, and check the church section to locate the greatest Bible scholars in that area. The choices were exciting! There was Chuck Smith at Costa Mesa, and 5,000 super-charged Calvary Chapelites singing their hearts out just before he preached for an exciting hour on God's Word. A bit inland, David Hocking taught thousands at his church. A little further south was Tim "Left Behind" LaHaye—a pastor of not one, but two churches. Chuck Swindoll offered three services (I remember taking numerous notes, and if I didn't get enough, I would go to his next service to take even more). Then there was Grace

4 MP3 CD Audio DYG-24:030810AM

Community Church's John MacArthur, whom I went to hear almost every week. What a summer it was! It was so fascinating to hear these men teach God's Word.

But who is the greatest Bible teacher of all?

As we turn our focus back to the 119th Psalm, the greatest Bible educator of all time is with us, right now, to teach us. We are sitting at the feet of the greatest Teacher of God's Word, the Author Himself—the Everlasting God of Gods, King of the Universe, who breathed out through His Holy Spirit the very Word of God!

This Almighty God expounded upon the wonders of His own Word by inspiring one unique man, Ezra, to capture a sermon by Him on the "Book of books." That sermon—Psalm 119—is a song about the importance of God's Word, the foundation of a Word filled life. This Psalm, longer than ten of Paul's thirteen epistles, represents a call by the Lord Himself to let Him unleash His Word into our lives.

After comparing all the historical data on Ezra's life, I have concluded not only did God inspire Ezra to capture the greatest commentary ever written on the Bible, but also used Ezra to bring about the Old Testament Scriptures in a written language God's people could understand. Let's look at some important history regarding how we got the Old Testament in the first place.

The Origin of the Old Testament

Do you know what Bible Jesus used? How do we know the Word of God we have today is the right one? The answer is in Luke 24:44-45: *Then He said to them, "These are the words which I spoke to you while I was still with you, that all things must be fulfilled which were written in the Law of Moses and the Prophets and the Psalms concerning Me." And He opened their understanding, that they might comprehend the Scriptures.*

In this passage Jesus testified to His disciples after the Resurrection, preaching a sermon in which He referred to the Bible from which He taught. The words Christ used in verse 44 are the exact three divisions of the Hebrew Bible: "... *the Law of Moses and the Prophets and the Psalms* ...." Did you spot the relationship between the three divisions

PSALM 119: THE FOUNDATION

and *"concerning Me"*? Jesus Christ was saying, "This Book, with three divisions, is the Book I have taught to you, and is the Holy Scriptures." How did Jesus get those Scriptures? Where did they come from?

This is where I, a former seminary professor of Church History, get to have the fun of giving you a little history on how we got the Bible. The first thirty-nine books, the Old Testament, were always in the custodianship of the prophets and the priests (the New Testament was always under the oversight of the apostles). In other words, the prophets spoke, and the priests held on to those scrolls, keeping the documents safe in the tabernacle and later the temple. But how did they get into the form we have now? And how do we know some of them aren't missing?

Although there are twenty-two books in the Hebrew Old Testament, they are exactly the same as the thirty-nine books we have today. Does this mean some are missing? No, because the Hebrews combined all twelve of the Minor Prophets into one book, and called that "Hosea and the Prophets"; 1 and 2 Samuel plus 1 and 2 Kings were called "The Book of Kingdoms"; 1 and 2 Chronicles were called "The Book of Chronicles." They also put other books together, but the same thirty-nine we have are contained verbatim in their twenty-two. But why are there only twenty-two? Why did Jesus refer to the Law, the Prophets, and the Psalms? Here is the history lesson behind that.

Because there are twenty-two letters in the Hebrew alphabet, there are also twenty-two books in the Hebrew canon. Those twenty-two books were decided by the council of 120 scribes headed by Ezra.[5] (Even though the last of the minor prophets was Malachi, the last voice in the Old Testament, Ezra was the contemporary with him who led the finalization of the canon). After Ezra had copied the letters of the entire Old Testament, he gathered a council of the righteous leaders and teachers of Israel. Together, they agreed upon the books of the Old Testament that had been in the care of the prophets and priests for a thousand years. They then arranged the books in the three-fold division we see in Christ's ministry. However, if you talk to Hebrew believers, they won't call these divisions the Old Testament; they call it the TaNaKh, because the Hebrew Old Testament is named by a word made from the first two letters of the three divisions of the original twenty-two books of the canonized Old Testament. Below are those three divisions and the books within each.

---

5 Melito (170 A.D.), in agreement with the original Jewish reckoning, gave the number of Old Testament books as 22. (Eusebius, Eccl. Hist., 4.26.14); Origen (210 A.D.), "It should be stated that the canonical books, as the Hebrews have handed them down, are twenty-two; corresponding with the number of their letters." (Eusebius, Eccl. Hist.); Hilary of Poitiers (360 A.D.), "The Law of the Old Testament is considered as divided into twenty-two books, so as to correspond to the number of letters." (Tractate on Psalms, prologue 15); Athanasius (365 A.D.), "There are then of the Old Testament twenty-two books in number ... this is the number of the letters among the Hebrews." (Letter 39.4); The Council of Laodicea (343-391 A.D.), Twenty-two books. (Canon 60); Cyril of Jerusalem (386 A.D.), "Read the divine scriptures, the twenty-two books of the Old Testament." (Cathechtical Lectures 2, 4.33); Gregory of Nazianzus (390 A.D.), "I have exhibited twenty-two books, corresponding with the twenty-two letters of the Hebrews." (Carmina, 1.12); Jerome (410 A.D.), "That the Hebrews have twenty-two letters is testified ... as there are twenty-two elementary characters by means of which we write in Hebrew all we say ... so we reckon twenty-two books by which ... a righteous man is instructed." (Preface to the Books of Samuel and Kings); Synopsis of Sacred Scripture (c. 500 A.D.), "The canonical books of the Old Testament are twenty-two, equal in number to the Hebrew letters; for they have so many original letters."; Peter of Cluny (1150 A.D.): Twenty-two books. (Edward Reuss, Canon of the Holy Scriptures, p.257)

THE LAW (Torah)

1. Genesis
2. Exodus
3. Leviticus
4. Numbers
5. Deuteronomy

THE PROPHETS (Nevi'im)

6. Joshua and Judges
7. The Book of Kingdoms (1-2 Samuel and 1-2 Kings)
8. Isaiah
9. Jeremiah
10. Ezekiel
11. The Twelve (Hosea to Malachi)

THE PSALMS (Kethubim)

12. The Psalms
13. The Proverbs
14. Job
15. Song of Songs
16. Ruth
17. Lamentations
18. Ecclesiastes
19. Esther
20. Daniel
21. Ezra-Nehemiah
22. The Book of Chronicles

When it was publicly proclaimed that the council of scribes believed these twenty-two books in the hands of the priests and prophets to be the holy manuscripts—starting with the Books of Moses all the way through the writings of the Psalms and the prophets—the people applauded and praised God saying, "Now we have the Word of God in its completion!" And almost 500 years later,

Jesus Christ acknowledged Ezra's work when He referred to the three divisions and books above as "the Scriptures" (Luke 24:45). After Ezra taught the writings of Moses to the people, I am convinced he sat down and wrote his testimony—the 119th Psalm.

Ezra Summarized God's Word

Ezra's testimony, Psalm 119, is the song of a Word filled life. A song of the never-ending grace of God offers as a new beginning every time we open our hearts to His Word. Through His Word we are sanctified, revived, and quickened.

Psalm 119, with its 176 verses, is the longest chapter in the Bible—like a book within the "Book of books." In its 176 verses, God is mentioned 176 times; His Word is mentioned in 173 verses; prayer requests are given 70 times; suffering is mentioned 66 times; and Ezra refers to himself 325 times, making Psalm 119 the most personal portion of the Scriptures.

If your Bible has the divisions, you will find Psalm 119 has twenty-two eight-verse stanzas divided according to the twenty-two letters in the Hebrew alphabet. By using such a division, it is like God is saying to us, "My Truth exhausts the capacity of human language to express it. Therefore, I am using up every letter of the alphabet to reveal Myself to you so you will know how much I love you, and want you to know Me."

Why are there eight verses in each of the twenty-two stanzas? The Hebrew people always thought in terms of why things were. For example, looking at Creation they saw God created the universe, put man upon earth, and then made the week to be seven days long. Seven is the number of completeness, or spiritual perfection. Its Hebrew meaning is to be full or satisfied, have enough of. God rested from His labors on the seventh day, blessing and sanctifying it unto Himself (Genesis 2:3). There are seven days and then the week starts over; with seven notes, the musical scale starts over; after seven colors, the spectrum of color begins again. In the Hebrew mind they looked at all those sevens and said, "Eight will be the number of new beginnings." So all the way through their feasts in the Old Testament, it would say, "And on the eighth day …." Did you ever think about the fact the Lord's Day, Sunday, is the eighth day after the last Sunday?

Christ rose from the dead on the eighth day, and the eighth day is when we celebrate what Communion is all about. So every Sunday is a day to worship with a new beginning.

The completion of seven, and the starting over again on the eighth, is the declaration of a new beginning. In each stanza of eight verses God is declaring: "I am using every means possible to express what I want to offer you—a new beginning, a new hope, a new peace, a new joy, and a new power to live!"

Psalm 119's Ten Synonyms Describing God's Word

As we meditate on Psalm 119, we are reflecting upon the greatest commentary ever written on the Bible. To me, the different synonyms, God used to describe His Word is probably Psalm 119's most fascinating point. In the Elizabethan, or Puritan times, biblical scholars found fourteen synonyms for the Word of God. However, most modern scholars identify ten, and they are the most well known to us. Here is an overview of these ten synonyms for God's Word, the Bible, as found in Psalm 119. (Emphasis is added to the verses that identify the ten synonyms.)

Synonym 1
WAY: Walking the Divine Path
Blessed are the undefiled in the way, who walk in the law of the LORD! ... They also do no iniquity; they walk in His ways. ...
Oh, that my ways were directed to keep Your statutes! ...
I have rejoiced in the way of Your testimonies, as much as in all riches (vv. 1, 3, 5, 14).

When God's Word is filling our lives, as the passage above describes, we are walking the divine path, with the Divine Guide, down the journey of life. In verse one, "way" refers to the divine path. It is a Hebrew word that occurs thirteen times[6] and is always translated as "the Way" in all four of the main versions (King James, New King James, New International, New American Standard). "Way" speaks of life as "following the Divine Guide through our sojourn

[6] For a complete analysis of the Hebrew words and occurrences see Appendix A.

here on earth." In fact, it hearkens to Psalm 16:11 which says, You will show me the path of life …. In other words, "This is the Way—the divine path."

I think about "the Way" every time I recall earlier years when we took our family to caves. I'll never forget visiting the Mammoth Caves in Kentucky when, fourteen stories underground, they made us all sit on benches. Then the guide reached behind one of the stalagmites and it was suddenly blacker than midnight. The nervous tour group became very quiet as the guide said, "It is pretty dark down here, isn't it? You are 140 feet underground, and there are passages you could fall into that are hundreds of feet deep. You can't find the way out of here without me." After we sat in total darkness awhile longer, he flicked the lights on again—and everyone began looking for a quick exit! However, we soon realized we couldn't get out without him, as the system had miles of caverns.

Just as we couldn't escape the cave's darkness without our guide, so we can't escape walking in darkness without our Divine Guide to show us His divine pathway. For Jesus said, … "I am the light of the world. He who follows Me shall not walk in darkness, but have the light of life" (John 8:12). We need to see life through our Divine Guide's description in the Bible, and then depend on Him to show us His divine path—the way to guide us safely through our journey.

Synonym 2
TESTIMONIES: Listening to the Divine Witness
Blessed are those who keep His testimonies, who seek Him with the whole heart! (v. 2).

When God's Word fills our lives, we listen to the Divine Witness testify to the Truth that is sure and makes us wise. The word "testimonies" is sometimes called "statutes" in the New International Version. "Testimonies" speaks of God's Word as a divine witness. God Himself is the Divine Witness, and He is testifying to the Truth about a matter. Think about that for a minute. Consider events where something occurs and an expert witness is called upon to give a testimony. In the case of the Scriptures, God Himself is the "expert witness" who is testifying.

There is only one Person who really knows your future. Others may claim to be able to predict what your future will be, but I am not talking about fakes. I am saying there is only one Person who for sure knows your future. There is only one Map that leads to the right direction and destination—God's Word. There is only one Witness who will always tell you the Truth, and that is the One who is speaking in Psalm 119.

The 119th Psalm contains God's testimony fourteen times. He says, "I want to testify about your origin—where you came from. I am the only One who knows, because I am the only One who was there. I want to testify about your purpose—because I know it, and designed it for you. I designed you for a purpose, and I am taking the witness stand. I am the Divine Witness, and want to testify to you about your destiny—where you are headed for eternity. Are you interested?"

Do you know what is so fascinating to me? We have the Divine Witness, God Himself, speaking in His Word about our origin, our purpose, and our destiny. Yet, sometimes we pay more attention to the non-divine witnesses about origin, purpose, and destiny than we do to the One who always tells the Truth—the Perfect One who has recorded His indisputable eyewitness testimony in the Holy Scriptures.

Synonym 3
PRECEPTS: Following the Divine Directions
You have commanded us to keep Your precepts diligently (v. 4).

When God's Word is filling our lives, we are following the divine directions for life that are right, and cause great rejoicing. The word "precepts," a synonym for God's Word, occurs twenty-one times. It is always translated in all four versions (KJV, NKJV, NIV, NASB) as "precepts," and it speaks of the divine directions that tell someone where to go, or how to do something.

Have you ever tried to assemble a desk or a child's bike without any directions? I recall getting a very good deal on a lawn mower that still needed some assembly. However, I did not receive instructions with it, so I ended up with several unused parts—and even installed the blade wrong-side-up!

What about directions for life? If you buy something that needs assembling, but there are no directions, you simply go back to the store and say, "I need directions in order to put this together properly."

Have you ever read all the divine directions for life—God's Word? What about God's directions for marriage?[7] Have you read His directions for parenting, or His directions for work? He even provides directions for getting old.

> [7] See what the Scriptures teach about marriage and family in my book The Joy of a Word Filled Family. Available at www.discoverthebook.org.

Twenty-one times Psalm 119 says, "These are My divine directions I want you to follow. They are right, and will cause great rejoicing if you will pay attention to them." Remember: Psalm 119 is a "book within a Book"—by the Author of all sixty-six books of the Bible. God's precepts throughout the Bible provide His divine directions for every man and woman through marriage, family, job situation, aging, and all other decisions in life. The divine directions are right there in God's Word. Thus we can say, with joy: I will never forget Your precepts, for by them You have given me life (v. 93).

Synonym 4
COMMANDS: Obeying the Divine Orders
Then I would not be ashamed, when I look
into all Your commandments (v. 6).

When God's Word fills our lives, we obey the divine orders, the decrees of our heavenly Captain, which are perfectly pure and enlighten our lives. Being filled with God's Word is what all the verses we have discussed are talking about, but they are talking about it in a different way. The first word, "way," in verse one, is the divine path we should walk. The second synonym, "testimonies," is the divine witness we should listen to. The third one, "precepts," refers to the divine directions. And now we have the fourth synonym for God's Word—"commands." The King James and New King James versions say "commandments"; the New International and New American Standard say "commands," but it is the same Hebrew word. These are the divine orders we should obey.

This word "commands" is a little different than "directions." Directions accompany something needing assembly and basically say: "If you want to put this together correctly, you need to follow these steps (or diagrams)." Commands, however, are different. These are actual orders. What I see here in the fourth synonym is we should obey the divine orders of our heavenly Captain because they are perfectly sure, with no evil intent. When God says, "I want you to do this," we don't have to wonder: Is He going to hurt me? Does He have some malicious intent? No, look again at verse 6: Then I would not be ashamed, when I look into all Your commandments. God says His commandments are the divine orders, His decrees for what He wants us to do. It is a wonderful blessing to know we are obeying the divine orders of our heavenly Captain!

When the Apostle Paul gave his end of life testimony, he reported: I have fought the good fight, I have finished the race, I have kept the faith (2 Timothy 4:7). In other words, he was saying, "I wasn't disobedient. As much as possible, I have obeyed what I was told to do. I followed the divine orders; I obeyed my heavenly Captain." The Lord spoke to the Apostle Paul, ordering him according to His perfect will, and he obeyed. Is that true in your life?

Synonym 5
WORD (Written): Reading the Divine Word
Your word I have hidden in my heart,
that I might not sin against You (v. 11).

When God's Word fills our lives, we read the divine Word to obtain the will of God. This Hebrew word for "word" is used nineteen times in Psalm 119. What it speaks of is "the record." It is not talking about spoken words, but is talking about the written words. So the emphasis of "word" in verse 11 says we should be reading the divine Word that contains the will of God. It is similar to a legal proceeding of reading a will. When a will is read, everyone is very interested; they can't wait to see what has been bequeathed. The deceased person's will says, "This is what I want to happen …" Those in the room want to know whether or not they are included in the will.

Speaking of wills, I have some good news for you! If you are a born-again believer, you are included in God's will. If you think it would be wonderful to inherit something here on earth, just wait until you see what God has in store for you in eternity![8] It is unfathomable to our finite minds! "My Word contains My will," God says. "Do you know it? Do you know how it impacts you? Are you following it and yielding? You must cooperate with it."

Ezra was saying in verse 11, "Your Word, the divine Word by which

[8] For more details, see my devotional on the book of Revelation—Living Hope for the End of Days. Available at www.discoverthebook.org.

I obtain the will of God, I want to be reading. I want to read it so I can understand it, and so I ask You to help me. And not only do I want to understand it, but I also want to discern Your will in order to do it." This is what God intends for each of us: "I want you to be reading My divine Word to obtain My will!"

Synonym 6
LAW: Receiving the Divine Instructions
Open my eyes, that I may see wondrous things from Your law (v. 18).

When God's Word fills our lives, we receive the divine instructions from the Ultimate Teacher who gives perfect instructions to restore and transform. In verse 18, the Hebrew word "law," used twenty-five times in Psalm 119, is always translated the same in all four main versions of the Bible. Interestingly, it speaks of God's Word as being the divine instructions from a Teacher.

Ezra was saying in verse 18, "You are the Ultimate Teacher who gives perfect instructions, and Your Word is the lesson. And when I read Your Book, I joyfully sit at the feet of the greatest Teacher of all—the Author Himself—who personally instructs me." That is the attitude Psalm 119 puts upon the student of God's Word.

You and I don't have to wait for a once-a-year Bible conference somewhere. Nor must we count the days until we can go to some mountain retreat. Each morning, as soon as our eyes can focus, and the fog is cleared from our heads, we can sit and have our own private retreat. For across from us sits the Author of the Book Himself—the One who never tires, is never impatient or weary—the Divine Instructor who longs to show us His Word. That is what this synonym "law" speaks of. We should be receiving the divine instructions, looking to the Lord Himself as our Ultimate Teacher, because He always gives us perfect instructions.

It is interesting how the modern-day church always tries to reinvent itself. To supposedly do things a little better, we think of new ways of packaging this thing called "church" so we can stir up greater interest in attending. Yet, when I look back over the centuries since the birth of the church, I see there have consistently been supernatural workings of the Lord God Himself which transformed whole societies. For example, the most famous athlete in England immigrated to the Congo in 1910. The Bible was his entire library. He moved to a hut and began preaching the Word of God daily. He didn't have any audio visuals, no big praise band, or anything special to attract the natives—he just preached the Word. Before he died twenty-one years later, through the simple daily preaching of God's Word, he witnessed to tens of thousands to repent of witchcraft, drug use, gross licentious immorality, cannibalism, bestiality, and every other form of sin.

I am talking about my old friend, Charles T. Studd, whom I can't wait to meet in heaven. If you have never read the immensely challenging account of his life, written by his son-in-law, I would urge you to do so.[9] His diary records a habit of getting up daily at 3:30 a.m. to spend time alone with God in the Scriptures. He studied until 6:00 a.m., went back to sleep for another hour, and then awoke when all the natives arrived outside his hut. He would subsequently preach until he was out of strength. He looked on the Word as God's divine instructions, and God Himself as the Ultimate Teacher who gives perfect instructions to restore and transform. And that is the meaning of "law" in verse 18.

Synonym 7
JUDGMENTS: Building Life Upon Divine Decisions

My soul breaks with longing for Your judgments at all times (v. 20).

When God's Word fills our lives, we build life upon divine decisions—judgments always true and vindicated. Here is another descriptive term: "Your judgments." The NIV calls it "laws," and the NASB calls it "ordinances," but this Hebrew word, no matter how translated, is used twenty-three times in the 119th Psalm. It speaks of God's divine decisions. In other words, it is what God has decided about something. Whenever you are under someone's authority, you would go to him and say, "What have you decided regarding the matter? What are you going to do about this?" If you are involved in a financial transaction, and are subservient to someone else's will, you would say, "What have you decided? How do you want me to proceed? After all, it is your money at stake." We all face such situations at one time or another. But God is the One in control, and the Bible

---

[9] Norman P. Grubb, C.T. Studd: Cricketeer and Pioneer (Oxford: Worldwide Revival, 1935), 259 pages.

contains His divine decisions.

You and I are servants to the "King of Kings." To be His good and faithful servants, we should regularly ask, "What have You decided about …? In what should I invest my life? With whom should I spend my life? How should I spend my strength, mind, time, and money? How do You want me to do that? I know You have already thought about these things, so what have You decided?" That is what this word "judgments" is—God's divine decisions. It is how to build our life upon the unchanging decrees of God, His divine decisions which are always true.

If you are at all involved in technology, you must constantly upgrade. You have to have the newest version, the latest edition. Another example is print and online editions of local newspapers. Something I've always wondered about my local daily newspaper, is whether there is a difference between the two editions? Did I read the right one? Should I read both? That is how life is. Every time you get something, you can count on there being a newer edition—an updated or revised version. But how does all this apply to the Bible? God's Word will never be upgraded. There will never be a later edition with a little more in it you didn't already have. God has given His decisions on everything and will never change them. Isn't that wonderful? So if you learn His decisions while young, you will still know them throughout your whole life. We should build our lives on these always true and unchanging divine decisions!

Synonym 8

FEAR: Practicing the Divine Condition of Reverencing God

Establish Your word to Your servant,
who is devoted to fearing You (v. 38).

When God's Word fills our lives, we practice the divine condition of fearing God that makes life clean and enduring. One of the greatest deterrents to sin in mature believers' lives is the awareness they are never alone—God always watches and waits to be acknowledged. A mature awareness of God is called "fear" in the Old Testament. This eighth synonym, "fear," is one of those the scholars talk about. It is only used once, and is therefore the least used of all the synonyms. It is from the 119th Psalm where it talks about the Word of God: The fear of the LORD is clean, enduring forever … (v. 9). But in Psalm 119:38, Ezra said he was devoted to fearing God. In this case, it is just the word "fear." So the ancients felt this was another synonym, and, in light of the 119th Psalm, I would agree this speaks of the Word of God as the divine condition of fearing God. If we look on His Word as the divine condition, and we practice it, our lives will be clean and enduring and will get us ready to … appear before the judgment seat of Christ … (2 Corinthians 5:10). This is the Bema Seat of Judgment where the whole life of a believer goes through a refining fire to see if anything done was pleasing to God, and thus considered by Him as eternal (see 1 Corinthians 3:10-13).

Consider this illustration: When I've traveled to the Middle East and visited Jerusalem, my favorite part, the Old City, always captivated me. I always bought spices there because I love the smell. On a trip a few years ago, after buying spices and other things, I threw them in my suitcase. You know how it is when you get home and unpack—you don't necessarily unpack everything, so I left that suitcase under the bed unopened. I didn't find it again until a few weeks later, and when I opened it up, worms were crawling through those spices! The worms had changed into moths, laid more eggs, and made even more worms. It was gross! Why did the spices do that? In the Old City, they don't add all the preservatives our country does. They sell the spices right off the plant, worms and all. If they are not consumed in a timely manner, they become polluted.

Unlike those spices, if you live in the divine condition of fearing God, it makes your life clean and enduring, and nothing in your life for Him will decay. Everything you do out of fearing God is going to last forever. It won't be ruined by worms, decay, or be burned up by the judgment fire.

Synonym 9
STATUTES: Using the Divine Plans

The earth, O LORD, is full of Your mercy;
teach me Your statutes (V. 64).

When God's Word fills our lives, we use the divine plans, or specifications, to build the ultimate life. "Statutes" ("decrees" in the NIV) are what I call "divine plans" or "specs" (specifications). This is another beautiful description for God's Word, occurring twenty-two times.

Growing up in a tool and die home provides a great illustration for this idea of "divine plans." My dad had the most beautiful set of real micrometers and calipers that went down to the thousandths of an inch. His team at General Motors, where he worked for forty-six years, made dies for the bumpers of all Oldsmobile products. He learned very quickly that if the huge press, with its tons of pressure, stamped the steel plate even a thousandth of an inch off from being "to specs" it would cause the process to go out of kilter. Pretty soon, the press would stamp crooked pieces, and they wouldn't fit at the next assembly point. So my father had to grind everything exactly to the manufacturer's specifications. And that is what it says here in verse 64: … teach me Your statutes [specifications for life]. In other words, "What are Your plans, Lord? What is it You plan for me to do in life?" The divine specs are all in God's Word for our personal lives, our public lives, our private lives, and everything else in life.

Before we move on to the last synonym, let's consider one more illustration on specs. When I toured the huge new Asbury United Methodist Church in Tulsa, Oklahoma, I found it to be absolutely amazing! The building is unbelievably well-built. But everyone who took part in the construction didn't just do their own thing. They had a master plan everyone agreed to follow. So, all the pipes and wires are connected as they are supposed to be, and everything works according to specs. Often, people wonder why their lives aren't working right. God's statutes are the divine plans and specs to build the ultimate life. Do you want the ultimate life? You can have it by building your life one day, one step, one obedient decision at a time as you follow your Manufacturer's specifications.

Synonym 10
WORD (Spoken): Hearing the Divine Voice
You have dealt well with Your servant,
O LORD, according to Your word (v. 65).

When God's Word fills our lives, we are hear the Divine Voice. Earlier, I talked to you about the written "word." But "word" in verse 65 is a completely different Hebrew word. It does not speak of the written revelation; it speaks of the Voice behind it. In our language, when we say "word" we aren't sure if it is written or spoken. But in the Hebrew language, they could tell the difference by the word used in the text. So Ezra was saying in verse 65: "I have been hearing Your divine voice; You have walked me all through life."

That reminds me of some of the stories about the World Trade Center and the 9/11 terrorist attacks in New York City. When the press interviewed people who had been inside the buildings at the time of the attacks, they asked, "How did you get out of there?" One group said, "Well, when we hit the exit doors, smoke was billowing up, and it looked like fire. But we heard a voice in the dark saying, "Follow me! Come this way!" Those brave firemen were faithfully guiding people down the steps, but the crowd was stampeding and people were going up the steps instead. However, the voice called out all the more: "Don't go up! Go down! Follow me!"

A lot of young people view life like that moment, as resembling the fire exit. They are confused and don't know which way to go. The crowd is going one way, but another is voice saying, "Go this way!" When God's Word fills your life, you can hear the Divine Voice walking you all the way through life: Your ears shall hear a word behind you, saying, "This is the way, walk in it ..." (Isaiah 30:21).

This Hebrew word for "divine voice" is used twenty-four times in this psalm. God wants to write upon our hearts, and record upon us His voice, so when we get into a situation where we don't know what to do, we cry out to Him and His Word comes into our minds. The voice of God reminds us of His revelation: His plans and specs, His judgments, His statutes, His testimonies. God says to us, "I know how to live life. I want to guide you through life. I will be the Divine Voice guiding you through all the dangers of life so you safely arrive at the right destination."

It is the most beautiful picture of what God wants because there is the book within the Book—describing what God wants to do with the Bible in our lives. So with ten different synonyms, God lovingly says to us:

- Walk My divine path.
- Listen to My Divine Witness.
- Follow My divine directions for life.
- Obey My divine orders, for I am your Captain.

- Read My divine Word, for it contains My will.
- Receive My divine instructions, for I am the Ultimate Teacher.
- Build your life on My unchanging decrees, for they are My divine decisions about life, and they are always true.
- Practice the divine condition of fearing Me so your life won't burn away at the judgment seat.
- Use My divine plans to build "to specs" so you can have the ultimate life, not one that is out of sync. You can have the ultimate life if you will follow My specifications.
- Hear My divine voice, and I will walk you all the way through life. And when you get to the end of life you can dwell in My house forever!

Truly, B*lessed are the undefiled in the way, who walk in the law of the LORD!* (Psalm 119:1). For God will show His path of life, give us joy in His presence—and pleasures forevermore at His right hand (Psalm 16:11). Hallelujah! Praise God for Psalm 119—His glorious foundation for living a Word filled life![10]

[10] NOTE: For those of you who enjoy a birds-eye view of topics like this, a chart of the ten synonyms for God's Word, the Bible, is provided at Appendix A.

My Prayer for You:

Oh Lord, I thank You that Your Word is forever settled in heaven. Your Word is not only Your divine plan and will for us, but it is also Your voice written on our hearts so we can hear You. I thank You that we can truly live what we sing: "And He walks with me, and He talks with me, and tells me I am His own." Lord, we know this is possible if we let Your Word be written on our hearts. Help us to love and yield to Your Word. Perhaps someone reading about Psalm 119 may not even understand what I am talking about, having never received the engrafted Word which is able to save souls. So I pray Your Spirit would convict and move and stir and draw any around me so he or she can realize faith comes by hearing the Word of God. May that person admit to being sinful and lost and separated from You, and come to You in faith for salvation! Lord, we always agree with Your invitation; it is always open that whosoever will come to You, You will not cast out. But You must draw that soul, and I pray You will. Then draw us daily into Your Word. Let it change us because we want to live the ultimate life according to Your specs. In the name of Jesus I pray. Amen.

3

> With my whole heart I have sought You; oh, let me not wander from Your commandments!
> —*Psalm 119:10*

A Word Filled Life Offers True Security

ONE OF OUR GREAT RESPONSIBILITIES as individuals is to protect those we love.[11] Thus, as husbands, one of our great duties is to protect our wives and children. We lock the doors at night, listen to weather advisories, remind our family to buckle up in cars and watch for suspicious characters—all because we love them, and want to protect them. Constant vigilance is needed to keep our freedom and safety secure.

This was vividly brought home to me during a family camping trip on the edge of the great Huron National Forest. This beautiful area, stretching across the northern third of Michigan, has nearly one million acres of trees with nine pristine rivers running 550 miles, and is crisscrossed by 330 miles of trails. On our last night camping, my wife and I sat under towering oaks and ancient jack pines watching the stars and enjoying the campfire. A short distance away, our children slept peacefully in three tents. The whole scene was idyllic and picturesque.

So, there we were, out in this vast wilderness, and Bonnie and I were ready to stop talking and head to bed. I switched on my flashlight and made a wide arc, hoping to see a grazing deer. Just as I finished the arc, Bonnie gasped: there in the distance, loping across the hillside was a pair of silver-dollar-sized glowing yellow eyes—heading straight toward our tents. Bonnie was sure it was some fierce carnivore, so this dad was dispatched with a stick and a flashlight to intercept the creature that could potentially harm our sleeping and unprotected children.

As parents we saw a danger coming toward our children. Having been entrusted by God with the care and protection of those small lives, we had to act. Lurking in the million acres of dark night shadows were creatures that could harm the lives we love so much. After quite a chase, I ran the forest "monster" up a tree, only to turn around and find two more sets of glowing yellow eyes headed out from another thicket. By rolling stones, banging sticks, and waving my flashlight, the next two were also warded off. Although the "monsters" were only harmless raccoons on their way to the camp trashcan, the memory of night creatures stalking our children was unforgettable.

Later, as I lay quietly listening to the forest sounds, my mind turned to something far more dangerous than a Huron National Forest wild animal. Those animals could only scratch and scare my children, but in the dark world in which we live there are creatures far more lethal than raccoons or anything else roaming the forest. I began to think: What can I do to protect and guard my life, and the lives of those I love, from dangers that lurk in the spiritual darkness? What does God say we need to do to stay safe and secure on earth? Constant vigilance not only keeps our freedom and safety physically secure, but also keeps our freedom and safety spiritually secure.

A safe, secure, and liberated life is described in the Scriptures as one which is Word filled. As the Apostle Paul said, Spirit-filled believers have the Word richly dwelling in and filling them. But how is this possible? Psalm 119 reveals how to maintain a Word filled life, the only sure protection in the dark spiritual forests we and our loved ones must walk each day.

A Word Filled Life Is Full of Holy Habits

I am persuaded Ezra, that Old Testament giant of the faith, left his life testimony in the 119th Psalm. In its 176 verses, he recorded his holy habits of scriptural responses and resolves toward the Lord. Psalm 119 is comprised of twenty-two stanzas of eight verses each. Each verse in the first stanza begins with "A" and the stanzas continue with successive Hebrew alphabet lettering. This is called an acrostic. (There are eight other acrostic Psalms: 9, 10, 25, 34, 37, 111, 112, and 145.) To best comprehend the acrostic concept let us go over the literal Hebrew translation.

In The Psalms Chronologically Arranged, compilers show how the 119th Psalm would look if the English alphabet were used in this way. Here is an example of Theodore Kubler's treatment within Psalm 119 reflecting the use of only Daleth (like our letter "D") at the start of each of the verses 25-32 (KJV, emphasis added). Each Hebrew letter would comprise a section of this psalm and have a particular theme.

- "**Depressed** to the dust is my soul: Quicken Thou me according to Thy word" (v. 25).
- "**Declared** have I (to Thee) my ways, and Thou heardest me: Teach me Thy statutes" (v. 26).
- "**Declare** Thou to me the way of Thy precepts: So shall I talk of Thy wondrous works" (v. 27).
- "**Dropping** is my soul for heaviness: Strengthen Thou me according unto Thy word" (v. 28).
- "**Deceitful** ways remove from me: And grant me Thy law graciously" (v. 29).
- "**Determined** have I upon the way of truth: Thy judgments have I laid before me" (v. 30).
- "**Deliberately** have I stuck unto Thy testimonies: LORD, put me not to shame" (v. 31).
- "**Day by day** I will run the way of Thy commandments, When Thou shalt enlarge my heart" (v. 32).[12]

[12] Theodore Kubler, The Psalms Chronologically Arranged (New York: MacMillan and Co., 1891), pp. 329-342.

What a beautiful confession! A wonderful expression of the Word filled life that enables us to vigilantly go through a sin-darkened world in safety and security. Such a Word filled life is one full of holy habits—habits cultivated out of a deep love for God. Holy habits are things we have thought about and practiced so extensively they become ingrained in our minds, and invoke an automatic scriptural response and resolve in us. Like Ezra, without even thinking about them, holy habits just flow from godly choices we routinely make.

Holy Habits Flow from Godly Choices

As we look into Psalm 119 again, notice the intensely personal nature of its verses. Ezra referred to himself 325 times as "I," "me," or "my" as he shared his life testimony in two areas: his holy habits of scriptural **responses** (the areas Ezra had given to the Lord) and scriptural **resolves** (the further areas he wanted to see the Lord work on). We will first look at the responses Ezra chose to make to the Lord, and then his resolves.

SCRIPTURAL RESPONSES—

Ezra wanted the Lord:
With my whole heart I have sought You; oh, let me not wander from Your commandments! (v. 10).

We all have habits; we want things. Do you know what Ezra's all-consuming holy habit was? He wanted the Lord. "That is my habit," Ezra said, "I am whole-heartedly a seeker of the Lord. All of me, every single part of me, wants God!"

Ezra wanted the Word:
Your word I have hidden in my heart, that I might not sin against You (v. 11).

Have you ever had a treasure so precious, a possession so fragile, or favorite food you wanted so badly you hid it away so no one else could take it? Ezra was saying, "That is what God's Word is to me. I want His Word so badly I have treasured it. I don't want anything to dispel His Word which keeps me from sin."

Ezra loved God's ways:
I have rejoiced in the way of Your testimonies,
as much as in all riches (v. 14).

I once sat with some people at a conference who couldn't stop talking about another attendee who owned a palatial home with fifteen bathrooms. From their conversation, I gathered he was rich and they weren't, but they wished they were. They went on about all the stuff he possessed, the trips he'd taken, and so forth. You might be tempted to look at the lives of the rich and famous and think it would be nice if you, too, could have the same. But God says, "I have something far better. Get to know Me and learn to love My ways more than all the world's riches!" That saves a lot of effort, doesn't it? We don't have to keep striving for more. We already have everything we could ever want or need in God Himself! That is what the psalmist said: "My holy habit is that I love God's ways more than all riches."

Ezra obeyed the Word:
Remove from me reproach and contempt,
for I have kept Your testimonies (v. 22).

Troubles can't stick to us and bog us down if we are obedient to the Lord. God said all who want to live godly can expect to suffer persecution (2 Timothy 3:12). That has been true throughout the Old and New Testament periods, and is still true today. Those who have holy habits are likely to, at one time or another, come under the brunt of mean-spirited criticisms and personal attacks. But since Ezra was suffering reproach for God's sake, having so faithfully obeyed Him, he could in good conscience appeal to the Lord to have that pain "rolled from off him," like a heavy stone lifted off a person. Although the timing and manner of doing so was up to the Lord, there is one thing Ezra could count on with certainty: God was in each situation working it for his good, and God's glory (Romans 8:28).

Ezra talked about God:
*I have declared my ways, and You answered me;
teach me Your statutes (v. 26).*

He didn't just obey God's Word; he talked about it. He couldn't stop talking about it!

America is unique in the history of the world. There has never been a wealthier, more powerful country. The armed forces are bigger than any other. There is nothing that compares to the sheer power and wealth of the country. But because there is so much power and wealth, Americans have grown accustomed to seeing things in life accomplished by professionals in all fields, including music and sports. This has lead to some negative fallout in many spheres of society.

No longer are amateurs respected in the sports arena. Instead, paying spectators demand professionals who can give the best possible performance. In the media and the arts, only professional musicians and actors are truly valued. This has even slid over into our church pews. Multitudes of believers prefer to be merely spectators in church since they feel they can't share the Word as well as professionally trained speakers. How might that affect their families? Many husbands and fathers are uncomfortable sharing spiritual beliefs with their wives and children. Furthermore, countless Christians fail to declare their belief to co-workers, neighbors, or classmates. But what did the psalmist say of his holy habit? Ezra said, "I have a habit of declaring my ways; I talk about God."

Talking about God, the One who should be your "Best Friend," ought to be as natural as breathing! You should be able to freely talk about the Lord to those you love by saying, "I met with the Lord, and I can't wait to tell you what I received and learned from Him! I want you to know how He is touching my life." You should no longer be content to live merely as a spectator who watches "professionals" do what God called you to do.

In many places overseas, it is a different story. When I served with a special team in Russia, we helped in the graduation of nineteen church planters and pastors in Volgadonsk, Russia. I spoke for hours at multiple services, visited small house churches, orphan and children's ministries, and drug and alcohol rehabilitation centers. At one service, after preaching an hour and a half, I was asked to continue with a "Question and Answer" session which went on for yet another hour. Those saints were very hungry and responsive to God's Word. On a different occasion, I had the privilege of ministering every week in various Eastern European churches behind the communist "Iron Curtain." A whole part of the service was open to anyone wanting to share a verse and tell what God had taught them that week. Sometimes those services went on for up to five hours because the people lived out Psalm 119:26. They rejoiced in declaring the ways of the Lord because they knew God heard and was teaching them.

Ezra followed the pathway of God:
I have chosen the way of truth;
Your judgments I have laid before me (v. 30).

God's Word is like a map to show us the correct path to follow. Ezra said, "Your Word, oh God, I have laid before me. I have chosen to go the way Your Map says I should go." This reminds me of the passage: But the path of the just is like the shining sun, that shines ever brighter unto the perfect day. The way of the wicked is like darkness; they do not know what makes them stumble (Proverbs 4:18-19).

On that threatening night in the Huron National Forest, when I headed out with a stick and a rock to intercept the yellow-eyed "monster" heading toward our camp site, I had to feel my way along—expecting at any moment to fall into a pit, or be bitten by a rattlesnake—in total darkness and not knowing what was around me. That is what wickedness is like. Spiritually speaking, our pathway either gets clearer and better and brighter every day, or darker and harder. If we are on God's path—the way of Truth—our way gets clearer. We can see further ahead, and we are more assured of what God wants. Should we stray onto the path of wickedness, however, our way gets increasingly darker, and we have no idea what is going to happen because our path is clouded by sin's blackness.

When I hear people talk about their lives, I often sense they are operating "in the dark." They don't know what is going on; they don't know why things are happening to them. Verse 30 tells us we must choose the way of Truth. We have to lay God's judgments before us, like a map, and say, "Lord, I want to follow Your path. I want to understand it more clearly. I want it to be ever brighter—like the shining sun!" The psalmist said his automatic response to the Lord is: "I choose to follow God's pathway!"

Ezra clung to the Word:
I cling to Your testimonies;
O LORD, do not put me to shame! (v. 31).

Ezra's life became inseparable from the Word of God. Initially, as a scribe, and the father of the scribes, this related to his copying of the ancient Egyptian and middle Phoenician-style Hebrew into Modern Hebrew. So, in a very real sense, being inseparable from the Word began because he clung to the Scriptures by copying them.

Do you know what happens if you stick to the Word of God long enough? I feel odd if I am not within reach of my Bible. You see, whenever I talk with someone, I automatically think in terms of what the Bible says about the situation, and instinctively turn to an appropriate passage. In fact, if someone has a question, or I am watching the news, or reading about something happening, God's perspective instantly comes to mind. The psalmist said, "My holy habit is that I cling to God's Word. I am stuck on it, and I can't do without it!"

Ezra was excited about God:
Make me walk in the path of Your commandments,
for I delight in it (v. 35).

Ezra didn't just cling to the Word; he was excited about God Himself. He said, "I want to follow Your road. I want to go Your way, and I am thrilled to do so!" Are you delighted in God and His Word? If not, could you have done something to squelch your excitement and taken away your spiritual appetite?

One of my constant prayers is for everyone who sees trashy movies on Saturdays to feel absolutely miserable on Sundays. Maybe then they will figure out that feeding on rubbish is death to their spiritual brain waves—to their spiritual fervor. If the Bible is not a true delight to you, and you're not excited about God Himself, ask yourself: "Have I wandered from God's true path? Have I allowed my mind to become so full of garbage my spiritual appetite has been deadened?" If the answer is yes, then know it simply is not worth it!

Ezra feared disappointing God:
> *Turn away my reproach which I dread,*
> *for Your judgments are good (v. 39).*

Both as a deliverance from criticism and as a desire to never displease God, Ezra cried out to the Lord. The way of love is learning the mature attitude that says, "I love God so much that, as this psalm says, I fear reproaching Him. It is not because I am afraid He is going to do something terrible to me, but I simply don't want to displease Him!" A mature child will respond in like manner to his parents. For example, I know of a teen who once demonstrated this spirit when his friends suggested going to a certain restaurant for a good time. "I'd rather go home," the teen said, "my parents don't approve of that place." "Are you afraid your father will hurt you?" one of the girls asked sarcastically. "No, I'm not afraid my father will hurt me, but I am afraid I might hurt my father." He understood the principle that a true child of God, one who has experienced the love of God, has no desire to sin against this love. Such is the mature view, and is the holy habit Ezra had.

Ezra longed after the Lord:
> *Behold, I long for Your precepts;*
> *revive me in Your righteousness (v. 40).*

Ezra said, "I longed after Your precepts, and You quickened me in righteousness." If you find living a godly life difficult, and your love for God and His Word is not as it should be, it is probably due to not longing after Him. Verse 40 speaks of a reciprocal relationship; when you long after God and His Word, in response, God will revive you to make you feel alive again. When you are quickened—filled with His life—it will increase your longing for Him even more.

SCRIPTURAL RESOLVES—

We have just seen some of Ezra's holy habits of scriptural responses (the areas Ezra had given to the Lord), now let's turn our attention to his scriptural resolves (the further areas he wanted to see the Lord work on).

Ezra sought to turn his life toward God:
*I thought about my ways, and
turned my feet to Your testimonies (v. 59).*

Like a person who hears or sees something, then stops and turns to go in that direction, Ezra examined his life, looked at the Word, and then went the way of the Lord. We each need to do the same, and come to a point where we examine our life and say, "Lord, there are a lot of things I could do in life, a lot of ways I could live, and a lot of areas I could emphasize. But after thinking about my ways, I have turned my feet to Your testimonies. I want Your way, not mine."

Ezra sought to hate evil in any form and used personal restraints to avoid those ways:
*I have restrained my feet from every evil way,
that I may keep Your word (v. 101).*

In Ezra's first resolve, he turned his feet to the Lord's way. He also restrained his feet when they were prone to go in all different directions. Either we get our marching orders from the Lord by learning to meditate, fixing our hearts to concentrate on seeking after the Lord, or we are tossed about with every wave, new doctrine, or cunningly devised plan someone else has for our lives. Ezra chose to hate evil in any form, to personally restrain himself to avoid the ways God's Word says displease Him. Ask yourself: "From what do I restrain myself?"

Ezra sought to lean God's way by obedience:
*I have inclined my heart to perform Your statutes forever,
to the very end (v. 112).*

I love this verse! It reminds me of the time I introduced one of my children to a former college student of mine. He immediately commented, "Oh, I knew he was your son because he walks just like you walk." This surprised me, so he explained, "That is how you used to walk to class. You leaned forward in the direction you walked, and walked fast. Your son does the same."

I thought about this conversation as I read Psalm 119:112: I have inclined [I am leaning toward] my heart to perform Your statutes forever, to the very end. In other words, "Lord, I am leaning Your way." You can tell the direction someone is going if they lean forward, and they plow a certain way. Ezra reported his heart was leaning God's way. Did you know that was a choice? God says, "I want you to incline; I want you to lean toward Me!" Ask yourself: What do I lean toward?

Ezra sought to set his hopes in the Lord:
You are my hiding place and my shield;
I hope in Your word (v. 114).

This message has been taught in the church throughout all the ages, and was what Paul asked believers to do in Romans 15:13: … May the God of hope fill you with all joy and peace in believing, that you may abound in hope by the power of the Holy Spirit. Paul wrote to the people in Rome who faced the flickering torches of Nero's persecutions. In this verse Ezra was saying, "I am doing this because I know it. I am doing this because I love it. I am leaning toward it because I want it." Ask yourself: Upon what do I have my hopes set?

Ezra sought to cultivate spiritual appetites:
I opened my mouth and panted,
for I longed for Your commandments (v. 131).

What do you really, really want? Most of us eventually get what we really want. In a general sense, one way or another, where you are and what you are doing right now is what you want. Some people wish they could have a little more of something, but most of us are right where we want to be, and have learned to be pretty good at maneuvering to get what we want. What did Ezra want? I love what he said: "I opened my mouth and panted, because what I want is Your commandments." Ask yourself: For what do I pant? If there is anything you can't fast from for a week, it may be too important to you.

Ezra sought to cultivate spiritual disciplines:
I rise before the dawning of the morning,
and cry for help; I hope in Your word (v. 147).

Ezra was growing in the spiritual discipline of saying, "Lord, I need You! Apart from You, I can do nothing." Look at the little tag he put on the end: "I hope in Your word." In other words, he was saying to the Lord, "I am cultivating the spiritual discipline of realizing I can't do anything that matters unless I do it in Your strength. Oh, Lord, I need You! Every hour I need You!" Thus, he practiced the spiritual discipline of rising up early to start his day with the Lord. Ask yourself: What spiritual disciplines am I cultivating?

Ezra sought to live a life of praise:
Seven times a day I praise You,
because of Your righteous judgments (v. 164).

This does not mean Ezra had a little timer that beeped when it was another prayer time. Since seven is the number of completion, he was simply saying, "Seven times throughout my day, I completely praise You because of Your righteous judgments." Ezra said, "God's Word is measuring my life, founding and filling my life, and I just want to stop all day long to say, 'God, You are so awesome! I can't help but praise You for how great You are!' " Ask yourself: How many times a day do I actually praise God?

Ezra was able to maintain a Word filled life because he formed habits of scriptural responses and resolves by consistently thirsting for God and longing to "drink in" His Word—longing for the "water of life" (the continual flow of eternal life) and "drinking in" freely from God in His Word. Amidst the arid, sun-baked, lifeless deserts of life, Ezra found a beautiful, ever-present oasis through communing with God in His Word. His habit of such meditation freed him to prayerfully ask the Lord for each character quality necessary to live fruitfully for the Lord.

Because Ezra faced a congregation saturated in all the worldly ways of Babylon and Persia, he had to have a workable plan to bring about lasting change in those he served. And that plan started with his own life, by learning to point his heart frequently toward doing God's will through scriptural responses and resolves. As a result of living such a Word filled life, Ezra was enabled to vigilantly go through a sin-darkened world in true security despite the many challenges and afflictions he faced. Isn't that the best plan for us as well?

My Prayer for You:

Father in Heaven, I pray Ezra's words from 2,500 years ago—the testimony of a man of God, a man who mastered Your Word, a man who lived in Your Word, who stuck to Your Word—will impact each reader forevermore! Ezra lived during a period of great decadence and evil, yet he radiated Your righteousness. He walked the walk; he talked the talk; he lived the life; and he worshiped You. Lord, we also live in a decadent and dying world. We live among many who slumber in their faith, but we ourselves want to walk the walk; we want to live a Word filled life. So I pray each of us would hear the heartbeat and passion of Ezra through the 119th Psalm. By Your Spirit, may we establish and maintain holy habits of scriptural responses and resolves like he had. As we look daily into Your Word, help us to see it, hear it, and do it! In the name of Jesus I pray. Amen.

4

But He answered and said, "It is written, 'Man shall not live by bread alone, but by every word that proceeds from the mouth of God.'"

— *Matthew 4:4*

Discipline One—The Scriptures:
God's Perfect Path for Us

"Only one life, soon will be passed—only what's done for Christ will last" was how a dying missionary to Africa's summed up of his lifelong, all-consuming desire to love and follow Christ.[13] He knew how to make time on earth count for eternity.

Think about it: time flows past like a 60-minutes-per-hour river! Although we can't stop the speed of flow, by God's grace we can channel our time into living in a manner that reaps eternal dividends. The way to be *"redeeming the time"* (Ephesians 5:16) is to *"walk in the Spirit"* (Galatians 5:16) by letting Christ's desires (His Word) fill our lives (Colossians 3:16-17)!

To help us settle on what the Lord desires for all His children, we must refresh our minds with God's plan for us. One key passage in that plan is 1 Timothy 4:7: … *Exercise yourself toward godliness.* We are called by God to intentionally and with volition choose to exercise, discipline, and direct our lives for godliness (2 Peter 1:5-11). God expects us to discipline our lives by making choices that lead to godliness.

In the remainder of this book, we will therefore learn how to practice what I call "the disciplines of a godly life." We will focus on seven spiritual disciplines: the Scriptures, Spirit-filled living, meditation, stewardship, simplicity, supplication, and suffering affliction. The first, and foremost, discipline is "the discipline of the Scriptures"—making time to listen as God speaks to us daily through His Word. All the disciplines toward godliness are built upon whether or not you and I faithfully listen to God.

The great necessity of our spiritual lives is time alone with God in the Scriptures. E. Stanley Jones once described such periods as a "time exposure to God." He used the analogy of life being like a photographic plate which, when exposed to God, and in keeping with the length of exposure to the Scriptures, progressively bore God's image. The greater the exposure, the greater we can discern His perfect path for our lives.

God Has a Perfect Path for Us

A Word filled life is God's perfect way of communicating with us, recharging our batteries, giving hope, cleansing us, providing weapons of victory, teaching discernment, helping us feel secure in Christ, and growing us to taste God's goodness. All those benefits of a Word filled life can be distilled down into one verse, Psalm 16:11

The Lord longs to arrange the best life possible for His children. In an earthly way, I am going to portray what a life arranged by Him can be like. It all started at Thanksgiving time in 1978. As a ministerial student in Greenville, South Carolina, I was assigned hospital visitation. When I neared a sick friend's hospital room, I glanced in the room next door and caught sight of one of the most forlorn faces I had ever seen in a hospital bed. After sharing Scripture and praying with my friend, I said I would see if I could cheer the sad man in the next room. Later, I stood by the man's bed and determined he was one of the loneliest Christians I had ever met. When I finished reading God's Word and praying for him, I asked, "Is there anything else I can do to encourage you?" To my surprise, he brightened up and said, "It would mean so much to me if you would bring me a Wendy's™ triple burger for my Thanksgiving dinner!"

Returning with the three-quarter pound burger, I shared a bit more of Christ's love to cheer him. Before I left, he asked for my name and address to keep in touch. But I had no idea how much that visit was going to impact my life.

To make a long story short, the man was a very wealthy heir to a Texas oil field family. He was alone, away from his family, and the Lord had sent me to his room at a moment he desperately needed comfort and hope.

Two weeks later, I got a call from him asking when we could go out to dinner. He arrived in a stretch limo, and we went to a place where the menu did not show prices and the meal was prepared at the table. That evening he asked if I would join him for a little trip with his friends. Being young and unencumbered in many responsibilities, I said, "Sure!" This started of one of the most amazing ten days of my life! I traveled with Carl and two friends, who are both now pastors of churches, on a whirlwind trip to England, Holland, France, Switzerland, Germany, and Italy—all expenses paid.

The point of this story is since I had never been to any of the places we went, Carl arranged everything. We were chauffeured to sites, museums, restaurants, and plays, an unbelievable experience of the way the rich and famous travel. More than that, however, it was a lesson for me that someone with greater resources, experience, and knowledge can do a better job of arranging events than I could.

The whole experience with Carl was certainly fun in an earthly sense, but what if you receive a similar offer—only from God—and not for only ten days, but for today and forevermore? That is precisely what the Lord longs to do. Psalm 16:11 thrills my heart, because in this verse God offers three incredible and priceless benefits from making time to listen to Him speak daily to us.

The first benefit is **you can trust God's arrangements for your life:** You will show me the path of life …. As impressive as Carl's actions were on the European trip, can you imagine what every day of life is meant to be when arranged by your Creator who knows you, designed you, and built you for a purpose?

The second benefit is **you can enjoy God's companionship through life:** … in Your presence is fullness of joy …. While traveling, Carl shared story after story of how his vast wealth was accumulated, and then concluded, "It is just money." Money can't buy happiness—only the ability to look for it. In contrast, Jesus offers His companionship throughout your life!

The third benefit is **you can rest in God's authority over your life:** ... at Your right hand are pleasures forevermore. Do you know what "right hand" means? It speaks of power and authority: being at the right hand of the Father means the Son has both the power and authority of the Father. Thus Jesus can say to us, "If you will listen to Me, let Me arrange your life and walk with you, you can live in My power. I want you to have the boldness that comes from knowing your life has been authorized by Me. I want to empower you to live My life here on earth." What an entirely different and powerful way to look at life!

God desires to *arrange, accompany, and authorize* your life as you discipline yourself daily in the Scriptures and respond to Him in prayer saying, "Speak, Lord! Your servant wants to obey You!" Don't you find it absolutely amazing the *Lord God of the Universe* wants to arrange your life, accompany you on your life's journey, and authorize all you ever need from now on? Isn't that the best life imaginable?

But what if your present life comes nowhere close to the kind God wants you to experience? Perhaps you undergo great stress at work or at home, and constantly struggle just to survive. How can you turn things around so you can experience God's best for your life? A good starting place is to learn from the examples of others who faithfully responded to God speaking through His Word and became overcomers as they followed His perfect path for their lives.

Scriptural Models of Overcomers Who Followed God's Perfect Path

Jesus wants to give us the greatest life possible—a Word filled life, which is an abundant life! In fact, He has clearly assured of this in John 10:10: "... *I have come that they may have life, and that they may have it more abundantly.*" Joseph, David, Jeremiah, and the Apostle Paul are wonderful models of men who disciplined themselves to spend time alone listening as God spoke through the Scriptures. As a result—in spite of abuse, stress, pain and danger—they each found the path to living the abundant life Jesus promised.

*God's Word is for people who have
an abuse-filled life like Joseph's.*

Psalm 105:17-19 describes the life of this man who was deserted by all: *He sent a man before them—Joseph—who was sold as a slave. They hurt his feet with fetters, he was laid in irons. Until the time that his word came to pass, the word of the LORD tested him.*

In Genesis 37-45, we find Joseph spoiled by his dad and hated by his brothers; he was abused, enslaved, sold, and deported for family members' financial gain. He was used, set up, unjustly accused, and imprisoned by his own employer, then chained, tormented, and forgotten in jail.

In spite of horrible abuse, Joseph (circa 1800 B.C.) is one of the Bible's greatest men. He was vindicated, elevated to one of the highest offices in one of the world's greatest empires, and was used by God. But what led to his high purpose? His life passed the test of God's Word.

God's Word has two life-transforming truths for everyone who has ever been abused. Look at Genesis 41:51-52: *Joseph called the name of the firstborn Manasseh: "For God has made me forget all my toil and all my father's house." And the name of the second he called Ephraim: "For God has caused me to be fruitful in the land of my affliction."*

If you, like Joseph, have suffered abuse, God can enable you to forgive and forget. Find a new beginning He alone can offer. For only God can give you a fresh start in life and make it worth living. Take God at His Word. Start over by allowing Him to help you forget the bitter memories of abuse. As Jesus offers: "Come to Me, all you who labor and are heavy laden, and I will give you rest. Take My yoke upon you and learn from Me, for I am gentle and lowly in heart, and you will find rest for your souls. For My yoke is easy and My burden is light"
(Matthew 11:28-30).

From Joseph's life we learn God can guide us even if we find ourselves in a bad work area, bad home situation, or bad school setting.

God's Word is for people who have a stress-filled life like David's.

He killed predatory bears and lions at a young age; while still a teenager, he killed a giant; and in his twenties slew "ten thousands." When he was king, David committed adultery and murder. And he was such a swordsman, slinger, spearman, and deadly warrior that God said he was too much a "man of blood" to be allowed to build His temple.

How did his life turn out after such stress? David (1040-970 B.C.) stands out above most others in the history pages—he was a man after God's own heart because he would do all His will (see Acts 13:22). How could a man with his background be considered so special by God? The answer, again, is simple: the Lord looked on his heart and saw the heartbeat of obedience (see 1 Samuel 16:7).

David's beautiful spirit is revealed in prayer: Search me, O God, and know my heart; try me, and know my anxieties; and see if there is any wicked way in me, and lead me in the way everlasting (Psalm 139:23-24). In these verses, he said, "I want You to arrange my life, and accompany me all the way through. I want to be under Your authority and power, and have You guide me into eternal pleasures." From David's life, we learn there is hope for us as well. No past stain or failure at home or marriage is too deep for the God of New Beginnings to forgive and heal.

God's Word is for people who have a pain-filled life like Jeremiah's.

Jeremiah (633-573 B.C.) was known as the weeping prophet—partly for his compassion, and partly for his condition of sadness. As an adult he wept more than anybody else we know of in Scriptures, but as a child his life must have been incredible. The Bible tells God chose him to be a prophet before his birth (Jeremiah 1:4-5). His family was distinguished in their service for the Lord, and life would have been exciting for the son of a high priest. As a prophet, however, his woes were unimaginable to our relatively peaceful lives.

As a prophet, Jeremiah endured and suffered through the death throes of the final generation of the nation of Judah. He watched the decay of God's chosen people, the destruction of Jerusalem, and the Israelites deportation to Babylon. Although he preached forty years, he had no converts. Instead, the countrymen he warned on God's behalf sought to kill him for preaching doom (Jeremiah 11:19-23).

In addition, Jeremiah had no one with whom he could find joy and comfort. His own family and friends plotted against him (Jeremiah 12:6). He never had the joy of establishing a godly home because God never allowed him to marry. Thus, he suffered an agonizing loneliness (Jeremiah 16:2).

Jeremiah lived under a constant threat of death, living in secret so no one would find him (Jeremiah 18:20-23). He suffered physical pain from severe beatings, and then being bound in wooden stocks (Jeremiah 20:1-2). He also lived with emotional pain from deceitful friends spying on him and seeking revenge (Jeremiah 20:10).

He was consumed with sorrow and shame, and even cursed the day he was born (Jeremiah 20:14-18). His life ended with no relief, as he was falsely accused of being a traitor to his own country (Jeremiah 37:13-14), arrested, beaten, thrown into a dungeon, and starved many days (Jeremiah 37:15-21). An Ethiopian Gentile interceded on his behalf or he would have died there (Jeremiah 38:7-13). In the end, having been exiled to Egypt, tradition tells us he was stoned to death by his own people. From an earthly perspective, Jeremiah's life was a failure.

By now you may be thinking: *How is that report supposed to give me hope? Jeremiah's life is just one big mess of gloom, despair, and misery!* Certainly, that is true if you merely look at his outward circumstances, but when you consider Jeremiah's heart in all this you will see a far different picture.

Look at his incredible testimony: *Your words were found, and I ate them, and Your word was to me the joy and rejoicing of my heart; for I am called by Your name, O LORD God of hosts* (Jeremiah 15:16). How was he able to persevere in such tragedies? The discipline of the Scriptures! This verse is offered whether you have an endless joy-filled life of pleasures, or an endless joy-filled life of trials.

Let's examine Jeremiah 15:16 further to better grasp what enabled Jeremiah to not give up in the miry pits. First, look at the beginning of the verse: **Your words were found** … This indicates Jeremiah was in the Word regularly, asking God to open his eyes to His Truth.

Now look at his attitude toward the Scriptures: … **and I ate them** …. The expression describes Jeremiah's devotional times. He made God's Words personal by incorporating them into his life. He didn't simply have devotions and say, "That's over with, so I can check off my Things-to-Do list." No, his devotional times were like a feast: he eagerly came expecting the Lord to open His "Basket of Treasures" and feed his soul with the richest, most delightful foods.

This is the key which unlocked the door to living the best life possible: … **and Your word was to me the joy and rejoicing of my heart** …. How could Jeremiah have joy in light of all he went through? Wouldn't you love to personally ask him: "What did you rejoice about Jeremiah? Your wife or children? You never had any. Your ministry? You didn't have one. What did you rejoice in?" He rejoiced in this truth: … **I am called by Your name, O LORD God of hosts.**

Because Jeremiah lived after David's time, he knew God's Word well, making me confident he trusted in the Lord's Psalm 16:11 promise to reveal the path of life, and make the best possible arrangements. God promises if we stay in His presence, He will give us fullness of joy. That became the testimony of Jeremiah's life. His passion for God and His Word was consistently and relentlessly demonstrated throughout his life as God's prophet.

God's Word is for people who have a danger-filled life like Paul's.

If you are experiencing the stress of a dangerous life, such as working in the military or law enforcement, or even living in a dangerous part of town, God can guide even then. Just as He guided the Apostle Paul, who was in constant peril, so He can guide in whatever difficult situation you face.

Paul (A.D. 5-65) lived one of the fullest lives of the first century. How did God view Paul's life? He saw him as a man who persevered in the midst of trials that would have caused many to quit. Paul was stoned, shipwrecked, and sleepless. He was hunted, hounded, and heckled, imprisoned and impoverished, bruised, beaten, and banished. He was hard-pressed on every side, yet not crushed; he was perplexed, but not in despair; persecuted, but not forsaken; struck down, but not destroyed (2 Corinthians 4:8-9). Yet, he never stopped hoping in God's Word. In all these things he was more than a conqueror through Jesus Christ (Romans 8:37)!

God gave us disciplined models like Joseph, David, Jeremiah, and the Apostle Paul to show us what living a Word filled life looks like so ... *we through the patience and comfort of the Scriptures might have hope* (Romans 15:4). Wouldn't you like to capture their same passion in your own life? You can by disciplining yourself to listen to God speak!

To help you start cultivating a disciplined "alone time" with God, we will now look at three areas: (1) reading God's Word daily, (2) memorizing God's Word, and (3) meditating upon God's Word.

Discipline Yourself in Reading God's Word

We can most readily get alone with God faithfully *reading* His Word.[14] Since the Scriptures are the very voice of God, we must discipline ourselves to listen to Him. It is amazing that Christians imagine they can live a fruitful Christian life without regularly reading the Bible. It's just not possible, because our minds do not retain what is necessary and must be refreshed again and again (2 Peter 1:12-15).

Some who have been believers for years have never read the Bible through even once. In contrast, Dr. Harry Ironside (1876-1951), a man with little formal education but great power, read the complete Bible fourteen times by age fourteen! Through individual lives transformed by his ministry, his mark is still on Chicago—and indeed, the entire world. It's only when we consider His Word to be even more important than our daily meals we can begin to get alone with God. If we never inconvenience ourselves enough to be disciplined in Bible reading, there are truths God has for us that will be missed. Such lives can't help but be spiritually void.

An outstanding example of a man who practiced "the discipline of the Scriptures" is Lt. General William K. Harrison (1895-1987). He was the most decorated soldier in the 30th Infantry Division, which General Eisenhower rated as the top infantry division in World War II.

General Harrison was the first American to enter Belgium, which he did at the head of the Allied Forces. Except for the Congressional

[14] This section is a paraphrased adaptation of R. Kent Hughes' Preaching the Word: Ephesians—The Mystery of the Body of Christ (Wheaton: Crossway Books, 1997), electronic edition, in loc Ephesians 5.

Medal of Honor, he received every other decoration for valor. When the Korean War began, he served as Chief of Staff in the United Nations Command and, because of his character and self-control, was ultimately President Eisenhower's choice to head the long and tedious negotiations of ending the war.

General Harrison, a soldier's soldier who led a busy, ultra-kinetic life, was also an amazing man of the Word. When he was a twenty-year-old cadet, he began reading the Old Testament once a year plus the New Testament four times, and continued to do so until the end of his life.

By age ninety, when General Harrison's failing eyesight no longer permitted his discipline of the Scriptures, he had read the Old Testament 70 times and the New Testament 280 times. No wonder his godliness and wisdom were proverbial, and the Lord used him to lead Officers Christian Fellowship (OCF)[15] for eighteen years.

Even to the busiest of us, General Harrison's story should serve as a challenge. No one could be busier or lead a more demanding life. His life demonstrates a mind programmed with the Scriptures. His closest associates say his domestic, spiritual, and professional life, as well as each great problem he faced, was informed by the Scriptures. People marveled at his Biblical knowledge and ability to bring its light to every situation. He lived the experience of the psalmist which tells us the attitude we need if we are going to have the discipline of the Scriptures.

Since it only takes eighty hours to read the entire Bible, General Harrison's commitment obligated him to just one-half hour daily to read God's Word. Let me ask you this: Can't you also spare thirty minutes per day to cultivate the mind of Christ as General Harrison did? How about fifteen minutes to read God's Word through in a year? Or, at the very least, are you willing to devote five minutes a day to read the New Testament in a year?

---

15 R. Kent Hughes, *Disciplines of a Godly Man* (Wheaton: Crossway Books, 1991), pp. 76-77.

		TOTAL HOURS	TOTAL MINUTES	DAILY MINUTES
THE BIBLE				
• OLD TESTAMENT	77%	62	3695	10
• NEW TESTAMENT	23%	18	1104	5
TIME TO READ BIBLE		80	3799	15
THE HARRISON PLAN				
• OLD TESTAMENT	1	80	4800	15
• NEW TESTAMENT	4	74	4419	15
MINUTES NEEDED		154	9219	30

At the rate of three and one-third chapters per day, an average Bible can be read in a year. In the One Year Bible, what our children work on, daily reading is just three pages—an Old Testament passage, a New Testament passage, a psalm, and a proverb. Fifteen minutes reading per day makes it through the Bible once a year, and a half-hour equals two times. On a CD or tape, listening to the complete Bible in a year requires the same amount of time. On your computer or digital device, get MP3s of God's Word for free and listen anywhere. Isn't God worth it?

This passage represents the heartbeat of a man of God: *Oh, how I love your law! I meditate on it all day long. Your commands make me wiser than my enemies, for they are ever with me. I have more insight than all my teachers, for I meditate on your statutes. I have more understanding than the elders, for I obey your precepts* (Psalm 119:97-100 NIV).

Now think with me: What would have happened if I had refused to fulfill Carl's hospital request for a simple Thanksgiving dinner because I was too busy, or too poor? In reality, I did only have two dollars. What if I had not answered the phone when he called my house and asked me out to dinner? What if I had turned down his offer to go on that European trip? Think of what I would have missed!

In comparison, what if you never take the time to know what God wants you to do, and therefore don't stay at His right hand? You will miss enjoying His pleasures forevermore! All earthly pleasures are as nothing if you miss out on God saying, "I want make arrangements for you, show the path of life, and teach you how to stay in My presence all the time. Even if you were to be in a dungeon or a pit like Jeremiah, I want to give you fullness of joy through pain and suffering and trials."

I encourage you to not miss out on God's best for you. Plan to make the discipline of the Scriptures your way of life. Feast with God every day. Set aside one-half hour and say, "Lord, speak to me. Show me Your arrangements. Help me to know Your presence, yield to Your authority, and stay at Your right hand." On the authority of God's Word, I can say if you do you will live an unbelievable life—the life God designed for you to live.

Remember, you can never have a Christian mind without regularly reading the Scriptures because you cannot be deeply influenced by what you do not know. If you are filled with God's Word, every part of life can be informed and directed by God—your domestic relationships, child-rearing, career, ethical decisions, and internal morality. The only way to have a Christian mind is through God's Word.

Discipline Yourself in Memorizing God's Word

Second on the list of cultivating time for getting alone with God is a discipline of *memorizing* the Scriptures. The depth of impact Scripture memorization can have upon ministry is profound. Donald Gray Barnhouse (1895-1960) is an outstanding example of one who understood the importance of such discipline. Because he loved and believed God's Word, early in life he memorized the Book of Philippians, a verse a day until he knew the entire book by heart, and then went on to other passages. The impact of his discipline of Scripture memorization is reflected by his answer to how long it took him to prepare a certain sermon. He replied it took both thirty years and thirty minutes. He then explained because he had immersed himself in the Bible from the age of fifteen, and never stopped memorizing God's Word, he did not just learn the words, but treasured them in his heart.

The pioneering missionary to Africa, C. T. Studd (1860-1931), is another of God's great disciplined servants. His life was like his grass hut with no doors to shut. He lived with, and for, his beloved pygmy tribes. How did he prepare to teach as many as 5,000 at a time, and ready himself to disciple the scores of church leaders who sat at the foot of his cot every morning so he awakened to a sea of black faces and white teeth waiting for him to open the Book of God? Beforehand, he memorized and meditated upon God's Word, so he would be ready at a moment's notice to minister to all whom the Lord brought to him.

Studd faithfully practiced time alone with God as is clearly evident by his diary entry of February 7, 1886: "The Lord is so good to give me a large dose of spiritual champagne every morning which braces one up for the day and night. Of late I have had such glorious times."

His family described these times as: "A Bible is taken down from the shelf, and Bwana [Swahili for "master" or "boss"] is alone with God. What passed between them in those silent hours was known a few hours later to all who had ears to hear."

He continued in his diary: "I find then what I read is stamped indelibly upon my heart all through the day; and it is the very quietest of times, not a foot astir, nor a sound to be heard, saving that of God. If I miss this time I feel like Samson shorn of his hair and so of all his strength. I see more and more how much I have to learn of the Lord. I want to be a workman approved of the Lord, not just with a pass degree as it were. Oh, how I wish I had devoted my early life, my whole life to God and His Word. How much I have lost by those early years of self pleasing and running after this world's honors and pleasures."[16]

Are you wasting precious time better spent listening to God? Will you have any regrets when you look back on life? If you begin by memorizing even one verse a week, you will know a total of fifty-two verses within one year!

16 C. T. Studd, Cricketeer and Pioneer (Oxford: Worldwide Revival, 1935), pp. 57 and 206.

Discipline Yourself in Meditating Upon God's Word

Third, and last on the list of how to begin cultivating a time alone with God, is the discipline of *meditating* on the Scriptures. Meditation is the spiritual discipline of practicing Christ's words in Matthew 4:4. At salvation, we became a soul that thirsts for God and longs to "drink in" His Word; a soul longing for the "water of life" (the continual flow of eternal life). Amidst the arid, sun-baked, lifeless deserts of life, we find a beautiful, ever-present oasis through communing with God in His Word. This is the secret of God's great warriors, and a spiritual discipline we need to practice.

Hudson Taylor (1832-1905), the founder of China Inland Mission, conquered immense hardships with daily meditation on the Scriptures. Dr. and Mrs. Howard Taylor recorded this in his biography:

> *It was not easy for Mr. Taylor, in his changeful life, to make time for prayer and Bible study, but he knew it was vital. Well do the writers remember traveling with him month after month in northern China, by cart and wheelbarrow with the poorest of inns at night. Often with only one large room for coolies and travelers alike, they would screen off a corner for their father and another for themselves, with curtains of some sort; and then, after sleep at last had brought a measure of quiet, they would hear a match struck and see the flicker of candlelight which told that Mr. Taylor, however weary, was pouring over the little Bible in two volumes always at hand. From two to four a.m. was the time he usually gave to prayer; the time he could be most sure of being undisturbed to wait upon God.*
>
> *Day and night this was his secret, "just to roll the burden on the Lord." Frequently those who were wakeful in the little house at Chinkiang might hear, at two or three in the morning, the soft refrain of Mr. Taylor's favorite hymn ["Jesus, I am resting, resting in the joy of what Thou art"]. He had learned that, for him, only one life was possible—just that blessed life of resting and rejoicing in the Lord under all circumstances, while He dealt with the difficulties, inward and outward, great and small."*

Meditating upon the Word brings us immediately into the intimate presence of God who promises: *Blessed is the man who does not walk in the counsel of the wicked or stand in the way of sinners or sit in the seat of mockers. But his delight is in the law of the LORD, and on his law he meditates day and night. He is like a tree planted by streams of water, which yields its fruit in season and whose leaf does not wither* (Psalm 1:1–3 NIV).

Another spiritual giant was George Mueller (1805-1898). His life may be distilled down to these words he wrote in a diary:

> *It has pleased the Lord to teach me a truth, the benefit of which I have not lost for more than fourteen years. The point is this: I saw more clearly than ever that the first great and primary business to which I ought to attend every day was to have my soul happy in the Lord. The first thing to be concerned about was not how much I might serve the Lord, or how I might glorify the Lord; but how I might get my soul into a happy state, and how my inner man might be nourished. … Before this time my practice had been, at least for ten years previously, as a habitual thing, to give myself to prayer in the morning. Now I saw the most important thing I had to do was to give myself to the reading of the Word of God, and to the meditation on it, that thus my heart might be comforted, encouraged, warned, reproved and instructed; and that thus, by means of the Word of God, while meditating on it, my heart might be brought into experiential communion with the Lord.*

Each of these great men of the Scriptures—Dr. Harry Ironside, Lt. General William K. Harrison, C. T. Studd, Hudson Taylor, and George Mueller—responded with joy to Jesus when He related to them, "If you will listen to Me, and let Me arrange your life for you, I will accompany you through life. I will empower you to live My life here on earth. I want you to have the boldness that comes from knowing your life has been authorized by Me. For I designed it, am leading it, and guiding it." What an entirely different and powerful way to look at life, and exactly what He offers if you joyfully pursue "the discipline of the Scriptures."

If you want to be great for God like these devoted men, then *learn* and *live* what He has to say, and *lead* others to follow God's way. This is the greatest possible plan for living with God written across every page of your life!

Get Started Today

Since the Scriptures are the voice of God, we must listen to His voice again and again. It is simply the way He wired us: our minds need to be refreshed regularly with the truths God longs to share; we need to establish regular "alone times" with Him.

If you are a saint, a born-again believer, will you, right now, say to the Lord: "Lead me; fill me; keep me?" In doing so, you are *choosing* to have a Word filled life, and choosing to pursue the daily discipline of the Scriptures by listening, praying, and obeying God.

Men, husbands, and dads, will you choose to humbly lead your wife, children, and family toward the Lord by seeking a Word filled life for their sake?

Women, wives, and moms, will you choose to follow the Lord in humility by seeking a Word filled life for the sake of your husband, children, and family?

Children, sons and daughters, will you choose to obey and honor your parents by seeking a Word filled life for the sake of your own personal growth?

You can start following through with your commitment to the Lord by spending a minimum of fifteen minutes each morning reading God's Word. Ask Him to give you at least one Truth to hold all day long. During your time alone with God, think through your entire day. Ask Him to show you what would be the best use of your life that day. I encourage you to also end your day with the Word. Personally, I love to follow this adage: "No Bible, no breakfast; no Bible, no bed."

It is important to also establish the habit of half-hour weekly times of evaluation to reflect on where you are, and where you are headed, in life and ministry. In addition, it is helpful to take several hours of spiritual retreat each month to strategically plan and truly reflect on life. With Bible in hand and your personal calendar, make a list of priorities for the next month. Pray over them; change them; decide upon them, and then do them.

Invite God Into Your Daily Life

A profitable study to aid your prayer life is to look up each of the Psalm 119 verses below that contain Ezra's prayers. Thirty-eight times, with these eleven different phrases, he cried out to the Lord. The secret of his fruitful life was his choice to invite the Lord each day into every part of his life. For a rich blessing, I encourage you to meditate on each of these verses.

- Teach me (vv. 12, 26, 33, 64, 66, 68, 108, 124, 135).
- Remove from me (vv. 22, 29).
- Make me (vv. 27, 35, 98).
- Give me (vv. 34, 73, 125, 144, 169).
- Revive me (vv. 25, 37, 40, 88, 107, 149, 154, 156, 159).
- Help me (v. 86).
- Save me (vv. 94, 146).
- Uphold me (vv. 116, 117).
- Redeem me (vv. 134, 154).
- Hear me (vv. 145, 149).
- Deliver me (vv. 153, 170).

This next group of verses from Psalm 119 could be considered as imperatives Ezra called out to God. These short prayers are examples of how he invited the Lord to impact and direct specific areas of his life. As you read each verse, ask the Lord to do whatever He wants to in your life, and prayerfully let the way God worked in Ezra's life become the guide for yours.

- Do not forsake me (v. 8).
- Deal … with me (vv. 17, 124).
- Open my eyes (v. 18).
- Strengthen me (v. 28).
- Not put me to shame (v. 31).
- Incline my heart (v. 36).
- Turn away my (vv. 37, 39).
- Let or not let [me, my or to me] (vv. 10, 41, 76, 77, 79, 80, 116, 169, 170, 173, 175).

- Let [others] (vv. 78, 122, 133)
- Take not (v. 43).
- Remember … to (v. 49).
- Be merciful to me (vv. 58, 132).
- Accept [from me] (v. 108).
- Not leave me (v. 121).
- Be surety (v. 122)—meaning "a basis of confidence or security."
- Deal with [me] (v. 124).
- Direct [my] (v. 133).
- Make your face shine (v. 135).
- Consider (vv. 153, 159).
- Seek Your servant (v. 176).

Remember: God wants to invade every part of your heart, mind, and life. But He can only do so if you will say, "By Your grace, Lord, I purpose to *learn* Your Book, to prepare my heart to *live* Your Book, and to *lead* others in living and learning Your Word." That is exactly what God has put you on earth to do!

What a difference a Word filled life can make! Are not your spouse, children, and family worth the little time it takes to invest in the discipline of the Scriptures to pursue a Word filled life? Is not your Lord and Savior worth *any* price to show Him how much He's worth to you?

My Prayer for You:

Father in Heaven, I thank You for all the models You have provided so we may learn what a Word filled life looks like, and thus how important it is to practice the discipline of the Scriptures. I thank you especially for Jeremiah's life! If he could have joy "eating Your Word" in the midst of dungeons, pillars, stocks, constant danger, adversities, abuse, loneliness—then we can likewise find strength for whatever You arrange in our own path of life. For You are the same God, and Your grace is more than sufficient for us! I praise You for wanting us to know Your presence so we can have fullness of joy, and stay at Your right hand of authority and power forevermore. I pray we will make decisions to that end for the days You have ahead for us. In the name of Jesus I pray. Amen.

5

"He who believes in Me, as the Scripture has said, out of his heart will flow rivers of living water."
—**John 7:38**

Discipline Two—Spirit-Filled Living:
An Overflowing Life

G OD DESIGNED US TO BE walking and talking "rivers of life-giving water."[19] Everywhere we go, each word we speak, all the deeds of our lives, are lived in the shadow of the cross and energized by the Spirit of God, and intended to bring life and light to those still in darkness.

19 MP3 CD Audio DYG-02:030105AM

How is your life example today? Are you refreshed, God-conscious, sin-hating, and self-denying? Are your words and deeds abundantly spilling over with His grace? For that is what the unhindered, unquenched, and ungrieved Spirit of God always does in our lives. This chapter is therefore a plea to discipline yourself to form habits leading to an overflowing and abundant life.

Life can be defined as "a collection of the results of our plans and priorities." Or, actions have consequences, and consequences shape the quality of our lives. We should regularly refresh our thinking with what the Lord God of the Universe desires for each of us: ... *Exercise yourself toward godliness* (1 Timothy 4:7). In other words, you and I are to discipline ourselves by making choices leading to godliness because that is what living a Word filled life is all about.

In this chapter, we will examine the second of "the disciplines of a godly life"—"the discipline of Spirit-filled living." Choosing to practice all seven of these disciplines is at the heart of living a powerful Word filled life.

The Holy Spirit Gives an Overflowing Life

Just as we must choose to discipline ourselves to daily get into the Word of `God, we must choose to discipline ourselves to stay filled with the Holy Spirit. Spirit fullness is a choice. To illustrate this, in dry climates like ours, swimming pools must be refilled regularly because the water evaporates. Many pool owners install a unit to automatically refill the water. Some think Christian life is like the automatic pool filler, but it isn't. When we become dry spiritually, there is no automatic refill by the Holy Spirit. We must choose to obey the command of God in Ephesians 5:18: empty ourselves of self-rule, and ask Him to again overflow our life.

In John 7:37-38, Jesus explained the Holy Spirit's fullness in our lives through the imagery of a strong river of water flowing out of us. In verse 37 Jesus first referred to salvation when He said ... *"If anyone thirsts, let him come to Me and drink."* Then, in verse 38, He spoke of the result of salvation: *"He who believes in Me, as the Scripture has said, out of his heart will flow rivers of living water."*

When first saved, the Holy Spirit flows out of our lives by making us joyous and thankful—excited all our sins are gone. The first time Bonnie and I celebrated communion together as a young married couple at Grace Community Church, I looked at my new bride and saw tears running down her cheeks. I asked, "What's wrong?" She replied, "Nothing's wrong ... I just can't believe the Lord forgave me ..." "But," I said, "why cry about it?" Then I thought: Yes! *The joyous streams of the Holy Spirit cause us to be that thankful because we are forgiven!*

As the Holy Spirit flows out of our lives, He not only causes us to rejoice about being forgiven, but makes Bible reading come alive so it's like God personally meeting and talking with us. When the

Holy Spirit flows out of our lives, prayer also becomes natural and uncluttered. Through the Holy Spirit, our lives fill to overflowing as we talk and walk with the Lord, and each day becomes a brand new beginning!

Our great God wants His mighty *"rivers of living water"*—literally, torrents of cascading, gushing waters—of the Holy Spirit flowing out of our lives. He longs to refresh, make us victorious and filled with delight, and help us serve Him joyfully. That is how He intends normal life to be for all of His children of faith.

While thinking about such a victorious and joyful Christian life, I recalled what it was like, not only when I became saved, but also when our family experienced a great event. Such an event can serve as a good illustration of the Holy Spirit's ministry in us.

Through the love, prayers, and hard work of so many friends, we moved into our first new home in 1995. One of the things which impressed us most was that the water lines were large and very strong. In fact, water poured with a roar and flow reminiscent of Niagara Falls.

Our new large dishwasher and washing machine worked well with the strong water pressure. The dishwasher practically started the instant we closed its door, and the roar of the swishing water was remarkable. The shower was quite an experience as well. With the simple turn of a handle, water gushed out, making us think of the famous geyser, Old Faithful. What a shower! And to have a bathtub as big as our old plastic swimming pool thrilled our little buddies! That tub easily held all three of them in an ocean of warm water—*plus all their toys.*

But enthusiasm over the powerful water pressure gradually dwindled over a couple of weeks. First, Bonnie noticed the washing machine slowing down. Before long, it took all day to do a single load. Then the dishwasher's complete cycle took three to four hours instead of thirty minutes. Next, our wonderful shower wilted until the only way to get wet was stand directly beneath the nozzle, and even then the water flow was pitiful.

What originally began as only a nuisance soon turned into alarm as the toilets, bathtubs, and washers slowed to nearly a stop. We were horrified that our fantastic new home might be ruined, and felt certain the problem was broken plumbing. As Bonnie and I phoned the builder, nightmare scenarios of backhoes and mud and a torn-up lawn flooded our minds. The builder, however, seemed quite undisturbed at our plight. We could even sense he was smiling when he said he knew exactly what was wrong.

Within fifteen minutes the builder arrived, whistling and still smiling. We, however, were wringing our hands while showing him all the non-functioning appliances and fixtures. He just continued to smile. After we'd poured out all our grief and disappointment, he quietly asked us to follow him. Chuckling, he walked to our coat closet (a.k.a. "under the stairs tornado closet" and a.k.a. "the kids hideaway"), and knelt down, asking, "Do you have any little children who play in here?" Without waiting for an answer, he instructed, "Go try the shower now." We ran to test the water flow and joyfully discovered "Niagara Falls" was back! When we returned, the builder's held the small round shutoff valve handle one of our precious little buddies had been slowly turning bit by bit each day until the "rivers of water" into our house had been choked, reduced, and shut out.

This new house story clearly shows the picture of what happens spiritually to many believers. Could you be shutting the Holy Spirit out of His "home" in you?

Are You Grieving the Holy Spirit?

If you are a born-again child of God, do you remember how incredible life was when you were first saved? As a new believer, you probably couldn't get enough of Bible reading, talking with God and fellowshipping with His people. Most likely, you told everyone who would listen that Jesus forgave your sins, and wants to forgive their sins as well. This is exactly how God intends His children to live—with mighty *"rivers of living water"* of the Holy Spirit flowing out of joyful lives.

Why then have so many believers strayed away from their first love, and Christians in today's church experience defeated lives? The answer is simple: when believers fail to discipline themselves toward godliness, a downward spiral results. Almost imperceptibly, interest in spiritual matters begins to wane. The water pipe of the Holy Spirit begins constricting—drop by drop. Scriptures once vibrant with God's voice soon seem strangely silent. Even prayers become lackluster. As spiritual sensitivity withers, the flow of the Holy Spirit is shut off, leaving waterless lives to become dry and barren.

That is what happens when sin closes the water valve of a believer's spiritual life. The Bible describes such a downward spiral as grieving the Holy Spirit. I wonder: Have you lost your first excitement over being saved and are now wondering whether you were even saved at all? Have you gone from overwhelming desire to flee sin and resist temptation to now being so discouraged you can't resist anything? Have you gone from voraciously reading your Bible—marking, underlining, memorizing, and meditating upon the Word—to preferring to sit and fall asleep in front of the television? If you answered yes to any or all of those questions, I recommend you contact your Builder to come by and check your "closet" to find out who or what has turned off your water valve to the Holy Spirit.

Look carefully (and prayerfully) at this passage:

Therefore, putting away lying, "Let each one of you speak truth with his neighbor," for we are members of one another. "Be angry, and do not sin": do not let the sun go down on your wrath, nor give place to the devil. Let him who stole steal no longer, but rather let him labor, working with his hands what is good, that he may have something to give him who has need. Let no corrupt word proceed out of your mouth, but what is good for necessary edification, that it may impart grace to the hearers. And do not grieve the Holy Spirit of God, by whom you were sealed for the day of redemption (Ephesians 4:25-30, emphasis added).

Ephesians 4:25-30 is an imperative, a direct command from God. Your responsibility is to not grieve the Holy Spirit who has sealed you for the day of redemption. What are some grievers? Look again at verses 25-29, and there are more in verse 31: *Let all bitterness, wrath, anger, clamor, and evil speaking be put away from you, with all malice.* In verse 32, Paul provided an insight into how to avoid grieving God's Spirit: … *Be kind to one another, tenderhearted, forgiving one another, even as God in Christ forgave you.*

Since God's Holy Spirit is our lifeline for all we need to make it here on earth, we are to stay filled with the Spirit, which simply means to be "controlled by the Spirit." Ephesians 5:18 tells us to ... *not be drunk with wine, in which is dissipation; but **be filled** [present passive imperative] with the Spirit* ... (emphasis added). We are to constantly look toward being filled, make it our regular endeavor to have the Holy Spirit fill and overflow our lives.

A Short Lesson on the Holy Spirit

To help you better discern whether or not you are disciplining yourself for Spirit fullness, we're going to look at a little theology of the Holy Spirit. This should reveal whether the Holy Spirit is cascading out of your life, or if you have just been standing beneath the "shower head" hoping to get something from God.

The Apostle Paul, that great training coach of the winning lifestyle for believers, had this to say about the Holy Spirit: *... Do you not know that your body is the temple of the Holy Spirit who is in you, whom you have from God, and you are not your own? For you were bought at a price; therefore **glorify** [aorist active imperative] God in your body and in your spirit, which are God's* (1 Corinthians 6:19-20, emphasis added). *Your body, the temple of the Holy Spirit,* is His headquarters, His abode, ministry center, home, and holy place where He comes and abides. Because the Holy Spirit makes His headquarters in you, do everything necessary to keep Him from being grieved.

You must not hinder the Holy Spirit in your life. Rather, actively follow the Lord, disciplining yourself to allow the working of the Holy Spirit in you by reading the Word, praying, and obeying His will: *... **Walk** [present active imperative] in the Spirit, and you shall not fulfill the lust of the flesh. ... If [you] live in the Spirit, ... also walk in the Spirit* (Galatians 5:16, 25, emphasis added).

Rather than couples who power walk and never get near each other, when Bonnie and I go for a walk we stroll hand in hand and talk as we go along. Spiritually speaking, many Christians are like power walkers who stride alone on the race course of life. They are no longer in step with the Holy Spirit; He has been put on the sidelines. Having been constricted to the role of Spectator, He now merely watches as they pass by in all their sportswear finery. But the Christian life is not meant to be lived that way. The Lord wants us to enjoy strolling hand in hand through life with Him, sharing daily heart-to-heart talks. In other words, He wants us to … *Walk* [present active imperative] *in the Spirit* …. *And if we do so, we … shall not fulfill the lust of the flesh* (v. 16). *If we live in the Spirit* [our body is His abiding place], *let us also walk in the Spirit* (v. 25).

We cannot possibly walk in the Spirit, however, unless we carefully guard our relationship with Him. We do that best by obeying His command: … **Do not grieve** [present active imperative] *the Holy Spirit of God* … (Ephesians 4:30, emphasis added). We should be on guard against whatever can harm or hinder His work in us. Close study seems to indicate this involves not just one, but two levels of sin. Grieving (the first sin level) is when we give in to lying, coarse talking, anger, wrath, malice, bitterness—all those things we saw in Ephesians 4. Right on the spot, those sins grieve the Holy Spirit.

Imagine yourself at dinner with a friend and you happen to say something you wish you hadn't. Picture the look of disappointment on your friend's face when his spirit is grieved. You would not leave the table, but sense your fellowship is just not the same. Because the Holy Spirit is a Person, with a personality capable of human emotions, He, too, can feel grieved. If we don't regularly remind ourselves He is a Person (and Friend) who can be grieved, we can eventually quench His Spirit, which is the second level of sin that can harm or hinder His work in us.

Quenching, goes beyond grieving. The long, drawn out grieving of the Holy Spirit is why God commanded: **Do not quench** [present active imperative] *the Spirit* (1 Thessalonians 5:19, emphasis added). An ongoing pattern of sin leads us further away from the vital ministry of the Holy Spirit. And when we quench or douse the Spirit, the fire of His warmth and the power in our lives is extinguished. As Warren Wiersbe has explained:

In using the word quench, Paul pictured the Spirit of God as fire (see Isa. 4:4; Acts 2:3; Rev. 4:5). Fire speaks of purity, power, light, warmth, and (if necessary) destruction. When the Holy Spirit is at work in our lives and churches, we have a warmth of love in our hearts, light for our minds, and energy for our wills. He "melts us together," so there is harmony and cooperation, and purifies us so we put away sin. The fire of the Spirit must not go out on our hearts' altar; we must maintain the devotion to Christ that motivates and energizes our lives."

To keep the "fire of the Spirit" burning in our hearts, remain alert to all the things that quench His work in us, such as the following: (Emphasis added.)

- **We quench the Spirit by saying no to something God directs us to do.** We choose our will over His. The Holy Spirit can do nothing to help and keep us in the center of God's plan and purpose if we willfully turn away from His leading and choose to pursue our desires and goals. He will not help us do something He knows is contrary to God's best for us.

- **We quench the Spirit by ignoring His presence.** Again, this is a matter of the will. We can go about living our lives and refuse to acknowledge, invite, or accept His help.

- **We quench the Spirit by sinning repeatedly.** Our sin causes the Holy Spirit to abandon any positive, forward-moving implementation for our blessing so He might convict us of our sin. When we sin, we evoke the chastisement and chiding of the Holy Spirit in our lives. He cannot reward our unfaithfulness or participate in our rebellion. We stifle His eager desire to produce good fruit in us, for us, and through us.[20]

20 Adapted from Charles Stanley's Relying on the Holy Spirit (Nashville: Thomas Nelson, 1996), electronic edition, in loc.

Byproducts of a Spirit-Grieved Life

What happens when the Holy Spirit has been grieved? There is an immediate impact upon these seven areas in our lives:

1. **Our victoriousness fades:** *The law of the Spirit of life in Christ Jesus has made me free from the law of sin and death* (Romans 8:2). We immediately lose our power to say no to sin. This is like being out of your home area and discovering your cell phone is dead; you have it on, but lack the necessary power to make it work.

2. **Our confidence wanes:** … *We are debtors—not to the flesh, to live according to the flesh … For as many as are led by the Spirit of God, these are sons of God* (Romans 8:12, 14). We have spiritual confidence when we walk in the Holy Spirit, but when we grieve Him the Bible says the unrighteous will run when no one is even chasing them (Proverbs 28:1). If you are afraid to speak up—to share your hope in Christ—you have not listened, not followed, or intentionally and repeatedly sinned and shut off the Holy Spirit's valve. When that happens, it takes away your confidence, victorious life in Christ, and spiritual boldness.

3. **Our assurance wavers:** *The Spirit Himself bears witness with our spirit that we are children of God …* (Romans 8:16). We lose our assurance we are even saved. Was there a time when you felt assured you were walking in Christ, and knew you loved Him, but now don't even feel like you belong to Him anymore? Does it mean you have lost your salvation? No, if you were truly saved, you still are. However, by ignoring the Holy Spirit, sinning against Him, and grieving His Spirit, the valve of His "rivers of living water" has been constricted to the point where you no longer feel it. The assurance of belonging to Him goes away.

4. **Our prayerfulness declines:** … *The Spirit also helps in our weaknesses. For we do not know what we should pray for as we ought, but the Spirit Himself makes intercession for us …* (Romans 8:26). We lose connection to heaven; our calls to the Lord feel as if they are "breaking up"—like bad reception on a cell phone—because the Holy Spirit is the Carrier of our call signals. The reason why people don't like to pray when not full of the Holy Spirit is because they have pushed the antenna down, unscrewed it, and taken it off. There is no way to commune when we grieve the Holy Spirit, the One who compels us to intercede.

5. **Our yieldedness ends:** *I beseech* [parakaleo, or "Paraklete," one of the names of the Holy Spirit] *you therefore, brethren, by the mercies of God, that you present your bodies a living sacrifice, holy, acceptable to God, which is your reasonable service* (Romans 12:1). When we fail to yield to the Holy Spirit, we stop the life of consecration and daily sacrificing for Christ's sake.

6. **Our fruitfulness drops:** ... *The fruit of the Spirit is love, joy, peace, longsuffering, kindness, goodness, faithfulness, gentleness, self-control* ... (Galatians 5:22-23). The Holy Spirit's production of attitude and action fruit through the power of God ceases.

7. **Our joyfulness stops:** ... *You became followers of us and of the Lord, having received the word in much affliction, with joy of the Holy Spirit* ... (1 Thessalonians 1:6). The springs of the joy of the Lord, which is to be your strength (Nehemiah 8:10), dry up!

Grieving the Holy Spirit does not mean He leaves us. We know because Jesus promised: "... *I will pray the Father, and He will give you another Helper, that He may abide with you forever—*" (John 14:16). In the Greek language, the word "another" has two different meanings: "another of a different kind" and "another of the same kind." In this verse it means "another of the same kind," so Jesus was saying, "The Holy Spirit is a Helper just like Me, and He will always abide with you."

How can you avoid quenching the Holy Spirit? As your Sword of the Word, constantly ask Him to help you walk in Him, live through Him, bear fruit by Him, and overcome sin with Him. By God's grace, choose to keep His commandments and lead a disciplined godly life. When you sin, confess the sin immediately and repent by changing your mind and behavior to conform to God's statutes. If you ask the Holy Spirit to lead you on a daily basis, He will keep your footing sure, and give courage to withstand temptation. Remember: God's Holy Spirit is your lifeline for all you need to make it here on earth. The first-century saints understood that incredible truth—and their lives were stained by the Holy Spirit's irresistible beauty!

Unleash the Power of the Holy Spirit Into Your Life

I pray you, like those time-honored, first-century saints, already behold the pure loveliness of the Holy Spirit. If you haven't, I encourage you to walk with God's Spirit through the New Testament to look for Him. What a priceless treasure hunt! To get you started, below is a path you can walk through Romans to discover more of the fullness of what the Holy Spirit wants to be in your life. If you follow this path, you will find Him absolutely amazing.

As you look up each verse, pause and reflect upon the characteristic work Paul identifies as the work of the Spirit. Then open your heart in prayer by inviting Him to witness Christ within you, liberate your heart from a particular sin, transform your mind, and fill you. Although the Holy Spirit longs to do this, you must first ask Him. Remember: the overflowing life in the shadow of the cross can be found in the energy of the Spirit alone.

- He is the witnessing Spirit of God. (Romans 1:3-4)
- He is the liberating Spirit of God. (Romans 8:1-4).
- He is the transforming Spirit of God. (Romans 8:5-8)
- He is the quickening Spirit of God. (Romans 8:9-11)
- He is the guiding Spirit of God. (Romans 8:14)
- He is the encouraging Spirit of God. (Romans 8:15)
- He is the assuring Spirit of God. (Romans 8:16-17)
- He is the hoping Spirit of God. (Romans 8:18-25)
- He is the interceding Spirit of God. (Romans 8:26-30)
- He is the sacrificing Spirit of God. (Romans 12:1-2)
- He is the gladdening Spirit of God. (Romans 14:17; 15:13)
- He is the sanctifying Spirit of God. (Romans 15:16)

I hope this path in Romans inspires you to worship anew this mighty and blessed second Person of the Trinity!

As we close this brief theology of the Holy Spirit, I encourage you to prayerfully examine your life by asking these questions: *Am I engaged in the discipline of Spirit-filled living? Am I living the Christian life God wants for me, and experiencing mighty "rivers of living water" of the Holy Spirit flowing out of my life? Am I truly refreshed? Am I a victorious Christian? Am I full of delight, and serving Him joyfully?* The Holy Spirit wants to flow through your life like the *"rivers of water"* which flowed in our new house. That is the life of a believer as God intended. So discipline yourself for the purpose of staying filled with the precious Holy Spirit!

My Prayer for You:

Father, you have told us Christ's sacrifice on the cross is sufficient to cleanse us even from the grieving and quenching of Your Spirit. For You have told us that if we will agree with You that we have not disciplined ourselves toward godliness, and have slowly allowed the valve of the water of Your Spirit in our lives to get shut off, You will forgive us and cleanse us of all unrighteousness. So help us to discipline ourselves to turn the Holy Spirit's "rivers of living water" back on by repentance and confession, through Your cleansing, and by purposing our hearts to say no to sin and yes to You, oh Savior. Thank you! In the name of Jesus I pray. Amen.

6

You will keep him in perfect peace, whose mind is stayed on You, because he trusts in You.
—Isaiah 26:3

Discipline Three—Meditation:
Finding Quietness in Ultra Busy Times

I F WE CAREFULLY EXAMINE JESUS' life in the Scriptures, we find He was always quiet, composed, and led by the Spirit even when living a super full, ultra busy, demanding life.[21] He perfectly lived the human life—even in the midst of a whirlwind of activity. Consider what daily life was like for Him:

21 MP3 CD Audio DYG-33:031026AM, MP3 CD Audio DYG-34:031102AM

He was constantly eating, walking, talking, and sleeping with twelve men who never seemed to leave Him alone.

Vast crowds and desperate individuals continually sought Him out.

His life was so full of people and ministry He often lacked sufficient time to stop and eat.

He was chided, rebuked, and even scoffed at by His own family.

He was the personal target of Satan who tempted Him, tried to derail Him, and even entered people to drive them to destroy Jesus.

He was attacked by every demon that could be rounded up to scream at Him, thrash around in front of Him, and bother Him.

Civil and religious authorities fiercely hounded Jesus, always plotting to catch Him and take Him off for punishment and execution.

Yet, in spite of all that, how was He?

Peaceful, calm, focused, and confidently following God's will.

What kept His human life so strong? What was His secret to finding quietness in His ultra busy times? He constantly spent time **alone with God**, in solitude, away from everything and everyone else.

Jesus had to be alone with God—Jesus wanted to be alone with God. Thus, He found **times** (no matter what was going on) and **places** (no matter where He was) to be alone with His Father!

Though we can never be sinless like Jesus, we can learn to follow His pattern for a perfect life, in step with God's will—beginning with choosing to … *exercise* [ourselves] *toward godliness* (1 Timothy 4:7). To experience the power of a Word filled live, this is absolutely essential. Remember: through the first step, establishing "the discipline of the Scriptures," God not only shows His perfect path for our lives, but He will also walk with us every step of the way (Psalm 16:11). "The discipline of Spirit-filled living" is then the "valve opener" to let the Holy Spirit's mighty *"rivers of living water"* flow freely through us (John 7:38).

The Holy Spirit is our lifeline to all we will ever need on earth. As the Holy Spirit helps us … *understand the way of* [God's] *precepts, and* … *meditate on* [His] *wonderful works* (Psalm 119:27), we can more and more follow Christ's words in Matthew 4:4: … *"Man shall … live by … every word that proceeds from the mouth of God."* Practicing Matthew 4:4 is the essence of "the discipline of meditation"—the third of "the disciplines of a godly life."

This will be our main focus for the next few chapters as we study three topics: (1) finding quietness in ultra busy times; (2) finding hope in fearful times; and (3) finding comfort in painful times. Understanding how to apply these timely topics to our lives is like a "survival kit" for this ultra fast-paced and highly stressful twenty-first-century. And finding quietness in the midst of busyness and other distractions is probably at the top of most people's "Wish List." So then, let's move on to discover how God can make that "wish" come true!

An Invisible Killer Is on the Loose

What happens to us as Christians when we are first gloriously liberated from sin's shackles? We ... *mount up with wings like eagles* ... (Isaiah 40:31)—and soar in the heavens with our God! But sadly, if we fail to remain alert to the dangers from natural predators, our wings are soon clipped, and we become earthbound again. As a result, our lives are anything but peaceful, quiet, and assured. We worry for our safety, future, jobs, health ... the list can go on and on.

Why does that happen? There is a deadly yet invisible predator—a killer on the loose! It first steals our joy, then our time, later our strength, and finally, even gives a fatal blow to any real purpose in life. What is the name of that invisible killer? OVERLOAD. What weapon is used to administer the fatal blow? STRESS. In his insightful book, *The Overload Syndrome*, Dr. Richard Swenson has a lot to say about this deadly problem.[22]

Prayerfully consider where you might show up on this diagnostic test that detects the critical condition "overload." Do you have any of these symptoms?

- **Activity Overload:** Often manifested by booking our lives weeks into the future, and often, in the desire to be more efficient, book several things into the same time period. But think on this: "Activity overload takes away the pleasure of anticipation and the delight of reminiscence." (See Psalm 46:10.)

- **Change Overload:** "... Nothing defines our age more than the furious and relentless increase in the rate of change," summarizes

[22] This section on "overload" has been adapted from Richard Swenson's The Overload Syndrome (Colorado Springs: NavPress, 1998).

historian Arthur M. Schlesinger, Jr. For thousands of recorded years of history, change came in a slow, controlled, and at an understandable rate, but we now brutally jerk forward at warp speed—whether we like it or not. (See Jeremiah 6:16.)

• **Commitment Overload:** Most of us make more commitments than we have available time. In his great book, *Balancing Life's Demands*, Dr. J. Grant Howard says, "Some people can't say no. They take on too many relationships and too many responsibilities. They enroll in too many courses, hold down too many jobs, volunteer for too many tasks, make too many appointments, serve on too many committees, and have too many friends. They are trying to be all things to all men all at once, all by themselves!" (See Psalm 27:4.)

• **Competition Overload:** This is part of the American dream. To compete is American, and is constantly emphasized in school, business, and athletics. But is it spiritually healthy? In the Sermon on the Mount, Jesus taught a non-aggressive, non-self asserting, non-self promoting lifestyle for His children. (See Matthew 5.)

• **Debt Overload:** From the White House to the bungalow on your street, most of America is awash in red ink, but this is debilitating and unbiblical. (See Romans 13:8.)

• **Decision Overload:** Every day we have more tough decisions to make and less time to do it in. The trivial ones are objectionable just because of how many there are [what flavor, which topping, mint or tartar control, low fat, low sodium, diet or regular ...]. But we also are facing new choices generations past never dreamed of: whether or not to wait to have children; whether to move and change jobs; whether both dad and mom should work outside the home; whether we should put grandma in a home or not. Too many decisions, trivial or not, in too short a time is vintage overload.(See Matthew 6:25-34.)

• **Education Overload:** Each decade the education level of the general populace rises. While agreeing education is important, we must ask the heretical question: how much is enough? (See Ecclesiastes 12:12-14.)

- **Fatigue Overload:** We are a tired society. Even leisure is often exhausting. With our generator indicator flashing "discharge," little wonder our batteries are drained. Our weary, withered state is not God's plan. It's not the fault of activities or friends, but the result of overload. (See Matthew 11:28.)

- **Hurry Overload:** Haste is a modern ailment. It is also fashionably American. Our lives are nonstop, lived at a breathless pace. We walk fast, talk fast, eat fast and then excuse ourselves by saying, 'I must run.' " Alexander Solzhenitsyn accusingly said, "Hastiness and superficiality—these are the psychic diseases of the 20th century." Wait patiently for the Lord! (See Psalms 25:5; 27:14; 37:7, 9, 34; 62:5; 123:2.)

- **Information Overload:** A single edition of The New York Times contains more information than a seventeenth-century Britain would have encountered in a lifetime.

- **Media Overload:** In America, 98 percent of our homes have a television. In fact, the average family in the United States has two TVs, and both are on seven hours a day.

- **Possession Overload**: We have more "things per person" than any other nation in history. Closets are full, storage space used up, and cars can't fit into garages. Having first imprisoned us with debt, possessions take over our houses and occupy our time. It begins to sound like an invasion. Everything I own owns me. Why should I want more? Jesus warned that the care of things will make our hearts grow cold!

Did any of those overload symptoms ring true in your own life? Most of us have either allowed or chosen to engage energies in filling up our lives with activities that take hold of and control our time. As a result, our activities begin to own, possess, and control us. The next time you tell someone how busy you are, you may be confessing even good activities have begun to take over and control your life—which may be fine, unless something or someone else suffers because of it.

Beware of a Shallow Family Life

I am particularly concerned about the "someone else" who may suffer due to our being ultra busy. Awhile back, a dear friend gave me a little article by Doug Morrell on how busy our families have become. Listen to his piercing insights regarding the impact being "too busy" can have on the relationships God has given us:

> *It seems that in a generation equipped with the most timesaving devices in history we have less time for building and maintaining relationships than ever before. Perhaps it's because we've substituted activity for intimacy, busyness for value.*
>
> *Though many people fuss about how busy they are, the simple truth is that each of us chooses to live this way. We enroll ourselves and our children in classes, clubs, and camps, all good things that can consume our schedules and leave no time for the best things—love, joy, peace.*
>
> *Busyness, like heroin, tobacco, or alcohol, is addictive. The "buzz" of a hectic lifestyle is intoxicating and like other addictive substances, reveals deeper underlying problems such as a low self image, the need to feel accepted and valued. We may also find it difficult to have genuine face-to-face relationships for the sheer joy of the relationship apart from some hidden agenda. In other words, we may have working relationships, but they are shallow and unsatisfying. It appears that many in today's generation do not know the blessing of simple fellowship. They have yet to discover the value of simple, unstructured time together. So we become human doings instead of human beings.*[23]

Being ultra busy destroys relationships—even though we tell ourselves, "It's the quality, not the quantity of time that counts." But there is simply no substitute for time spent with those we love. It takes time and sacrifice on our part to maintain: a healthy, growing relationship with our spouse; loving nurture, caring admonishment, and play with our children; and fellowship with friends. Busyness robs us of

---

23 Doug Morrell, Disciples Corner e-mail letter, October 11, 2003.

time to reflect, meditate, and live.

More importantly, busyness also destroys our relationship with God. To have a relationship with Him, we must make time to meditate, worship, listen and talk with Him. For that reason, He tells us: *Be still, and know that I am God …* (Psalm 46:10). Yet, He's so often told, "Sorry, but I have a meeting to attend." When we lose sight of who God is, we start reshaping Him into our image, making Him into something to fit *our* lifestyle.

Why do we repeatedly allow ourselves to be entrapped by an ultra busy lifestyle? Morrell shares this simple observation:

> *Busyness makes us feel important, too. Ask anyone how their jobs are going and they'll immediately say how busy they are. This appears to offer some sense of job security. If we're busy, we must be needed. Similarly, busy family and church lives convince others that we must be important. After all, we reason, people are depending on me. I'm working hard for God.*[24]

Another way we commonly busy ourselves is through distractions. Perhaps Morrell's conclusion may apply to your own life:

> *Sometimes we stay busy because we don't really want to have time to think about how busy we are. We think if we don't talk about all the problems we have, because we don't have time to discuss the problems we have, they'll simply go away. But we have beautiful homes and talented children, so everything must be ok, right?*[25]

Tragically, everything is often not as okay as we may think it is—we just aren't allowing ourselves to take enough time to see reality. Therefore, we keep looking for something else to do, then we don't enjoy it when we find it, because we're thinking about something else. That is *distraction*, and is the grave malady of our twenty-first century culture.

On a Friday evening some time ago, I was with our little buddies at a food-and-games place called Chuck E. Cheese's™. They were very excited and having a blast. For a few moments, I looked at the other parents, many of whom appeared to still be at the office. Their children loved running gleefully from game to game. The parents,

[24] Ibid.

[25] Ibid.

however, held game token cups and looked dazedly off into the distance. One thing seemed clear to me: their minds were not at Chuck E. Cheese's along with their youngsters. That image was riveted in my mind because it is a picture of our distracted culture in general. We hold "tokens to life," and those around us are spending them, but we aren't even paying attention.

Hand-in-hand with distraction is dissatisfaction. Part of the reason so many people in our world are dissatisfied is they are completely distracted by something else they *think* they want to do. We live in a distracted world, among distracted people, with distracted minds, families, and lives. And distraction can only lead to aimlessness, hopelessness, and powerlessness.

For a believer, the only safeguard against ensnarement by an ultra busy and distracted life is to pursue a focused life filled with God's Word. That is the only protection to escape the invisible killer OVERLOAD from stealing our joy, time, strength, and purpose in life.

God wants our lives aimed at His glory as we follow His perfect path—one filled with hope—an endless life of quietness in His power! How can we best do that? Read on!

How to Think Deeply About God in a Shallow World

> *… Exercise yourself toward godliness. … These things command and teach. … Be an example to the believers in word, in conduct, in love, in spirit, in faith, in purity. … Give attention to reading, to exhortation, to doctrine. Do not neglect the gift that is in you ….* **Meditate on these things;** *give yourself entirely to them, that your progress may be evident to all. Take heed to yourself and to the doctrine. Continue in them, for in doing this you will save both yourself and those who hear you (1 Timothy 4:7, 11-16, emphasis added).*

In this passage, Paul instructed Timothy to devote himself entirely to Jesus Christ. He gave him a simple list of items to follow. Timothy was to first discipline himself in godliness, and then he was to teach that truth to others. Paul commanded him to be an example in everything he did, get focused, and to use his gifts. In verse 15, he told Timothy: *Meditate on these things* …. Paul was telling him to think deeply, to *digest* the things he'd just said in verses 7 and 12-14, and then apply them to his life.

In the New Testament world, the word Paul chose in verse 15 for "meditate" carries the idea of "being in something" and "giving yourself totally to" that. Some Bible versions translate the word "meditation" as "take pains with," and meditation can also be described as "the digestive faculty of the mind." Biblical meditation is thinking deeply upon something; the process of digesting what we have been learning through "the discipline of the Scriptures." Just as a napkin draws water to itself, so a believer draws the Word of God into his or her life.

When we meditate we are taking God's Word, examining and turning it over in our minds. That is the only way to have proper spiritual nutrition in an unhealthy world. There is a terrible spiritual condition I call "biblical anorexia," or a lack of hunger for God's Word. Its twin sister, "biblical bulimia," takes in the Word but soon loses it, because it was never digested in the first place. Both are the result of a severe deficiency of biblical meditation.

When we are surrounded by confusing voices, twisted paths, and hurried lives, God has the cure: meditation. Through "the discipline of meditation," He wants to control our thinking, and help us to achieve the maximum possible life on Earth. To do so we need to stay focused on God, in spite of all the lures of busyness and distractions around us. That is what living the Word filled life is all about.

In the midst of a multitude of challenges, let's look at men who modeled how to keep ultra-busyness and distractions from robbing their lives of quietness.

God's Word Filled Team Shared the Same Habit

There is a collection of individuals I like to call "God's Word filled team." They were all ordinary people who lived extraordinary lives. As far as we can see from God's Word, the only unique aspect each shared was the fact they had what I call a "Word filled life."

We will meet four persons from ancient times who had very contemporary problems nearly everyone can relate to completely. After we see what these men had to deal with in their world, amazingly, we will find each shared a simple habit. They all chose to follow the same path through the multitude of handicaps, misfortunes, and successes they experienced in life. One simple habit set each of them apart from the rest of the world. They practiced "the discipline of meditation," which is the strength of character shared by all of God's great warriors.

How did they do it? These men grasped the simple truth that knowing the Lord is a choice, a lifestyle, a habit we can either make or neglect. So they continually pointed their ordinary everyday lives toward God, and never let go of Him. As a result, they each reaped extraordinary results!

Enoch had a Word filled life—
even as a dad.

The Scriptures indicate Enoch's walk with God started after the birth of his son: *After he begot Methuselah,* **Enoch walked with God** *three hundred years, and had sons and daughters. And Enoch walked with God; and he was not, for God took him* (Genesis 5:22, 24, emphasis added). He didn't use his family as an excuse to neglect the Lord, but as a prompt to seek the Lord daily, even while living in a world so wicked God had to drown every person, except the eight in the ark.

How did Enoch find quietness in the midst of his challenging parental and other responsibilities? **Meditation:** Enoch "walked his talk" with God each day by inviting Him into every part of his life. All day long—at every meeting, every stop, every call, and every situation—the Lord Himself was a part of it all.

Enoch was on God's Word filled team because he chose to include the Lord in everything; what the Lord said continually went with him. If you want to be great for the Lord, learn to walk through life with God. Have you ever walked around wearing headphones and listening to something? That is similar to what Enoch did, and it made him a hero on God's team; he continually walked through life with his "spiritual headphones" on—listening to the Lord.

Noah had a Word filled life—
even though he was consumed by his job.

He felt compelled to finish the ark: *Thus Noah did; according to* **all that God commanded him, so he did** (Genesis 6:22, emphasis added). For 120 years, Noah faithfully labored in the wickedest work location of all history! He worked among people whose every imagination was filled with evil; they were demonic, murderous, and immoral.

How did Noah find quietness under such adverse conditions? **Meditation:** Noah *did* whatever the Lord asked, even if it sounded impossible. He remembered what God said, thought about it, and obeyed. That is both simple and powerful; Noah knew what the Lord had told him, and he did something about it.

Noah was on God's Word filled team because he both listened and obeyed. The next time you read God's Word, ask yourself: *What did the Lord just say to me? What does he want me to do, and how can I do it in such a way that I please Him?* You become a person of God by meditating upon His Word as you live life, like Enoch, and then do something to respond obediently to the Lord, like Noah.

Abraham had a Word filled life—
even while experiencing complete turmoil in his personal life.

His whole life was turned topsy-turvy. Abraham had to pack up and move across the continent from one coast to the other, which was no easy matter in those days. He lost his job in the city and took up outdoor work as a cattleman, moved away from his family and raised his brother's son, and gave up a two-story home in the city to live in a goat-hair tent out in the hills of Canaan. Yet, in spite of it all, Abraham still lived a Word filled life.

Look at Genesis 12:7: T*hen the LORD appeared to Abram and said, "To your descendants I will give this land." And there* **he built** [established; constructed] **an altar to the LORD**, *who had appeared to him* (emphasis added). Therein lays the secret to how Abraham maintained a Word filled life. **Meditation:** *Abraham built an altar to the LORD*—a place to meet with God wherever he was.

If you really think about it, Abraham's habit of making altars was profound. He did everything possible to not forget. When God Almighty took the time to reveal something to him, Abraham was bound and determined not to lose whatever God had to say. Abraham invested in special time-consuming efforts to never forget what God had done, what God had promised, and what God expected of him. He went out of his way to raise a vivid marker: he rolled and piled stones into an altar, chose a special animal, and gathered a rope, knife, and wood for a fire; then he bloodied and blackened those rocks with the sacrifice. Abraham heard from God and offered a sacrifice, thereby declaring the Lord was indeed worthy of his time and attention.

By choosing to never let the Lord down, and by remembering everything God said to him, Abraham was on God's Word filled team. Are you that focused? Do you take the time to set up markers at the spots where God has revealed himself to you? Here is a simple place to start:

- Decide you will read God's Word until you hear Him speak.
- Make a note of what He says.
- Jot a word of reminder in the margin of your Bible, and draw an arrow to that verse.
- Bow and offer a sacrifice to the Lord by saying, "I will remember You today!"

Altars marked the big events of Abraham's walk with the Lord. Do you listen and clearly mark God's plans for you as well, making it a habit to remember what the Lord has said? Or do busyness and distractions crowd out His voice? By the power of the Holy Spirit of God living inside of you, I pray you will choose to walk through life with God (like Enoch), seek to obey what you remember He said (like Noah), and set up special markers or altars of remembrance (like Abraham).

Moses had a Word filled life—
even when responsible for 600,000 families.

In that incredible sea of stress, what was the habit of Moses? We find it in Exodus 33:7-11 (emphasis added):

> *Moses took his tent and pitched it … far from the camp, and called it the tabernacle of meeting. …* **Everyone who sought the LORD went out to the tabernacle** *of meeting which was outside the camp. … Whenever Moses went out to the tabernacle, … each man stood at his tent door and watched Moses until he had gone into the tabernacle. … When Moses entered the tabernacle, … the pillar of cloud descended and stood at the door of the tabernacle, and the LORD talked with Moses. All the people saw the pillar of cloud standing at the tabernacle door, and … rose and worshiped, each man in his tent door. So the LORD spoke to Moses face to face, as a man speaks to his friend. And he would return to the camp, but his servant Joshua the son of Nun, a young man, did not depart from the tabernacle.*

Moses had a Word filled life while living away from home and going to a very pagan, secular university in Egypt. He also maintained that life while recovering from manslaughter charges which drove him away from his home for forty years. He cultivated a Word filled life while working from dawn to dusk out in the blazing heat of the desert sun by day, and in the bone-chilling cold of its starlit nights. And, incredibly, Moses never forsook his Word filled life in spite of a forty-year career filled with 600,000 families' opinions, problems, and sins. His Word filled life endured: the defection of his family—wife, brother, and sister; attempted murder plots by his employees and friends; plagues, poisonous snakes, fierce attacks from marauding armies; and no water or food in the desert.

To further feel Moses' pressures, zoom back in your mind to 3,500 years ago in the Sinai Wilderness where 600,000 men and their families encamped over eighty-one square miles. Moving that crew was nothing less than miraculous.

How big was the task? The Israelites had an unbelievable need! For nearly forty years of their wilderness sojourn under Moses' leadership, they wandered through the dry, sun-baked arid wastelands of the Sinai. There were no lush green gardens, no stores and grain elevators to draw from, and feeding three million people would have required 1,300 boxcars of food *each* day—or a train *nine and one-half miles long!* Wow!

How did Moses find quietness in the midst of such overwhelming responsibility? **Meditation:** Moses went out to meet the Lord wherever he was, regardless of what might be going on around and in him. Consider how he prayed: " ... *If I have found grace in Your sight, show me now Your way, that I may know You and that I may find grace in Your sight. And consider that this nation is Your people*" (Exodus 33:13).

Moses was on God's Word filled team because he chose to: "... *Seek the LORD your God, and you will find Him if you seek Him with all your heart and with all your soul*" (Deuteronomy 4:29). Because Moses sought the Lord with all his heart and soul, he found and knew the Lord like no one else. Do you, like Moses, have a regular place for meeting with the Lord?

These ordinary men led such extraordinary lives because they shared the same secret: **meditation.** What a team! And what a lesson for us! All too often, we neglect hearing the voice of the Lord in His Word because we claim our twenty-first century lives are too full and too complex to find the time. Is that truly the case, or have we just failed to adopt God's plans and priorities as our own? Remember: actions have consequences, and consequences shape the quality of our lives. If we pause to examine our own lives in light of that statement, it can be very revealing.

I exhort you, therefore, to ask God to help you honestly answer this question: *Whose plans and priorities am I really pursuing—God's or my own?*

Is the Clock Your God?

In a commentary entitled "World View and the Clock," Prison Fellowship President Mark Earley shared these insights about full and complex lives:

> *In Jonathan Swift's classic book Gulliver's Travels, when Gulliver arrives in Lilliput, the Lilliputians see his pocket watch and conclude that it must be Gulliver's god. After all, Gulliver told them that he never did anything without consulting it first. I often feel like that.*

Is the clock your god? I believe that there is probably no other part of our lives so thoroughly co-opted by a secular worldview as our notion of time. We say time is a gift from God, but most of the time we treat time as a club rather than a gift—something that we chase, and once we catch it, it beats us up. It's a notion of time that is contrary to a Christian worldview. … We need biblical language that reflects the God who grants us life hour by hour, minute by minute.

Time in the global economy is what I call "head-banging time." There are no more days; there is simply productivity—24/7. Time in the global economy never slows down, never rests, and has no rhythm but the relentless beat of commerce.

That is not the biblical idea of time. God has built a rhythm into the world and into human beings. … In the Bible a day doesn't begin with sunrise. It begins with sunset. The day begins when we go to sleep and God works. We wake up and join Him in the work of the day He began while we were sleeping. We don't begin the day, but rather we wake up and step into God's rhythm of grace, a day already in progress.

This idea that day begins when I go to sleep is a vital worldview concept. Life, success, and productivity don't, in the final analysis, depend on us. They depend on God.

And that understanding allows us to rest—to rest in our sleep knowing that God is at work, and to rest on the Sabbath. Because we believe in the providence of God, we can affirm that we have enough time, and we can then receive the day as a gift.

There are at least four applications for this biblical view of time. First, we should honor our bodies by keeping sensible schedules and getting the rest we need. We have enough time to work, rest, love our families and friends, worship, and exercise.

Second, prayer and meditation on God's Word must be built into our schedules. Keeping God and His Word at the forefront of our minds helps us develop the biblical notion of time.

Third, we can say no. Our overscheduled lives are testimony that our notion of time has not been formed by a biblical worldview.

And finally, we can enjoy the freedom of the Sabbath, that foretaste of our eternal rest with God. … So the next time you look at your watch, take a moment to remember who your God is and how He has providentially given you all the time you need.[26]

26 "Worldview and the Clock," Break Point with Charles Colson, July 31, 2003. (Note: This commentary was delivered by Prison Fellowship President Mark Earley.)

God sits day after day ready to speak as long as you will listen. Just pick up the "receiver"—open the cover, turn your eyes onto the pages of God's Word, and hear His voice. Are you seeking Him with *all* your heart—or have you reserved large portions for yourself? Make the choice to clear a special site in your life for the Lord!

How to Find Quietness in an Ultra Busy Life

Jesus also had a full and highly pressured life, with long days and nights that were often short. He was sought out by individuals, hunted by friends, and invaded by crowds. At times, He had hurried or no meals, and collapsed in fatigue to the point of sleeping through a severe storm.

Yet, in the midst of the constant pressures all around, He maintained an aura of constant peace. He lived and breathed the fragrance of a world of heavenly tranquility. To His dying hour He was brave, bold, and confidently aware of God's plan and priorities—and He had made them His own. Finding quietness in an ultra busy life can thus be found in Christ himself.

Here are some basic principles to help you find quietness midst a multitude of stresses in life:

• **SURRENDER:** Be fully dedicated to God—holy, separated from, and distinct from the world.

- **SEEK:** From God's Word, seek out the way He wants you to live, and then practice those principles so your life pleases Him. (See Matthew 4:4.)

- **MEDITATE:** Habitually memorize God's Word to fill your consciousness, allowing it to change your behavior so you are not conformed to world standards, but transformed by a renewed mind. (See Romans 12:1-2.)

- **RENEW:** Faithfully meditate upon God's Word. Think of all of the applications a certain verse or passage could have for you, and then apply that Word to your life. (See Psalm 119:127; 1 Timothy 4:15.)

- **RECHARGE:** Choose to be continuously full of the Holy Spirit's overflowing presence and power. Realize when you choose an action, you also choose its consequences. (God cannot bless disobedience and unfaithfulness.)

- **LISTEN:** Never forget God will most often speak to you in what the Bible describes as a *still, small voice.* (See 1 Kings 19:11-12.) Most of the time, God speaks in a whisper, not a roar, and you must be *still* to hear Him. (See Psalm 46:10.)

- **REST:** As 1 Thessalonians 4:11 says: *Make it your ambition to lead a quiet life …* (NIV). If you are ambitious, your life will probably not be quiet. But the emphasis is on quietness of mind and heart, the inner peace that enables a man to be sufficient through faith in Christ. (See Isaiah 26:3, 12; 32:17; 48:18; Matthew 11:28-30.)

- **WALK AWAY:** Learn when to stop life's fast lane, pull over, and take a break. It is vital to learn to walk away when necessary. (See Mark 1:35-39; Luke 5:16).

Our Shepherd is not in the rat race; He will lead you beside quiet waters and restore your soul. (See Psalm 23:2-3.) So I encourage you to humbly return to a life of quietness and rest in the presence of your Lord Jesus! It begins by saying no to busyness and yes to God, for *"In returning and rest you shall be saved; in quietness and confidence shall be your strength …"* (Isaiah 30:15).

My Prayer for You:
Father, thank You for the discipleship manual Paul wrote to Timothy that commands us to establish "the discipline of meditation" by thinking deeply on Your Word, relating it to our own lives, rather than to other people's lives. May we faithfully meditate—not for biblical fact or trivia and questions—but for the purpose of obediently practicing Christ's words in Matthew 4:4. Oh Lord, again we ask that You help us to get absorbed in Your Scriptures, to think deeply about You, and then powerfully live a Word filled life for Your glory! In the precious name of Jesus I pray. Amen.

7

... Men's hearts [will] fail ... them from fear and the expectation of those things which are coming on the earth, for the powers of heaven will be shaken.
—**Luke 21:26**

Meditation:
Finding Hope in Fearful Times

JESUS TOLD US A DAY is coming when humans expire because they are so afraid of what is happening all around them.[27] (The Greek word for *"expire," aposucho*, literally means "their souls pop out.") This account in Luke 21:26 is part of Christ's promises and predictions of the end of the world. In verse 36, He instructed His saints to *"watch"* and *"pray"* (Luke 21:36), and expects His children to be disciplining themselves for godliness by meditating on His promises rather than the world's ever-growing problems.

Most people are great at meditation. However, meditation becomes anxiety and worry if it focuses on fears, problems, and the unknown. Endlessly mulling over of a fear or problem can grow it to such a size it dominates both mind and emotion. That is the power of meditation—on the *wrong* object.

But the opposite is equally true. With the *right* object—God's Word and His glory—your mind can be harnessed to produce perfect peace, great prosperity, and a Godward-focused life. The choice is

27 MP3 CD Audio DYG-35:031109AM

simply a matter of what we discipline or train our minds to do.

What are you focusing on today—God or the problems of this world? More and more we see the reflection of society's fears in apocalyptic-themed films. From early global disaster movies in the 1980s and 1990s to recent ones like "Day After Tomorrow," fearful themes are watched and thought about by people on this doomed planet. Just reading those titles is enough to scare anyone grounded in the Word of God!

As frightening as the apocalyptic-themed films may be, they are nothing compared to the realities of what Jesus said is coming to this unrepentant world: "... There will be great tribulation, such as has not been since the beginning of the world until this time .... And unless those days were shortened, no flesh would be saved ..." (Matthew 24:21-22).

There truly are fearful times coming. But if you compare our American news with papers of the world's industrialized nations, you can easily see our news lacks much foresight and discernment. Why is that? Other nations' news reporters look at the entire world while we Americans usually focus on ourselves. Unless the news is of a catastrophic nature, like the 2004 Tsunami, major American news sources do not generally report on global events other than the usual happenings in the Middle East. But sticking one's head in the sand when it comes to discerning the global signs of the times will not hold back God's ultimate plan for mankind. All events foretold in His Word will happen exactly as predicted, and precisely on schedule.[28]

Is there any way we can know Christ's second coming is actually close at hand? I believe there is. While studying a series I was preparing ("What's Next for Planet Earth?"), I examined just how much information God left about coming events. As a result, I found J. Barton Payne's series of numbers regarding prophecy to be quite enlightening:

> The Bible has a total of 31,103 verses, 8,352 of which are prophetic. All biblical predictions about the future can be grouped into 737 different predictions. Of the 8,352 verses, 6,312 (or 522 different predictions) have already happened *exactly* as God's Word said they would. About 2,040 verses, with 215 specific predictions from God about the end of the world, are in process of being fulfilled.[29]

---

[28] This chapter has been adapted from "Signs the End of Days Is Near" and "Fear Not! For I Am With You!"—two weeks of daily devotionals from my encouraging book on Revelation entitled: Living Hope for the End of Days. The book is available at www.discoverthebook.org.

[29] J. Barton Payne, Encyclopedia of Biblical Prophecy (Grand Rapids: Baker, 1980), pp. 631-675.

By the timing of the events, those prophecies can be further divided into eighteen chronological categories, five of which are yet to be fulfilled: (1) church prophecies, (2) Second Coming prophecies, (3) millennial prophecies, (4) final judgment prophecies, and (5) New Jerusalem prophecies.

Each prophetic sign Christ and His apostles gave is very specific. But the biblical signs of Christ's return will not be complete until the actual Tribulation, after the Rapture of the church occurs. Each signs, Jesus said, is a trend. These trends are accelerating in our generation; the countdown clock's last seconds before Christ's return are clicking away. The prophetic picture Christ painted grows clearer daily as signs captured by the apostles and prophets between 2,000 and 3,500 years ago are now happening in our lifetime.

In all history, *only* our generation has seen every one of these events start to unfold. Jesus said in Matthew 24, when you see these things happening know the end of days is near. All of the yet-to-be-completed prophecies fit within specific major events. Probably most exciting are the dozens of signs of Christ's second coming, many Jesus described in incredible detail. But here is what I want you to see: Jesus said these signs will not suddenly appear. Rather, becoming a trend that amplifies and strengthens until it's overwhelming, like a woman about to give birth.

Jesus' warning leaves us better prepared to deal with anxieties and fears. Whether from daily activities or apocalyptic events, God prepares us to deal with fear from a Word filled perspective.

Signs of the Times

Jesus has told us Jerusalem will be a focal point globally in the end times. He said, "… *When you see Jerusalem surrounded by armies, then know that its desolation is near. …* **And Jersualem will be trampled by Gentiles** *until the times of the Gentiles are fulfilled*" (Luke 21:20, 24, emphasis added). At the end of Luke 21:24, He was referring to where history is right now. After A.D. 70, Jerusalem ceased to exist as it had previously, so Jews could no longer worship God as before. In fact, Revelation reports there would be an abomination upon the

Temple Mount, and it is there today—the Dome of the Rock!

Jesus spoke of wars and rumors of wars, famines, earthquakes, pestilences (deadly diseases), and changes in climate. He spoke of Israel as a literal place in the last days and of Jerusalem's rise to global prominence. Have you ever considered that Jerusalem has the second or third largest press corps in the world? Jerusalem has less than one million people, so why do they have more reporters there than anywhere, except New York City and Washington D.C.? Because the whole world is fascinated with Israel! Other nations do not like Israel being there, and are afraid because Israel is so disproportionate in its influence and attention.

Now let's look at some of the "signs of the times" Jesus foretold. You may be startled to learn every one of the signs Jesus gave are present today. You and I are in the first generation in history to experience the following signs all at once:

- **The Sign of Global Travel:** Daniel was overwhelmed when he glimpsed the number and speed with which people would move about the planet in the end days. So God told him, *"... Daniel, ... seal the book until the time of the end;* **many shall run to and fro***, and knowledge shall increase"* (Daniel 12:4, emphasis added). The Bible said there would be many involved in travel, and today's transportation industry is one of the largest segments of the global economy. Prior to the industrial revolution, few traveled beyond their community, with foot, horse and boat the only modes of transportation. Yet, in our day, millions travel *"to and fro"* great distances every year.

- **The Sign of a Global Explosion of Knowledge:** God said *"knowledge shall increase"* in the end days (Daniel 12:4). We've recently seen the introduction of a new generation of computer chip. Each generation has basically doubled processing speed and power, but the newest chip—the "Cell"—multiplies everything the computer does by sixty times! God says in the last days men will be ... *lovers of pleasure rather than lovers of God,* ... **always learning** *and never able to come to the knowledge of the truth* (2 Timothy 3:4, 7, emphasis added). We live in a fast-paced world where many frantically search for whatever seems missing in their lives. Yet, nothing satisfies: what is "hot" today is quickly "ho hum" tomorrow!

- **The Sign of Global Weather Gone Wild:** Jesus predicted there would be a time when weather would be so bad that not just a few, but the whole world, would be troubled and fearful as many thousands are killed by the prevalent chaotic weather. Jesus foresaw "… *the sea and the waves roaring*" (Luke 21:25) in the last days, like the 2004 Tsunami and Hurricane Katrina, and likened these trends to birth pangs—"… *the beginning of sorrows*" (Matthew 24:8). The Greek word *odin*, often translated as *"sorrows,"* literally means *"birth pangs."* Paul said the Creation is under the curse of sin but it … will be delivered from the bondage of corruption … (Romans 8:21). While the Creation likewise awaits the coming of the Liberator, Christ the Lord, the universe itself will travail in intensity and frequency as the time of its delivery draws near: *For … the whole creation groans and labors with birth pangs …* (Romans 8:22). Of course chaotic weather has always existed, but there are indicators we are witnessing an unusual surge in strange and devastating weather around the globe.

- **The Sign of Global Telecommunication and Television:** God's Word explicitly specified the whole world would simultaneously be able to see and hear globally: … *Nations will see their dead bodies three-and-a-half days, and … will rejoice over them … because these two prophets tormented those who dwell on the earth* (Revelation 11:9-10). In the Apostle John's day, news traveled at "the speed of horseback." But due to the invention of television and global satellite networks during the twentieth century, news can travel the world at the speed of light.

- **The Sign of Global Evangelism:** Jesus told us before the end of days, the gospel would be preached to all nations. Today, Christ's sacrifice on the cross can be preached anywhere on earth through television, travel, radio, and email. My website alone, (www.discoverthebook.org) has visitors from over a hundred different nations! The Christian gospel is now "… *preached in all the world as a witness to all the nations, and then the end will come*" (Matthew 24:14). Portions of God's Word or the entire Bible have been translated into over 2,300 languages and dialects covering more than 90 percent of the world's population.

- **The Sign of Global Pestilences:** Despite an increase in scientific knowledge, the Bible predicted deadly diseases still being prevalent in the end days: "… *There will be famines, pestilences [deadly diseases], and earthquakes in various places"* (Matthew 24:7). Emerging diseases such as AIDS, Ebola virus, Hantavirus, West Nile, SARS, avian flu, and so forth, underscore this fact. Ironically, only a few decades ago some scientists forecasted that medical advances might soon eradicate deadly diseases.

- **The Sign of Global Tracking and Positioning:** The Bible foretold technology capable of tracking the world's population and commerce: He causes all … *to receive a mark on their right hand or on their foreheads, and that no one may buy or sell except one who has the mark or the name of the beast, or the number of his name* (Revelation 13:16-17). Such sophisticated tracking already exists. For VIP patrons of the Baja Beach Club in Barcelona, Spain, like a scene out of a science-fiction movie, all it takes is a syringe-injected microchip implant for the beautiful men and women of the nightclub scene to get the recognition they've come to expect. Conrad K. Chase, director of the Club, explains, "By simply passing by our reader, the Baja Beach Club will know who you are and what your credit balance is. From the moment of their implantation they will also have free entry and access to the VIP area." [30]

30 "Technology–Club-Goers in Spain Get Implanted Chips for ID, Payment Purposes," April 14, 2004, www.worldnetdaily.com.

- **The Sign of Weapons of Mass Destruction:** The term "weapons of mass destruction" is commonly used these days, but often without the somberness it warrants. God warns that at the end of the world mankind will be capable of destroying all life: "… *There will be great tribulation, such as has not been since the beginning of the world until this time …. And unless those days were shortened, no flesh would be saved …"* (Matthew 24:21-22). When Jesus made this prediction swords and spears comprised the armaments of the day. However, with today's nuclear, biological, and chemical weapons, it is not only possible to wipe out all flesh on Earth, but also plausible.

- **The Sign of the Return of the Wandering Jews to the Promised Land:** Over twenty-six centuries ago, God promised that at the end of the world Jews would again gather together in Israel:

> "... 'Thus says the LORD God: "Surely I will take the children of Israel from among the nations, ... and will ... bring them into their own land; and I will make them one nation ...; they shall no longer be two nations, nor shall they ever be divided into two kingdoms again" ' " (Ezekiel 37:21-22; see also Ezekiel 38:8 and Jeremiah 31:7-10).

Since 1948 the world has witnessed the call of God deep within the hearts of 5.4 million Jews who have done all they could to emigrate to the Promised Land. And more arrive each day!

There Shall Also Be Signs in the Sun

Events like the scientific community's flurry of concern over the solar explosion on Tuesday, October 28, 2003 (reported only in overseas papers) are but another example of troublesome times ahead.

For seven days, scientists around the world were completely focused on space weather. Then, that Tuesday, they sat up, rubbed their eyes, and started to sweat in of anticipation of what might happen. The sun bulged with a buildup of energy, and then they saw the sun explode a cloud of superheated gas equivalent to a million hydrogen bombs! It all happened at once, in a small area, going out from the sun's surface to head across the solar system, and away from the earth.

That explosion was the greatest solar event ever measured, so big scientists didn't have descriptions to explain its magnitude. And they didn't even get to see the fullness of the explosion because, as the sun turned, it just floated off in the opposite direction—almost as if the Lord did not want it to be seen.

Just as Jesus warned, we are starting to witness **"... signs in the sun ...."** (Luke 21:25, emphasis added). And I believe the marked increase in sunspot activity and solar flares is only the beginning of many such horrors. Paal Brekke, Deputy Project Manager of the SOHO spacecraft (the big solar orbiting heliosphere study observatory which looks at the sun), had this to say about solar explosions that occurred October 28, 2003: "I think the last week will go into the history books as one of the most dramatic periods of solar activity we have seen in modern time."³¹ He, an unbeliever, was trying to come to grips with the significance of three additional bursts on top of the two back-to-back monster flares.

Scientists now know there is an eleven-year cycle of events on the sun, such as sunspot activity and solar flares. Since 1755, everything for twenty-one eleven-year cycles has been recorded by solar observatories. The sun has observable patterns; it will have numerous solar flares and then be quiet for a season. At the moment (2007), we are five years into the quiet side, but, according to Mr. Brekke, there are signs the sun is revving up like never before in history.

As these ominous tribulations on the horizon multiply, this will cause a "panic attack" in many healthy humans. For Jesus said we are headed toward such trying days people will "expire" due to fear of things to come: *"... Men's hearts [will be] failing them from fear ... of those things which are coming on the earth, for the powers of the heavens will be shaken"* (Luke 21:26, emphasis added). It is not that some fearful disaster happens, and then people react by becoming afraid. No, they see it coming *toward* them and die at the *thought* of what is going to happen. He is talking about healthy people who see Great Tribulation events coming—and are literally scared to death!

To a science fiction enthusiast, a paraphrase of Luke 21:25-26 might read like news reports in a futuristic series: "The end of the world is upon us! There are troubles with the sun, moon, and stars! On earth there is distress of nations, with mass confusion, and the waves are roaring! All over the planet men and women are dying from fear!" From a Christian perspective, however, look at what Jesus says when all that happens: *"... When these things begin to happen, look up and lift up your heads, because your redemption draws near"* (Luke 21:28).

There are two separate Greek verbs in verse 28. Not only are we to lift our eyes, but also to turn our whole body toward Christ because His coming is near. Every time I hear of a major solar event, catastrophic earthquake or hurricane, or unprecedented tidal wave, I am grieved for those snatched into eternity without knowing Christ. Yet, my heart is also thrilled because our redemption is getting nearer. And in Luke 21:31-33, Jesus says the generation which is alive when these things begin will be the final generation, and will see His coming—if they survive.

---

31 http://www.space.com/scienceastronomy/solarsystem/solar_storm_000713.html

Joshua: How to Conquer Fear

Enoch, Noah, Abraham, and Moses could identify with what it is like to be living in fearful times. These ordinary men led extraordinary lives, and are all members "God's Word filled team." Now let's meet the next team member—Joshua.

Joshua is a wonderful example of how to live the Word filled life in fearful times. In his youth, he began a lifelong habit: … *[Moses'] … servant Joshua the son of Nun … did not depart from the tabernacle* (Exodus 33:11). What was that habit? He loved to spend time at the Tent of Meeting (similar to church and Sunday school), which was the representation of God's presence. Today, you could say Joshua formed a habit of hanging around church and the fellowship of God's saints. He was different than the typical young person, as he did not hang around with the crowd, but preferred his Creator, the Lord God of the Universe. As he matured, the habit of investing time for God to the exclusion of other activities never left him.

When God commissioned Joshua to be the head of His army on earth, He promised: *"Every place that the sole of your foot will tread upon I have given you, as I said to Moses. …. No man shall be able to stand before you all the days of your life; as I was with Moses, so I will be with you. I will not leave you nor forsake you"* (Joshua 1:3, 5, emphasis added).

Because it is natural to be afraid when facing what Joshua was facing, God further encouraged him: ***"Be strong and of good courage,*** *for to this people you shall divide as an inheritance the land which I swore to their fathers to give them. Only be strong and very courageous, that you may … do … all the law which Moses My servant commanded you … that you may prosper wherever you go"* (Joshua 1:6-7, emphasis added).

God not only commanded Joshua to not fear, but He also told him the secret of being successful: *"This Book of the Law shall not depart from your mouth, but you shall **meditate in it day and night**, that you may … do … all that is written in it. For then you will make your way prosperous, and … have good success"* (Joshua 1:8, emphasis added).

The Lord expected Joshua to absorb His words into his mind and his heart, and to be constantly saying or thinking upon them. Joshua never let his ultra busyness, heading to and from battles, to deter him from spending time with the Lord twice daily. Having formed a habit of loving God's presence, he immediately obeyed when the Lord said, "Let My Word be in you so full it overflows!"

In Joshua 1:9 God again reminded him: *"Have I not commanded you? Be strong and of good courage; do not be afraid, nor be dismayed, for the LORD your **God is with you wherever you go**"* (emphasis added). When the Lord God the Son, the Commander of the Hosts of the Lord, came and spoke to Joshua, He called him to lead the nation, and to perform all the conquests ahead.

Think about this monumental task—Joshua led an untrained army of three million into hostile territory and did frontal attacks on established armies, cities, and walled towns! Imagine coming up to a forty-foot-high wall with simply a bow and arrow, and saying, "Alright you guys, you might as well surrender now. We're here to take over your city!" Joshua's army didn't have sophisticated weapons; the Israelites had only arrows, sling shots, and spears.

How did Joshua find comfort in such fearful times? **Meditation:** Joshua continually let God's Word spill over in his heart. God had told him: "I don't want you to be dismayed or afraid. I want you to know that I, the Lord, am with you. Experience My presence and peace in fearful times by meditating on My Word."

Joshua continued his spiritual discipline of meditation to the very end, as seen in his testimony before the Israelites: *"... Choose for yourselves this day whom you will serve .... **But as for me and my house, we will serve the LORD**"* (Joshua 24:15, emphasis added). Do you know why Joshua could make such a majestic statement that we love to hang on our walls? Because, from his youth, he purposed he would always love God and linger in His presence, even to the neglect of the crowd. Thus, no matter what any other family did, Joshua and his family were determined to stay faithful to the Lord.

Whom do you serve? Ask yourself these questions: *Am I lingering in God's presence? Am I writing His Word on my heart so that I don't fear? Am I committed to saying, "As for me and my house, we will serve the Lord"?*

Joshua was a godly leader of both nation and family. The most powerful form of leadership is not the leadership of position: *I am the manager.* It is not the leadership of expertise: *I know more than everybody else*. It is the leadership of character, living a life people want to follow. That is what Joshua had.

What made Enoch, Noah, Abraham, Moses, and Joshua so special? After all, they were just ordinary men. The only unique aspect of their lives was that they shared the same secret of success: meditation. Let's look again at how regular meditation made each man so special:

- **Enoch** was on God's Word filled team because he chose to take the Lord into every part of his life.
- **Noah** was on God's Word filled team because he listened and obeyed.
- **Abraham** was on God's Word filled team because he chose to never let the Lord down by forgetting Him.
- **Moses** was on God's Word filled team because he continually sought the Lord.
- **Joshua** was on God's Word filled team because he continually let the Scriptures overflow in his heart and mind.

Just ordinary men—with extraordinary lives—and what God offered to each of them, He offers to you and me as well!

How to Find Hope in Fearful Times

Just as the Lord repeatedly encouraged Joshua, He will also speak hope to us when we need Him most. His tender "Fear not!" can calm the storm in our hearts regardless of circumstances around us. Consider how He assured these great saints: (Emphasis added in the verses below.)

- **Abraham**: ... *The word of the LORD came to Abram in a vision, saying, "**Do not be afraid,** Abram. I am your shield, your exceedingly great reward"* (Genesis 15:1).
- **Isaac:** ... *The LORD ... said, "I am the God of your father Abraham; **do not fear**, for I am with you ..."* (Genesis 26:24).
- **Jacob:** ... *He said, "I am God, the God of your father;* ***do not fear***

- **Daniel:** ... *"O man greatly beloved, **fear not!** Peace be to you; be strong, yes, be strong! ..."* (Daniel 10:19).
- **Mary:** ... *The angel said to her, "**Do not be afraid**, Mary, for you have found favor with God"* (Luke 1:30). Do you know what the word "favor" is? It is grace. If you are saved, you have been graced with grace, and there is no need to fear.
- **Peter:** ... *Jesus said to Simon, "**Do not be afraid**. From now on you will catch men"* (Luke 5:10).
- **Paul:** *"... '**Do not be afraid**, Paul; you must be brought before Caesar; and indeed God has granted you all those who sail with you' "* (Acts 27:24). That was when he was in the storm.

I love highlighting verses like these in my Bible, so when frightening times come I have an instant source to remember God's promises. The next time you are afraid, or feel defeated, claim by faith the Lord's presence. Isaiah 41:10 is a wonderful promise: *"Fear not, for I am with you; be not dismayed, for I am your God. I will strengthen you, yes, I will help you, I will uphold you with My righteous right hand."* Have you caught the connection that "fear not" always comes with an *"I am with you"*?

Do you recall Hebrews 13:5—*"I will never leave you nor forsake you"*—is from Joshua 1:5? God never changes: *Jesus Christ is the same yesterday, today, and forever* (Hebrews 13:8). God said to Joshua, "I have been with you in the past, and will never leave you. I am right by you, and I want you to experience My presence. Feel My presence and you will not fear." He says the same to us today!

During frightful storms in the night when my little ones have felt insecure, I have comforted them by saying, "Daddy's here!" I remember a precious time when my youngest, Elizabeth, was troubled about something, so I went into her room and said, "I am here, Elizabeth!" I loved when I saw her relax, crawl back in her tiny little bed, and snuggle up to her blanket. Once reassured, she could again rest.

As a child of God, when you, too, are afraid in the frightful storms of your life, you can cry out, *"...Abba, Father!"* (Romans 8:15). Since "Abba" is the equivalent of the English words "Daddy" or "Papa," listen for His comforting voice saying, "Fear not! Daddy's here!" Your heavenly Father offers His own presence and influence to fill you. So, although fearful times are coming, don't get swept up by the prevailing spirit of fear because fear is not from the Lord: ... *God has not given us a spirit of fear, but of power and of love and of a sound mind* (2 Timothy 1:7).

Meditation Is the Secret of Success

Whether it is business, the arts, homemaking, relationships, a military campaign, or whatever, "the discipline of meditation" is God's prescription for success. You need not pay for a seminar to inspire you—just learn to meditate faithfully on the Scriptures. You will always succeed if God is with you, like He was with Joshua, filling your mind and heart with His Word.

The Word filled life is meant to be your anchor when the whole world seems to be falling apart around you. The God of heavens wants you to constantly live in touch with Him, so no matter what happens you can walk in boldness. This is what Paul described in Ephesians 5 as a Spirit-filled life, and in Colossians 3:16 as letting ... *the word of Christ dwell in you richly in all wisdom* ....

Finding hope in fearful times comes from the living and written Word of God. As you read and meditate upon the Scriptures, the Holy Spirit will apply His truths to your heart, filling you with His wonderful peace. Being a Word filled believer will keep you from fearing things like terrorist attacks, ill health, lack of security, and an unknown future. There is only one solution for facing trouble: take God with you. And only one antidote for fearfulness: experience God's overflowing presence as you live out the Word filled life.

Jesus is saying right now: "Do you want to find hope during fearful times, and have serenity of mind and spirit? Choose to live a Word filled life, and experience My presence as never before—for I am your eternal Refuge and Hope!"

Are you listening to His voice? Here's what He promises: ... *The God of hope [will] fill you with all joy and peace in believing, that you may abound in hope by the power of the Holy Spirit* (Romans 15:13)!

My Prayer for You:

Father in Heaven, this is Your message: we are to have a Word filled life in fearful times. We are not to fear terrorists, or terrorism, cancer, stalkers, intruders, the future, a new job, or whatever it is. I pray we would see that Your prescription for not fearing is meditation—a Word filled life. For when we meditate, we know You are with us always to the end. So help us to have a Word filled life even in fearful times. Help us to truly understand and grab hold of that reality! In the name of Jesus I pray. Amen.

8

... He said to me, "My grace is sufficient for you, for My strength is made perfect in weakness." Therefore most gladly I will rather boast in my infirmities, that the power of Christ may rest upon me.

—**2 Corinthians 12:9**

Meditation:
Finding Comfort in Painful Times

W<small>E ALL SHARE THIS TRUTH</small> in common: our Christian lives will sometimes be painful and full of problems.[32] Job said this is unavoidable; Paul said to expect it as part of God's plan; and Jesus said, "Don't fear! Even if I don't take the problem away, I promise to go with you through it!"

God designed pain with specific purposes in mind—for good, and not evil. Pain serves as a warning system. Pain protects our bodies from further damage or reflects past damage. Pain is a constant reminder of our brevity and weaknesses. From birth to death, it is as much a part of life as breathing, eating, and sleeping.

Although a gift from God, pain is a gift no one really wants. To escape painful afflictions, North Americans, who represent only five percent of world population, consume over 50 percent of all manufactured drugs, one-third of which work on the central nervous system. In fact, over thirty thousand tons of aspirin alone are consumed each year by Americans! We are the most advanced society in the

32 MP3 CD Audio DYG-36:031123AM

world in terms of suppressing pain, yet the more we try to shut it out, the more pain seems to surround our lives.

Rather than less pain, we need a better solution for dealing with it. I am persuaded "the discipline of meditation" is the solution to not only be successful in finding quietness in ultra busy times, but also to find hope in fearful times and comfort in painful times. Of all the lessons on living the Word filled life we've studied so far, this chapter may be the most relevant to you.

From the constant challenges that filled the lives of Enoch, Noah, Abraham, Moses, and Joshua, we saw the secret to living a Word filled life—one in which God offers His presence and influence to surround every part of our lives. In this chapter, we will learn from more members of "God's Word filled team"—beginning with Ruth, who found it is possible to live the Word filled life even in painful times. She was an immense spiritual figure in God's Word. If anyone has ever experienced pain, she did.

The Book of Ruth opens during the period of Judges when apostasy, decadence, violence, anarchy, and warfare were the norm. The first five verses of chapter 1 introduce the initial cast of characters who set the stage for the beautiful story of Ruth. As I studied this portion of Scripture, I was fascinated to discover from the *Encyclopaedia Judaica* some explanations of the Hebrew meaning of their names. You see, in Bible times, parents picked out a name that characterized either what they hoped for the child, or what characteristics were seen in the child.

Meet the opening cast of characters in the Book of Ruth:

- **Elimelech** (husband) means "my God is King."
- **Naomi** (wife) means "pleasantness and favor."
- **Mahlon** (son) means "joy or song."
- **Chilion** (son) means "ornament or perfection."
- **Orpah** (Moabite daughter-in-law) means "stiff-necked, double-minded."
- **Ruth** (Moabite daughter-in-law) means "satisfied, fullness."

Background and Setting: When famine struck Bethlehem, Elimelech seemed to depart from the plan and desires of God. He took his wife, Naomi, and their two sons, Mahlon and Chilion, away from Israel and the covenant people of God, and into Moab, the land of Israel's enemies. The Moabites, descendants of Lot, worshiped Chemosh, a god of human sacrifice by burning. The sons seemed to have also stepped out of the revealed will of God in His Word because they married pagan, Gentile Moabite women.

Elimelech, Mahlon, and Chilion all died while living away from the Land of Promise. After ten years of great hardship, Naomi changed her name to Mara, meaning "bitterness". Since all she had ever loved were buried beneath the sod of Moab, Naomi finally looked back at Israel because food had again become available in Bethlehem. As she set off to return home, Naomi instructed her two daughters-in-law to return to their families and find a new life. Orpah departed for her people in Moab, but in one of the most touching moments of the Scriptures, Ruth clung to Naomi and the God of Israel.

Two widely respected references for extra-biblical history on this period provide additional background. The *Encyclopaedia Judaica* and the *Jewish Encyclopedia* record the historical note[33] that Orpah and Ruth were descendants of Eglon, King of Moab. When Orpah left Naomi, and forsook the God of Israel, she embraced the gods of Moab, married, and bore a child through a marriage with a Philistine nobleman. From her descendents came Harafu, mother of four Philistine warrior giants, one of whom became famous—Goliath. It is captivating to think David, Ruth's grandson, met and destroyed Goliath, Orpah's grandson. What a great difference a simple turn in life's path can make!

[33] Quoted from Israel my Glory, Feb/Mar 1993, p. 10.

Ruth Conquered Pain

With this background and setting in mind, let's turn to the first chapter of the Book of Ruth, and how Ruth dealt with a painful life.

Ruth knew the pain of having a stained past.

She was the result of a line of people from an incestuous relationship (Lot and his daughter), a line cursed by God to the tenth generation. To make matters worse, such information was written down and kept in print by God's Word so it was inescapable. Wherever she went, when she introduced herself as Ruth the Moabitess, people instantly knew her past.

Ruth knew the pain of prejudice.

She was an immigrant from a marked ethnic background, her type publicly singled out as unacceptable, and purposefully excluded from being comfortable in Jewish society. Why? God had said the Moabites were not to be welcomed into the assembly for ten generations. She experienced prejudice, which many can identify with in our own society.

Ruth knew the pain of poverty and financial pressures.

She was widowed, homeless, and left to care for her mother-in-law. Ruth felt compelled to enter the job market, but could only find temporary entry-level work at the lowest wage. She had to accept welfare via public assistance, but received just half the funds because she was caring for Naomi. In Israel, fields were harvested in a circular manner so the four corners were left untouched. That was the public welfare system, whereby the poor of the land could go in, cut down those corners, and thresh the remaining wheat. So Ruth had the financial pressures of working at a low-level job plus accepting public assistance.

Through the emotional pain, physical weariness, and stress of unknowns, Ruth shined as a monumental woman of faith, a woman of the Word, a woman who clung to the God of Israel, and knew Him personally. She was one of the godliest of Old Testament women because she lived a life of faith, hope, and love. When Ruth faced her greatest moment of truth—stay in Moab or leave to follow Naomi and her God—she chose the right path. A fateful decision that led to one of the most beautiful and often-quoted passages in Christian wedding vows:

> ... Ruth said: "Entreat me not to leave you, or to turn back from following after you; for wherever you go, I will go; and wherever you lodge, I will lodge; your people shall be my people, **and your God, my God.** Where you die, I will die, and there will I be buried. The LORD do so to me, and more also, if anything but death parts you and me" (Ruth 1:16-17, emphasis added).

Ruth chose to "hang on for dear life" because she had found the Truth. Though only a little portion of the Word was available to her, she met the God of heaven! Family, friends, future, and everything else peeled away, and just one thing remained—the revelation of God. She sought and clung to it!

How did Ruth find comfort in her painful life? **Meditation:** Ruth practiced the Word filled life by clinging to the Lord in good times and bad, never letting go even when life, people, and her days were hard, lonely, empty, and long. Can you see why God made her the great–grandmother of the *man after God's own heart*—David? We can thus say, as the New Testament records, that Jesus is the son of David. And if so, then Jesus is the great-great-grandson of Ruth.

Just think of all the marvelous things God did through Ruth because she clung to Him. He wants to do great things through you as well (Ephesians 2:10).

Hannah Conquered Pain

Many have heard the story of Hannah, but it is fascinating to study her life. Hannah means "gracious" in Hebrew, and truly reflects her character as she lived through one of history's most difficult times.

Hannah faced the pain of a difficult home situation.

Her husband, Elkanna, had two wives: Penninah and Hannah. First Samuel 1:6 tells us Hannah's rival ... *provoked her severely, to make her miserable, because the LORD had closed her womb.* Hannah lived in the same house with Penninah. Every day she had to cook meals, do housework, and try to please her husband while Penninah constantly sought to make her feel wretched. Because they lived far from the tabernacle in Shiloh, and could only go there once a year, Hannah had no real spiritual help available. But she had God, and found He was enough!

Hannah faced the pain of being childless.

Every time she looked at happy mothers enjoying their children, Hannah ached inside because she was missing her greatest joy of life. Penninah cruelly took advantage of this pain. Look at 1 Samuel 1:7: *So it was, year by year, when [Hannah] went up to the house of the LORD, that [Penninah] provoked her; therefore [Hannah] wept and did not eat.*

Hannah faced the pain of limited resources.

She had limited time to do her work, and limited exposure to God's Word. The latter limitation amazes me because of what God did through Hannah. Back then, the holy scrolls of the Word of God were kept in the tabernacle tent. Outside of the priests, the only person we know in the ancient world who had a copy of the Bible was the king. However, it was the time of the Judges, so there was no king. Hannah's only exposure to God's Word was to go annually into the presence of the priests. Thus she had to maximize her time while there.

Hannah chose to live a Word filled life by memorizing and meditating upon God and His Word in the Old Testament—especially seven verses in particular. On her yearly trips, instead of feeling sorry for herself, angry, and embittered because she had no children, a bad husband, and a miserable home life, what she meditated upon spilled over into her prayers. How do I know this? Her prayer in 1 Samuel 2:1-10 is one of the most beautiful in the Bible. In fact, Hannah's meditations were so wonderful Mary quoted from her prayer in the "Magnificat" (Luke 1:46-55)—a joyous song in the Christmas story.

Now let's look at the wonderful portions of Hannah's prayer

that specifically overflow from having meditated upon seven Old Testament verses. (Emphasis added in the verses below.)

> **Verse 1:** … "My heart rejoices in the LORD; my horn is exalted in the LORD. I smile at my enemies, because I rejoice in Your salvation." Though Penninah tried to provoke Hannah and make her life miserable, Hannah said she smiled at enemies. She rejoiced in God's salvation instead of focusing on her trials. You wouldn't believe how powerful it is when facing pain to meditate on your salvation, to know Who you belong to and where you are going!
>
> **Verse 2:** "No one is holy like the LORD, for there is none besides You, nor is there any rock like our God." This part of her prayer was an overflow from having memorized and meditated upon these verses (emphasis added)—
>
> • "Who is like You, O LORD, among the gods? **Who is like You, glorious in holiness**, fearful in praises, doing wonders?" (Exodus 15:11).
> • "To you it was shown, that you might know that the LORD Himself is God; **there is none other besides Him**" (Deuteronomy 4:35).
> • "**He is the Rock,** His work is perfect; for all His ways are justice, a God of truth and without injustice; righteous and upright is He" (Deuteronomy 32:4).
>
> **Verse 6:** "The LORD kills and makes alive; He brings down to the grave and brings up." Also look at Deuteronomy 32:39: " 'Now see that I, even I, am He, and there is no God besides Me; **I kill and I make alive**; I wound and I heal; nor is there any who can deliver from My hand.' " Hannah meditated on that verse and said, "Lord, You are in charge of my life. You can bring me down to the grave, and You can raise me up!"
>
> **Verse 7:** "The LORD makes poor and makes rich; He brings low and lifts up." And in Deuteronomy 8:17: "… Then you say in your heart, 'My power and the might of my hand have gained me this wealth.' "
>
> **Verse 8:** "He raises the poor from the dust and lifts the beggar from the ash heap …." Who is that beggar? Job! God

purposed "… to set them among princes and make them inherit the throne of glory. For the pillars of the earth are the LORD's, and He has set the world upon them." Where did Hannah get that? From these verses (emphasis added):

- "He does not withdraw His eyes from the righteous; but **they are on the throne with kings, for He has seated them forever, and they are exalted**" (Job 36:7).
- "Where were you when I laid the foundations of the earth? Tell Me, if you have understanding. Who determined its measurements? Surely you know! Or who stretched the line upon it? To what were **its foundations fastened?**" (Job 38:4-6).

By immersing herself in God and His Word, this simple woman became the role model, heroine, and mentor of the greatest woman of the Bible—Mary, the mother of Jesus!

Of what relevance are those verses in our twenty-first-century? God wanted to show how a godly woman experienced a pain-filled life and found comfort. She struggled with being childless and had to deal with a misery-causing partner in her home, but her pain did not defeat her. It drove Hannah to grasp what she could during those yearly visits to the tabernacle—to write the verses on her heart.

What an impact Hannah's meditation on even seven verses had! She digested those words for so long they simply spilled out into her prayers. And beyond that, the truth she discovered by her meditation was captured by the Spirit of God and recorded in God's Word. **The lesson:** today's Christians don't need breadth as much as they need depth!

Are you immersing yourself in God's Word? Is God's Word spilling over into your prayers and life?

- Like Ruth, do you know the pain of a stained past?
- Like Ruth, do you know the pain of prejudice?
- Like Ruth, do you know the pain of poverty?
- Like Ruth, do you know the pain of financial pressure?
- Like Hannah, do know the pain of a difficult home situation?
- Like Hannah, do you face the pain of being childless?
- Like Hannah, do you face the pain of limited resources,

limited time, and limited exposure to God's Word?

Through emotional pain, physical weariness, and stress of unknowns—Ruth and Hannah lived lives of faith, hope, and love. They shine as some of the godliest women of God's Word filled team.

More Members of God's Word Filled Team

Elijah lived a Word filled life—
even with all the demands, defeats,
and discouragements that we have.

He was in a full-time, vocational ministry. In fact, James tells us he was subject to the same passions we experience (James 5:17). He knew the power of God so strongly he could make the Jordan River dry up and stand still, but he also knew such great fear he turned and ran from it.

Elijah, who was fearless and able to call down fire from God, also became so discouraged he wanted to die. After standing in front of an entire nation on Mount Carmel, he quit the ministry to hide from people in a cave. Yet, God rescued him from his fears, refreshed his soul from the darkness, met and spoke to him face to face, and even transported him to his heavenly home in a fiery chariot—without Elijah tasting death. What amazing grace!

How did Elijah find comfort to overcome his fears, his depressions, his insufficiencies, and rate such a powerful ministry and prayer life in God's sight? **Meditation:** Elijah listened to the Lord's … still small voice (1 Kings 19:12) and then faithfully followed Him in troubles and triumphs.

- When in the pits of life and all seemed dark, Elijah listened to the Lord and faithfully followed Him.
- When on the mountain tops of life, Elijah listened to the Lord and faithfully followed Him.
- When at the end of life and the Lord said, "I am done with you, and it is time for you to go home," Elijah listened to the Lord and faithfully followed Him.

Elijah had the same passions and problems as us, but formed a habit of listening to God, and never stopped. As we open God's Word, we can likewise form the habit of listening to God, and never stopping. We can hear the voice of Jesus Himself, "My sheep hear My voice, and I know them, and they follow Me" (John 10:27)!

Job lived a Word filled life—
even while suffering excruciating pain.

Job maintained a Word filled life when he was a wealthy businessman, farmer, rancher, influential citizen. Job lived a Word filled life as a faithful husband, busy dad with ten children, and a man with close friends. He preserved his Word filled life even when he suffered immense financial reversal, lost his job, learned his children were killed in a tornado, lost his wife's companionship and affection, and even became an shut-in invalid with open sores that smelled sickeningly of death. And, in an effort to pin down the cause of Job's painful condition, his three false-comforting friends attached an accusation of sin upon him!

How did Job find comfort in his agonizingly painful times? Meditation: Job chose to focus on trusting God—even unto death, if the Lord willed: "Though He slay me, yet will I trust Him ..." (Job 13:15). How did God view Job's life testimony? Look at Job 1:8: ... The LORD said to Satan, "Have you considered My servant Job, that there is none like him on the earth, a blameless and upright man, one who fears God and shuns [turns away; puts aside; departs from] evil?" Job knew what God wanted and did it; he knew what God hated and avoided it.

Job summarized his whole attitude in painful times: "... [God] knows the way that I take; when He has tested me, I shall come forth as gold" (Job 23:10). Are you filling your mind and heart with the Scriptures, and doing whatever God asks?

David lived a Word filled life—
even when experiencing a multitude of painful trials.

David is probably the easiest person for us to relate to in God's Word. He experienced nearly every emotional pain you and I could ever feel:

- David knew the pain of a lost child.
- David knew the pain of a murdered son.
- David knew the pain of a wayward son.
- David knew the pain of a raped daughter.
- David knew the pain of a traitorous family member.
- David knew the pain of an unfaithful wife.
- David knew the pain of a hateful father-in-law.
- David knew the pain of a bitter employee.
- David knew the pain of jealous brothers.
- David knew the pain of disqualification from spiritual ministry ... and countless others.

How did David find comfort in these painful times? **Meditation:** David longingly and continually sought the Lord. His worshipful prayer in Psalm 63:1-2 reveals a beautiful spirit: *O God, You are my God; early will I seek [to seek early, earnestly, or diligently] You; my soul thirsts for You; my flesh longs for You in a dry and thirsty land where there is no water. So I have looked for You in the sanctuary, to see Your power and Your glory* (emphasis added). The word longs means "to long for, faint, faint with longing; the word seems to mean 'has gone blind,' or 'gone dark.' How vivid Hebrew poetry is! Then seek is a most revealing verb, basically meaning to long for the first light of the dawn."[34]

David didn't only know pain, but also experienced nearly every imaginable emotional joy:

34 Psalm 63 notes by George F. Knight, Daily Study Bible: Psalms, Volume I (Louisville: Westminster John Knox Press, 2001, © 1984).

- David knew the joy of falling in love and marrying a woman he deeply admired.
- David knew the joy of having children that were bright and gifted.
- David knew the joy of excelling in his career as a songwriter and worship leader.
- David knew the joy of earning an immense amount of money.
- David knew the joy of giving sacrificially to the Lord.
- David knew the joy of earning the deep respect, admiration, and undivided loyalty of his friends and co-workers.

Among the greatest individuals of ancient history, David was the most well-known songwriter of all time. He wrote words to more songs in more languages than anyone else. His poetry is the most widely known of any poet in history. His public and personal life is a matter of public record, more so than nearly anyone from the public sector. His royal line is the longest surviving lineage of any nation ever to exist on Earth, and he is the only person God promised would have a family to actually survive the Tribulation and be enthroned as the earthly ruler of the nation of Israel in the Millennium.

From youth to old age, David's life was captured in wonderful psalms that still bless others to this day. As a shepherd boy, he chose to follow the Lord as his own personal Shepherd (Psalm 23). As a man of strength and accomplishment, he gave all his trophies to the Lord (1 Samuel 21:9). When he reached old age, he gave entire credit to the Lord for any good accomplishments in his life (Psalm 18).

Do you, like David, longingly and continually seek the Lord? Do you focus your thoughts on Him rather than the circumstances of your pain and suffering? If so, you will find true comfort because His *"... strength is made perfect in weakness." You will find ... when [you are] weak, then [you are] strong* (2 Corinthians 12:9, 10). This is a lesson we all need to remember: our great God of All Comfort has an ultimate loving purpose for our suffering: He *... comforts us in all our tribulation that we may be able to comfort those who are in any trouble, with the comfort with which we ourselves are comforted by God* (2 Corinthians 1:4). *God never lets you down because He does "... all things well ..."* (Mark 7:37)!

Daniel lived a Word filled life—
even in the bright spotlight of negative public scrutiny.

He was a career politician; everywhere he went, everyone he met, and everything he said could be—and was—used against him. For over sixty-six recorded years, he lived in this "glass house," and ended with one of the most profoundly influential lives ever recorded in the Bible.

How did Daniel find comfort in spite of all the continual scrutiny and ill will? **Meditation:** Daniel had made it a habit from his youth to get alone with the Lord three times a day (Daniel 6:10). While still in his teens ... *Daniel purposed* [to put in place, set, appoint, make; to direct toward] *in his heart that he would not defile himself* ... (Daniel 1:8).

So many qualities flowed from the choice Daniel made as a teenager to point his heart toward God. He started a habit of seeking the Lord by regularly thinking about Him and His Word. This led to an amazing prayer life in all the flurry of the height of his career. Daniel, one of the busiest Old Testament administrators, devoted himself to a lifelong study of the Bible. To the very end of his life, Daniel was faithful to his purpose, always pointing his life toward the Lord!

So what is the secret shared by all of God's great warriors? Meditation! Have you committed yourself to joining God's Word filled team?

My Prayer for You:
Dear Father, thank You for offering a Word filled life, even as we go through pain-filled times. As we let Your Word fill our lives, we pray You will give us strength to go through pain as more than conquerors through Christ, who loves us! Right now, this very minute, we turn all our pains over to You, the God of All Comfort, knowing when You have tried us, like Your servant Job said, we will come forth as gold! In Jesus' precious name I pray. Amen.

9

> … You were bought at a price; therefore glorify God in your body and in your spirit, which are God's.
> —**1 Corinthians 6:20**

Discipline Four—Stewardship:
Living Totally for Jesus

J ESUS CALLS MEN AND WOMEN, boys and girls, to pledge to follow Him at all costs—never turning back—always seeking Him more than anything or anyone else![35]

35 MP3 CD Audio DYG-36:031123AM

As recorded in Acts, the early church met regularly to renew such a pledge. Called "the Lord's Supper," this act of dedication was a sacramentum, or oath of loyalty like that made by the Roman soldiers of Caesar's Legions—the most powerful institution in the first century. Spread across the ancient world, these soldiers were the Emperor's personal representatives. They were seen daily in Israel, and in all the New Testament cities. Bound together with a life or death allegiance, these soldiers were invincible.

When a man entered the Roman Legion, his pledge of allegiance was a declaration of loyalty above which nothing could be more far reaching. From start to finish, by affirming his personal commitment to the general, that oath became a solemn promise of absolute and even sacrificial fidelity. When the early Christians gathered together to celebrate the Lord's Table, they faithfully pledged loyalty to Jesus Christ—the King of Kings and Lord of Lords.

A Roman soldier vowed: I will always obey the commands of my general.

Jesus commanded: *When He had called the people to Himself, with His disciples also, He said to them, "Whoever desires to come after Me, let him deny himself, and take up his cross, and follow Me. For whoever desires to save his life will lose it, but whoever loses his life for My sake and the gospel's will save it. For what will it profit a man if he gains the whole world, and loses his own soul? Or what will a man give in exchange for his soul?" (Mark 8:34-37).*

A Roman soldier vowed: I will always serve my general to the best of my ability.

Jesus commanded: *I beseech you therefore, brethren, by the mercies of God, that you present your bodies a living sacrifice, holy, acceptable to God, which is your reasonable service. And do not be conformed to this world, but be transformed by the renewing of your mind, that you may prove what is that good and acceptable and perfect will of God (Romans 12:1-2).*

A Roman soldier vowed: I will always follow the written words of the Counsel (Roman Imperial Warfare Guide).

Jesus expected: *... Jesus said to those Jews who believed Him, "If you abide in My word, you are My disciples indeed" (John 8:31).*

A Roman soldier vowed: I will never leave the gathered regiment and flee from any battle.

Jesus commanded: *"My sheep hear My voice, and I know them, and they follow Me. And I give them eternal life, and they shall never perish; neither shall anyone snatch them out of My hand. My Father, who has given them to Me, is greater than all; and no one is able to snatch them out of My Father's hand. ... They went* *out from us, but they were not of us; for if they were of us, they would have continued with us; but they went out that they might be made manifest, that none of them were of us (John 10:27-29; 1 John 2:19).*

A Roman soldier vowed: I will always hold the Emperor's well-being as most important—dearer than myself or even my children.

Jesus commanded: *"... Seek first the kingdom of God and His righteousness, and all these things shall be added to you." ... I have been crucified with Christ; it is no longer I who live, but Christ lives in me; and the life which I now live in the flesh I live by faith in the Son of God, who loved me and gave Himself for me (Matthew 6:33; Galatians 2:20).*

"He who loves father or mother more than Me is not worthy of Me. And he who loves son or daughter more than Me is not worthy of Me. And he who does not take his cross and follow after Me is not worthy of Me. He who finds his life will lose it, and he who loses his life for My sake will find it" (Matthew 10:37-39).

Every time first-century Christians celebrated the Lord's Supper together, it was a fresh renewal of supreme loyalty to their Master, Lord, and King as they offered their pledge of absolute allegiance to the Lamb of God!

Have you given your pledge of allegiance to the Lamb of God? Have you committed to disciplining yourself for godliness to please Him? How can you best do that? Read on!

The Stewardship of Life

In an inspired letter to Timothy, the young pastor of the church at Ephesus, Paul instructed his son in the faith: ... *Exercise yourself toward godliness* (1 Timothy 4:7). *We see this same attitude expressed by Ezra in Psalm 119:2: Blessed are those who keep His testimonies, who **seek Him with the whole heart!*** (emphasis added). When we first seek the Lord "with the whole heart" as we practice "the disciplines of a godly life" the result is great blessings as the Holy Spirit empowers us to live a Word filled life.

Through "the discipline of Spirit-filled living," letting the Holy Spirit's mighty *"rivers of living water"* flow freely through us, God will call us to consecration. As we practice "the discipline of meditation," the Holy Spirit enables us more and more to follow Matthew 4:4.

What a wonderful growth process in the Lord! A process the Holy Spirit will use to prompt us to give our whole hearts to Him. Living totally for Jesus is what the fourth discipline—"the discipline of stewardship"—is about, which is what we'll study in chapters 9-11. Exercising godly stewardship involves total dedication—pouring ourselves out in loving, glad devotion by how we live and give for Jesus.

This excerpt from a letter forwarded to Billy Graham is a remarkable example of having such total dedication:

> There is one thing, which I am in dead earnest about .... It is my life, my business, my religion, my hobby, my sweetheart, my wife, my mistress, and my bread and meat. I work at it in the daytime and dream of it at night. Its hold on me grows, not lessens, as time goes on; therefore, I cannot carry on a friendship, a love affair, or even a conversation without relating it to this force which both drives and guides my life. I evaluate people, looks, ideas, and actions according to how they affect the ... cause, and by their attitude toward it. I've already been in jail because of my ideals, and if necessary, I'm ready to go before a firing squad.[36]

How does your dedication and devotion to God measure up to this young man's loyalty? Would it surprise you to discover the author was a communist—and the letter written to his fiancée to break off their engagement because there was no room in his life for anything other than the communist cause?

Communism triumphed largely because of its followers' complete devotion to one man: Vladimir Ilyich Lenin (1870-1924). In 1903, having put the teachings of Marx, Engles, and others into a political system, Lenin began training seventeen people in this philosophy and ideology—and set out to conquer the world. Sixty-two short

---

36 http://www.plymouth-brethren.org

years later (1917 to 1979), two-thirds of the world was under the domination in one form or another of Communism. Billions of people were under communist control, and the leaders brutally held on to their power.[37] If communists can be so dedicated to their cause, how much more should Christians pour themselves out in loving, glad devotion to their glorious Lord!

[37] Adapted from William MacDonald's True Discipleship (Kansas City, KS: Walterick Publishers, 1975), p. 33.

Learn Godly Stewardship

While the Apostle Paul lived and ministered in the city of Corinth, commercial hub of the ancient world, he was planting a church. During the time he taught there, he wrote a letter to a church in the city of Rome. The letter was called The Epistle of Paul to the Romans. This is a portion of what he preached in Corinth as he wrote to the Romans:

> … *We make known to you the grace of God bestowed on the churches of Macedonia: that in a great trial of affliction the abundance of their joy and their deep poverty abounded in the riches of their liberality. For I bear witness that according to their ability, yes, and beyond their ability, they were freely willing, imploring us with much urgency that we would receive the gift and the fellowship of the ministering to the saints. And not only as we had hoped, but they first gave themselves to the Lord, and then to us by the will of God (2 Corinthians 8:1-5, emphasis added).*

After giving themselves first to the Lord, as the Holy Spirit worked through them, these impoverished saints gave far more financially than Paul had ever hoped. As a result, they experienced great joy in spite of their deep poverty. We find the 2 Corinthians 8:5 context in Romans 12:1-2 as well.

"By the mercies of God" was how Paul summarized the heavy doctrine of the first eleven chapters of Romans where God intervened via the cross in a world sin-sick, fallen, and totally immersed in willful pride. On that basis, Paul said, "This is what I want you to do: give yourself wholly to God as a spiritual living sacrifice. Do so, and you

will no longer be conformed to the world's way of thinking because your mind will be continually renewed through God and His Word."

Stewardship is about life itself. Time and life are far greater treasures than money and possessions. First and foremost, God wants you. Look at 2 Corinthians 5:15: [Because] ... *He died for all ... those who live should live no longer for themselves, but for Him who died for them and rose again.* I think that verse is Paul's personal testimony as he explains life, and sums up how he got saved. It is important to be able to, in a brief way, explain how you know you are saved—how you know you have been born again and have eternal life.

What is salvation? Sin is such a powerful force in this universe that the only remedy was for God Himself to give His life—God the Son dying in the place of the sinner. That's how powerful sin is! Only God could break the power of sin. Through Jesus Christ's sacrifice on the cross, you receive the free gift of His substitution atonement. He died in your place, taking your sin upon Him. That is how you know if you are saved—if you have trusted Jesus died in your place, and received forgiveness from Him.

A godly steward understands this truth: your life was purchased by the Lord Jesus Christ. Because He did everything for you, the one thing you should do for Him is to lovingly give yourself back. What an overwhelming concept—that you and I should no longer live for ourselves—but for HIM!

Bought at a Price

We are to acknowledge God owns us. He purchased us when He saved us, and everything we have now belongs to Him. When he bought us, part of God's work is a growing awareness of His ownership. Just as God gives all things we need in Christ, so we give all we are back to Him. What does such total commitment to the Lord produce?

Godly stewards have an unrivaled love for their Master:
"*He who loves father or mother more than Me is not worthy of Me.*

And he who loves son or daughter more than Me is not worthy of Me" (Matthew 10:37).

The way Randy Alcorn describes this truth in The Treasure Principle reminds me of the heart behind that young communist's letter expressing total dedication and devotion to his cause:

> God wants your heart. He isn't looking just for "donors" for His kingdom, those who stand outside the cause and dispassionately consider acts of philanthropy. He's looking for disciples immersed in the causes they give to. He wants people so filled with a vision for eternity that they wouldn't dream of not investing their money, time, and prayers where they will matter most. Of course, giving isn't the only good thing we can do with money. We need to feed, clothe, house, and transport our families. But when the basics are taken care of, why shouldn't the rest go toward treasures in heaven?[38]

[38] Randy Alcorn, The Treasure Principle (Sisters, OR: Multnomah Publishers, 2001), p.43.

Godly stewards acknowledge their Master's right of disposal:
… *"If you want to be perfect, go, sell what you have and give to the poor, and you will have treasure in heaven; and come, follow Me"* (Matthew 19:21).

God is the Owner; we are only employees. Christ therefore asks that He be cherished above all treasures on earth, regardless of the form they take. These great saints of the past understood this vital principle:

- **Martin Luther**—"I have held many things in my hands and I have lost them all. But whatever I have placed in God's hands, that I still possess."
- **John Wesley**—"I value all things only by the price they shall gain in eternity."
- **David Livingstone**—"I place no value on anything I possess except in relation to the kingdom of God."
- **J. H. jowett**—"The true measure of our wealth is how much we would be worth if we lost all our money."

Godly stewards resist the temptation to cheat their Master:
> "... God said to him, 'You fool! This very night your life will be demanded from you. Then who will get what you have prepared for yourself?' This is how it will be with anyone who stores up things for himself but is not rich toward God"
> (Luke 12:20-21 NIV).

Jesus was teaching that some people hold on to their money and possessions with clenched fists and end up losing them. Exercising godly stewardship means we resist Satan's strategy. Since money is an essential of the work of the kingdom, it is not surprising God's great adversary does all in his power to prevent it from finding its way into the Lord's treasury. Satan has thus deceived many of God's children through schemes like these:

- **Satan tricks us into spending.** He encourages spending more than one can afford, using credit, so little is left over to give to God.
- **Satan tricks us into upgrading.** He plays on competitive instincts and incites us to constantly upgrade our standard of living so income increases are already committed. When John Wesley earned thirty British pounds a year, he lived on twenty-six and gave the rest to God. When his salary was raised to sixty British pounds, he still lived on twenty-six and gave the rest to God.
- **Satan tricks us into waiting.** He dries up the fountains of the heart's generosity by suggesting giving be postponed to a future time.

Stifling a generous impulse today makes it easier to do the same tomorrow.

- **Satan tricks us into leveraging.** He arranges things so the assets of the generous man become frozen or overcommitted and cannot be given as he genuinely wishes. Expanding business too rapidly often demands reinvestment on a scale that leaves little for giving.
- **Satan tricks us into keeping it too long.** We live in an age of great uncertainty. Many elderly fear savings will be exhausted before they expire. Others want to pass wealth on to children.

This causes some to be guilty of undue stacking. We need to give all we can in our lifetime, and have the joy of seeing our money work for God. God promises a reward for "deeds done in the body," not out of it. To be generous with God from right motives brings its reward here as well as hereafter.

Godly stewards obey their Master and give:
"Sell your possessions and give to the poor. Provide purses for yourselves that will not wear out, a treasure in heaven that will not be exhausted, where no thief comes near and no moth destroys. For where your treasure is, there your heart will be also"
(Luke 12:33-34 NIV).

To be giving and sacrificing is to be Christlike and blessed. Get Christ's heart for this world, be moved with compassion, and ask for the grace of giving. You will be surprised to see the Lord work wonders through whatever size of treasures you give Him!

Godly stewards unreservedly surrender to their Master:
"… Whoever of you does not forsake all that he has cannot be My disciple" (Luke 14:33).

Francis Ridley Havergal's (1836-1879) timeless hymn, "Take My Life, and Let It Be Consecrated," reflects godly stewardship. We often sing her lines without due seriousness of commitment: "Take my silver and my gold, Not a mite would I withhold." This hymn was autobiographical. This is her personal written testimony:

> "Take my silver and my gold" now means shipping off all my ornaments—including a jewel cabinet which is really fit for a countess—to the Church Missionary Society. … I don't think I need to tell you I never packed a box with such pleasure.[39]

39 Kenneth W. Osbeck, 101 Hymn Stories (Grand Rapids: Kregel Publications, 1997), electronic edition, in loc.

Godly stewards confess that all they have came from their Master:
… Who makes you differ from another? And what do you have that you did not receive? Now if you did indeed receive it, why do you boast as if you had not received it? (1 Corinthians 4:7).

The Lord created and gifted each of us uniquely. Babies do not hold anything in their hands at birth; they don't have title deeds, cars, or degrees. Everything in life is received from the Lord: *Every good gift and every perfect gift is from above, and comes down from the Father of lights ...* (James 1:17). God is saying to us, "Since you have received everything from Me—your breath, looks, talents, spiritual giftedness, and eternal life—why do you act like it is yours? Why do you show it off and glory in it?" This is such a humbling verse!

When Daniel confronted Belshazzar, the king of Babylon, he reminded him of his father Nebuchadnezzar's fate that because "... *his heart was lifted up, and his spirit was hardened in pride, he was deposed from his kingly throne, and they took his glory from him*" (Daniel 5:20). Then Daniel rebuked King Belshazzar for not humbling his heart, though he knew all about his father: "... You have lifted yourself up against the Lord of heaven. ... *And you have praised the gods of silver and gold, bronze and iron, wood and stone ...; and the God who holds your breath in His hand and owns all your ways, you have not glorified*" (Daniel 5:23).

Did you catch that God is the One who "holds your breath," your heartbeat? He can stop it in an instant, if He wishes! To be a godly steward, we need to confess all we have came from our Master, as 1 Corinthians 4:7 tells us.

Godly stewards seek to grow as givers:
> ... *May He who supplies seed to the sower, and bread for food, supply and multiply the seed you have sown and increase the fruits of your righteousness, while you are enriched in everything for all liberality, which causes thanksgiving through us to God*
> (2 Corinthians 9:10-11).

Paul was talking to saints living in a time similar as ours. The twenty-first century hold the wealthiest and most consumptive societies in history. What does God require of us who have so much? If you watch prosperity television shows, you may hear a preacher say, "God gives you wealth so you can be rich. If you give $5 to the church, God will give you $500 in return!" But that isn't how verse 10 ends. Paul doesn't say "so we might live in wealth, showing the world how much God blesses those who love Him." Paul finishes by saying this:

"You will be made rich in every way so that you can be generous on every occasion."⁴⁰ That's why God makes us rich, why He says everything comes from Him—because He wants us to grow in our giving as generous people.

40 Alcorn, pp. 72-73.

Philippians 4 contains some of the most quoted verses in the New Testament, so I want to show you what is between them. It reminds me of when my children have a sandwich; sometimes they take off the top bread and just eat what is in the middle. That is what happens with a lot of people's lives, only in Philippians 4 they eat the bread and leave the middle. Look at Philippians 4:13-20 (emphasis added):

> *I can do all things through Christ who strengthens me.* Nevertheless you have done well that you shared in my distress. Now you Philippians know also that … when I departed from Macedonia, no church shared with me [finances] concerning giving and receiving but you only. For … you sent aid once and again for my necessities. Not that I seek the gift, but I seek the fruit that abounds to your account [the more you give, the more God is blessing you with spiritual riches]. Indeed I have all and abound. I am full, having received … the things sent from you, a sweet-smelling aroma, an acceptable sacrifice, well pleasing to God. *And my God shall supply all your need according to His riches in glory by Christ Jesus. Now to our God and Father be glory forever and ever. Amen.*

These saints gave so much it caused them to be in need. Did you grasp what Paul was saying in verse 19? He was telling the Philippians, "God shall supply all your need because of your generosity. You don't need to send anymore because you are not supposed to be giving so much—but it is truly wonderful you did so."

We know all about that, but in our century we think God is making us rich as a testimony to the world of how great God is blessing us. In reality, God blesses us so we will grow as givers, and be generous. We should be the most caring, sensitive, giving, most sacrificial, and abundantly willing to respond to needy people in the world. We are to lovingly transfer the title of all we have back to God, the rightful Owner, and say to Him, "Lord, the more You bless me, the more I want to be generous and give to your kingdom. As Philippians 4:18 says, I want to be … *a sweet-smelling aroma, an acceptable sacrifice, well pleasing to God ...."*

Godly stewards choose to point their lives toward heaven:
For our citizenship is in heaven, from which we also eagerly wait for the Savior, the Lord Jesus Christ ... (Philippians 3:20).

In Hebrews 11 we learn: *These all died in faith, not having received the promises, but having seen them afar off were assured of them, embraced them and confessed that they were strangers and pilgrims on the earth. ... But now they desire a better, that is, a heavenly country. Therefore God is not ashamed to be called their God, for He has prepared a city for them* (Hebrews 11:13, 16). The greatest deterrent to giving all we are and have to the Lord is probably this: the illusion earth is our home.

The Lord wants us to realize that earth is a passing stop in our pilgrimage. Giving our moments and days back to the Lord means we finally understand. Nothing on this planet lasts, it all will pass away. At the end of each person's life is a landfill, a junkyard—the final resting place for the things in our lives. Sooner or later, everything we won ends up here. Christmas and birthday presents. Cars, boats, and hot tubs. Clothes, stereos, and barbecues. The treasures that children quarreled about, friendships were lost over, honesty was sacrificed for, and marriages broke up over—all end up here.[41]

Godly stewards invest their hearts in heaven:
This hope we have as an anchor of the soul, both sure and steadfast, ... where the forerunner has entered for us, even Jesus, having become High Priest forever according to the order of Melchizedek (Hebrews 6:19).

Moses left Egypt's treasures because he looked [ahead] to the reward (see Hebrews 11:24-26). That is what God honors, is the life of faith, and pleases the Lord.

---

[41] Alcorn, p. 47.

Are You Ready for the Inevitable?

Not only are we to live for Christ, but we should prepare ourselves for the inevitable—our home-going celebration—death. This truth really struck home on a trip with my family across central Florida. While we drove between the coasts, the scenery was pretty monotonous for a couple of hours. However, topping one hill, something new confronted us. Acres and acres of lined up mobile homes, as far as the eye could see. The fenced entrance said: Pre-Owned Mobile Home Liquidators.

One of our children asked, "What does 'Pre-Owned Mobile Homes' mean?"

Bonnie quietly responded, "It means many of the senior citizens in Florida who lived in them have died and now their former homes are for sale." And there were thousands of them.

Those acres of "previous-owner-deceased" mobile homes reminded me of one of the most amazing facets of pastoring Christ's church. As a pastor, I often get the joy of standing by people as they prepare to face death. For many, it is a dear time of helping get them ready to see the Lord face-to-face. Did you know the death of His saints is precious in the sight of the Lord (Psalm 116:15)?

Psalm 116 is one of the most practical places in God's Word for getting ready for our going home. That psalm teaches eight simple habits to keep us in robust spiritual health until death—regardless of whether it is imminent or distant.

1. **Believe in God:** *I love the LORD, because He has heard my voice and my supplications* (v. 1). Love requires you trust and believe someone is really there. So choose to believe He is listening and watching, and then respond to Him in love. That is really what salvation is about. I was reading in an earlier psalm how the wicked have death as their shepherd. They are merely marching to the grave. But for the Christian, Psalm 23:1 says: *The LORD is my shepherd* …. Our Shepherd will lead us through life according to our level of belief in Him.

2. **Cry out to God:** *Because He has inclined His ear to me, therefore I will call upon Him as long as I live* (v. 2). Pour out your

heart, fears, and woes—share all with Him. Cry out to the Lord not just when things go wrong, or even when death is imminent, but make it a habit to talk to the Lord in the good and bad times.

3. **Follow God through your daily life:** *I will walk before the LORD in the land of the living* (v. 9). The psalmist wants the Lord to be the One who oversees his daily life as he walks in the shadow of the Almighty (Psalm 91). That distills down to this: form the habit of following Christ daily because He is our Good Shepherd and we are His sheep. We, therefore, need to walk in His presence throughout our lives.

4. **Drink God:** *I will take up the cup of salvation, and call upon the name of the LORD* (v. 13). He is our cup of salvation. Only the Lord can satisfy our thirst, which is an internal deep need. I could be swimming in the greatest body of fresh water in the world, Lake Superior, yet die of thirst unless I, personally, drink it. A lot of people are dying of thirst though the *Water of Life* is all around them. They go to church but never drink Him themselves. Let the Lord into your life to meet your deepest needs!

5. **Obey God:** *I will pay my vows to the LORD now in the presence of all His people* (v. 14). Give in and submit to the Lord. Make it a habit to lovingly do whatever He says. Jesus said, "If you love Me, keep My commandments" (John 14:15).

6. **Serve God:** *O LORD, truly I am Your servant; I am your servant …; You have loosed my bonds* (v. 16). In Hebrew, to emphasize something they repeated it. That is why one of the most important statements in the Bible is "Holy, holy, holy." That is a *trisagion*; what they don't want to forget, they emphasize by the threefold repetition. Verse 16 has the second most emphatic way. The psalmist was emphasizing: "I want to serve You!"

Every night I pray this same little prayer with our youngest child: Dear Father in Heaven, I love You, Lord, and I want to serve You. I want to be a godly woman like Mama." She repeats each phrase after me. We should also say to the Lord with our lips: *I am Your servant; I am Your servant. Say it aloud and offer it to Him as an offering.*

7. **Thank God:** *I will offer to You the sacrifice of thanksgiving, and will call upon the name of the LORD* (v. 17). As sacred as Jews offering their little yearling or the firstling of the flock to God,

you and I can give Him a similar offering—a sacrifice of thanksgiving. Do you know why a lot of people dread getting old and dying? Because they have lost the art of thanking God. They've forgotten how to thank God for His faithfulness through all the years—for His loading them up with manifold blessings.

If you are having trouble knowing what to thank God for, get around some young children and listen to them pray. The earliest moment of the day, when I am in my home office, most often the first ones out of bed are my little ones. They find me for morning prayers, and I love hearing what they say. Usually, they thank the Lord for things like eyes to see, warm "blankies" to sleep under, food to eat, and a host of other simple and sweet life blessings. A child looks at life innocently and thankfully. Regularly offer such sacrificial praise and thanksgiving to the Lord!

8. **Live for God:** *I will pay my vows to the LORD now in the presence of all His people, in the courts of the LORD's house, in the midst of you, O Jerusalem* (vv. 18-19). Give this offering to the Lord, "As long as I have life I am going to come into Your presence, and live for Your glory. I am going to be in Your church—worshiping and adoring You. I am going to talk of Your blessings and testify of You in the presence of others. I am going to fulfill my vows because I love You and want to serve You!"

So then, what are the eight spiritual habits we should be cultivating for the Lord? Believe in Him; cry out to Him; follow Him; drink Him (make sure you have personally received and partaken of the water of salvation); obey Him; serve Him; thank Him; and live for Him!

- Those who lay up treasures on earth spend their lives backing away from their treasures. To them, death is loss—so they have reason to despair.

- Those who lay up treasures in heaven look forward to eternity and move daily toward their treasures. To them, death is gain—so they rejoice.

We often miss something in missionary martyr Jim Elliot's famous words, "He is no fool who gives what he cannot keep to gain what he cannot lose." We focus on his willingness to go to the mission field, a willingness started when he relinquished his hold on things as MINE![42]

Giving your life back to the Lord as an offering is the essence of godly stewardship, which is not only about money, but life itself. Time and life are far greater treasures than money and possessions. God wants you first and foremost! I therefore exhort you to prayerfully read the poem of consecration below—and then make a commitment by faith to live totally for Jesus. Whether this is your first time, or a renewal of your dedication to the Lord, worshipfully offer to Him, "Take my life, Lord—I want to give it wholly to You!"

Take my life, and let it be consecrated, Lord, to Thee.
Take my moments and my days; let them flow in ceaseless praise.
Take my hands, and let them move at the impulse of Thy love.
Take my feet, and let them be swift and beautiful for Thee.
Take my voice, and let me sing always, only, for my King.
Take my lips, and let them be filled with messages from Thee.
Take my silver and my gold; not a mite would I withhold.
Take my intellect, and use every power as Thou shalt choose.
Take my will, and make it Thine; it shall be no longer mine.
Take my heart, it is Thine own; it shall be Thy royal throne.
Take my love, my Lord, I pour at Thy feet its treasure store.
Take myself, and I will be ever, only, all for Thee.

—**Francis R. Havergal, 1836-1879**

My Prayer for You:

Father in Heaven, I pray this would be one of the most captivating thoughts in each of our hearts: *Have I fully given myself first to You?* Before we serve You in any other way, before we give You anything else, before we try to do something for You, we know You want us *first*. I pray You would impress on our hearts the necessity of giving and renewing that giving of ourselves to You. Open our hearts, our eyes, our wills, and help us to give ourselves throughout each day, every moment, unreservedly to living totally for Jesus—our Lord, our Master, and our purpose for living. Thank you, Lord Jesus! In Your precious name I pray. Amen.

---

[42] Adapted from Randy Alcorn's Money, Possessions, and Eternity, http://www.epm.org/articles/monnewma.html

10

> ... Not only as we had hoped, but they first gave themselves to the Lord, and then to us by the will of God.
>
> **—2 Corinthians 8:5**

Stewardship:
Giving Freely to Jesus

Have you ever reflected on what life must have been like for God's people in ancient Israel?[43] Bible times were hard!

43 MP3 CD Audio DYG-05:030202AM, MP3 CD Audio DYG-06:030209AM

Like much of today's non-industrialized world, Israelite men awoke at dawn, trudged to the fields, and picked away by hand at the soil, rocks, and weeds. They plowed with wooden yokes and plows tied to oxen with rope and leather. Planting, plowing, pruning, and harvesting were all done by hand. At sundown, they trudged back home where the women had also labored all day to gather and prepare food. They ate by the dim light of a smoking lamp, and slept the sleep of the laborer.

Harvested food was carefully stored for dormant long months. Pests, rodents, and mold constantly threatened the food supply, and drought and locusts could spell famine at any time. Herdsmen fared no better. They faced similar long, hard days, and often slept with the flock in caves and stone enclosures.

Archaeologists have discovered a lot about life in ancient Israel.

For example, Old Testament burial customs where bones were stored for generations in the back of extended family burial caves in special crypts. One fascinating discovery was in a cave in the 1970s where 762 human teeth were found among the bones. An American dental school examined those teeth, and found they represented fifty-one different individuals. Of them, thirteen (about 25 percent) never lived to age ten; only four in fifty-one (or 8 percent) lived to the age of sixty. The teeth of all the individuals showed they ate almost complete diets of rough grain.

Why the history lesson? Because that was the world of Israel, and the people of God's Word. Considering the hardships they faced, what do you think was expected under the strict code of the Law? What do you think the Lord God Almighty demanded from these hard-working farmers and herdsmen? Now ponder this question: "God, do You really expect less of me—who has Your Holy Spirit within and lives in the wealthiest society in human history—than You demanded of the poorest Israelite?"[44]

Those thought-provoking questions and more will be answered as we examine what God's precious Word has to say about our stewardship of money; a challenging, but wonderful lesson for us all.

44 Randy Alcorn, The Treasure Principle (Sisters, OR: Multnomah Publishers, Inc., 2001), p. 61.

The Bible Is About Giving

Living totally for Jesus is what "the discipline of stewardship" is about—pouring yourself out in loving, glad devotion for our glorious Lord by how you live and give for Jesus. Your overall heart's response to that challenge is a good indicator of how well you are learning to experience the power of a Word filled life.

If you are not quite there yet in your understanding or acceptance of "the discipline of stewardship," be encouraged! Over the next two chapters, we continue to examine this vital subject "... *precept upon precept, ... line upon line, ... here a little, there a little*" (Isaiah 28:10). In this particular chapter, I want you to grasp the difference between giving under the Law versus giving under grace. Comprehending that principle is the key to giving freely to Jesus and with great joy.

Now then, let me ask you *this* question: Do you realize, from Genesis to Revelation, the Bible is about *giving* through and through?

- *Genesis honored the first hero of the faith, Abel, for giving the offering that pleased the Lord. Enoch gave his fellowship to God, walking with Him faithfully. Abraham gave God his faith and trust. Joseph gave God his life, thereby overcoming his hurts and fears.*

- *In Exodus, the heroes of faith, the Israelites, gave God what He wanted on Passover. By putting blood on their doorframes, they became the only people to escape His death angel.*

- *Leviticus is about the freewill offerings of the proper type, kind, and character of giving that would satisfy God's desire for a substitution offering.*

- *Numbers tracks the lives of the few who never stopped giving to the Lord.*

- *Deuteronomy shows Moses as God's man who was giving to the Lord all of his days.*

- *Joshua pronounced doom upon those taking from God instead of giving back what He said belonged to Him.*

- *In the Historical Books, the Lord traced the lives of great givers. At the head of the list was David, a man after God's own heart, who gave his life, his trophies, and his treasures totally to the Lord. Look at this wonderful account in 1 Chronicles 29:1-9:*

> … King David said to all the assembly: "My son Solomon, whom alone God has chosen, is young and inexperienced; and the work is great, because the temple is not for man but for the LORD God. Now for the house of my God I have prepared with all my might … Moreover, **because I have set my affection on the house of my God, I have given … over and above** all that I have prepared for the holy house, **my own special** treasure of gold and silver: three

thousand talents of gold [300,000 pounds] ... and seven thousand talents of refined silver [700,000 pounds] ... for all kinds of work to be done by the hands of craftsmen. **Who then is willing to consecrate himself this day to the LORD?"** *Then the leaders of the fathers' houses, leaders of the tribes of Israel, the captains of thousands and of hundreds, with the officers over the king's work, offered willingly. They gave for the work of the house of God .... And whoever had precious stones gave them to the treasury of the house of the LORD ....Then* **the people rejoiced, for they had offered willingly,** *because with a loyal [faithful] heart they had offered willingly to the LORD;* **and King David also rejoiced** *greatly (emphasis added).*

What a picture of David! His whole focus was on pleasing the Lord. His own special love offering was used to call God's people to further consecration. That is what giving is about—*worship.* And what was the response of the leaders to David's call to consecration? They offered to God willingly, and rejoiced because of it.

Not only are you and I to freely give our hearts to God in devotion, our prayers as a fragrant sacrifice, and the fruit of our lips in praise to God, but we should give tangibly to God. As we see our eternal activity portrayed in the Book of Revelation, it appears we are going to be offering such loving stewardship to the most High God as an act of worship—forever!

Grace Giving Versus Law Giving

By God's grace, the first step toward exercising "the discipline of stewardship" is demonstrated by giving ourselves totally to Jesus (2 Corinthians 8:5). The next step is to freely give Him our resources, our possessions, and our finances. Note what Jesus told His apostles after they had been performing the kingdom miracles (healing the sick, cleansing the lepers, raising the dead, and casting out demons): **"...** *Freely you have received, freely give"* (Matthew 10:8, emphasis added). That simple statement, which is called **grace giving** because it is of God's grace, should be the theme of our lives.

No one ever explained giving as well as did God the Son, Jesus Christ. In the Sermon on the Mount (Matthew 5-7), what is probably the greatest sermon ever, Jesus gave the most wonderful expression of what we are supposed to do with earthly treasures. In Matthew 6:20 He said: *"... Lay up for yourselves treasures in heaven ...."* We can send all our treasures to this heavenly treasury, and accrue "compound interest" in the form of eternal rewards. What a beautiful thought!

Treasures are treasures, and money is money. Jesus' theology of material possessions is this: "Freely give Me all of your treasures as an offering and an expression of your love!" We have a choice on where to invest. Godly stewards will heap them up in heaven's treasury, but poor stewards will hoard them on earth.

What Jesus taught His apostles is what came out in the teachings of the New Testament church—we are the descendants. James,[45] the pastor of the first church in the Bible, located in Jerusalem, wrote the first New Testament epistle. Look at what Pastor James preached in this monumental Church of the Lord Jesus:

> *Come now, you rich, weep and howl for your miseries that are coming upon you! Your riches are corrupted, and your garments are moth-eaten. Your gold and silver are corroded, and their corrosion will be a witness against you and will eat your flesh like fire. You have heaped up treasure in the last days (James 5:1-3).*

What was James talking about? Gold can't corrode. James was pointing out that hoarded money will be a witness against us in the Court of Heaven. Picture yourself standing before Almighty God as He asks, "What did you do with your earthly life?" If you confess, "I heaped up a lot of stuff while I was there, but I hoarded it for myself," that attitude reveals "wood, hay, and straw" which will be burned up in the judgment (see 1 Corinthians 3:9-15).

In James 5:3, God brought a very convicting time to His church. He was saying: "You spend your life for what you are going to lose because you have heaped up treasure in the last days." Actually, the grammatical form of this is "for the last days." Isn't that the American dream? Go for it! Accumulate treasure for your retirement years! They did the exact same thing in the Jerusalem church.

---

[45] Jesus had four earthly brothers and two or three sisters; two of the brothers wrote books of the Bible—James and Jude.

There is a marked difference between being prudent, preparing for winter times as God tells us to do, and merely acquiring more treasures for ourselves. Their wrong attitude led even to the point of cheating employees who should have shared in some of those treasures: *Indeed the wages of the laborers who mowed your fields, which you kept back by fraud, cry out; and the cries of the reapers have reached the ears of the Lord of Sabaoth* (James 5:4).

It will help us to better understand stewardship teachings of the New Testament church by first referring back to the Old Testament—to the world of Israel, the people of God's Word. Under the strict code of the Law, what did God expect from these hard-working farmers and herdsmen? Close Old Testament examination reveals the Lord insisted on two types of giving:

- **Required Tithes:** This tithing was three-fold. The first required tithe was called the **Levites' tithe** (Leviticus 27:30-33), which kept the whole worship system going. They gave 10 percent tithes to the Levites who were in charge of the tabernacle, the worship, and all the offerings. The second 10 percent was called the **festival tithe** (Deuteronomy 12:6-7), to keep their whole national life going, funding all the festivals, the government, and national events. The third 10 percent tithe was called the **poor tithe** (Deuteronomy 14:28). Dan Belcher asks: Every third year? This was for the welfare of the handicapped and the unfortunate; that is how they took care of them. **All three of these were demanded, like taxation, and were not freewill offerings to God.** In addition, there was profit sharing on the corners of the fields (Leviticus 19:9) and not reaping to the edges, a temple tax (Nehemiah 10:32-33), and the Sabbath land rest (Exodus 23). They gave about 25 percent of income for funding their government and for the caring of the land—10 percent for worship and another 15-plus percent for the national economy. God demanded all of that under the Law.

- **Freewill Offerings:** In addition to the three required tithes, God said, "I also desire freewill offerings." Such voluntary giving was a matter of willingly giving Him the best. That is what God wants from us—the choicest things in our lives. Exodus 25:1-2 says: Then the LORD spoke to Moses, saying: "Speak to the children of Israel, that they bring Me an offering. From everyone who gives it willingly with his heart you shall take My offering." God has repeatedly emphasized in the Scriptures He desires gifts out of willing hearts, with the beauty of that being it provides more than enough. Required giving was always taxation; freewill giving always came out of the devoted heart. Those who truly love God want to obey: Honor the Lord with your possessions, and with the first fruits of all your increase … (Proverbs 3:9). Giving with that attitude is what caused God's people to rejoice when … with a loyal heart they had offered willingly to the LORD: and King David also rejoiced greatly (1 Chronicles 29:9).

So then, as Jews under the Law, it was demanded—almost like our own taxation—they give their percentage. But when they came to Christ under grace, He said, "What I want from you is not the taxation of the Law, but for you to look at your treasures as something like David in 1 Chronicles 29: "… You can willingly and joyfully give to Me!" What a magnificent picture of grace giving!

New Testament Principles of Grace Giving

Through "the discipline of stewardship," by devotedly and freely applying New Testament principles of grace giving, we lay up treasures in heaven rather than on earth. To further understand this second stewardship concept, examine several New Testament passages concerning God's principles of grace giving, which should be the theme of our lives.

Giving to the Lord is commanded—

> Now concerning the collection for the saints, **as I have given orders to the churches** of Galatia, so you must do also: on the first day of the week let each one of you lay something aside, storing up as he may prosper, that there be no collections when I come (1 Corinthians 16:1-2, emphasis added).

The giving the Apostle Paul ordered churches to do was not like again being under the Law, because no specific percentage was demanded. Rather, he said, "I am not ordering you to give a certain amount, but I am ordering you to give to the Lord—and with a proper attitude." What was that attitude? Obedience. They were to acknowledge because Paul had ... given orders to the churches ..., they were to do as he said. Nowhere in Scripture is giving an option; giving is always commanded by God.

In the second verse, Paul directed the command to give in this way: ... let each one of you lay something aside .... Who was supposed to give? Everyone. Paul wanted all the saints to give. Giving should be individual. "Each one of you" is all-inclusive—even if you are poor like the widow Jesus spoke about in Mark 12:41-44:

> No Christian is excepted or excused. We are stewards of whatever the Lord has given us, no matter how little it may be in economic terms. As Jesus observed different people putting their offerings in the Temple treasury, He did not discourage the widow from putting in her "two small copper coins, which amount to a cent," nor did He chide Temple officials for accepting money from someone so destitute. His reaction was to use her generosity as a model of spiritual giving.[46]

46 Quoted from sections of John F. MacArthur's The MacArthur New Testament Commentary: I Corinthians 16 (Chicago: Moody Press, 1983).

No matter how little or how much we have in economic terms, all of us are to be participants in grace giving. But sadly, I have heard people say, "I don't have anything to give right now—I'll give later." Such thinking reveals a lack of understanding of this stewardship principle: *"He who is faithful in what is least is faithful also in much; and he who is unjust in what is least is unjust also in much. Therefore if you have not been faithful in the unrighteous mammon [money], who will commit to your trust the true riches?"* (Luke 16:10-11). Those who faithfully give generously out of their poverty can be trusted to also faithfully give generously out of their prosperity.

Giving to the Lord is to be regular.

Paul instructed first-century saints to give on ... *the first day of the week ...* (1 Corinthians 16:2). Not only is giving not optional, but is to be planned and regular. You see, Paul wanted their giving to be systematic, not haphazard. When they came together for worship and the Word, as part of the service they were commanded to receive an offering. And Paul taught the appropriate period for giving was on the first day of the week, the Lord's Day.

What Paul was saying is the worship of the risen Christ included regularly giving money. In Revelation 1:5, Jesus identified Himself as having risen as ... *the firstborn from the dead* .... Think about it: since Jesus rose on Sunday, Sunday is actually Christ's birthday. When invited to celebrate someone's birthday, the normal custom is to give a gift. Well, the Bible says when you come to Jesus' celebration of His resurrection from the dead, He expects to receive gifts. Sunday giving is thus a mandated part of worship. Look at the beautiful picture Peter painted of this:

> *Coming to Him as to a living stone, rejected indeed by men, but chosen by God and precious, you also, as living stones, are being built up a spiritual house, a holy priesthood, to offer up spiritual sacrifices acceptable to God through Jesus Christ. Therefore it is also contained in the Scripture, "Behold, I lay in Zion a chief cornerstone, elect, precious, and he who believes on Him will by no means be put to shame"* (1 Peter 2:4-6).

In those verses, Peter talks about the church and Christians as being individual pieces of the church, the body of Christ. He calls it a holy temple built up of little stones, with Jesus as the Chief Cornerstone. So you and I are each a living stone—uniquely chosen, formed, and gifted by God to have our place in this special house, this temple built for God, His church. As a part of the body of Christ, He wants us to offer up acceptable spiritual sacrifices to Him.

Do you know what "acceptable spiritual sacrifices" are? When we sing, lifting our voices in worship to God, we sing in the power of the Spirit. When we pray, as our prayers are energized by the Holy Spirit, they are like a fragrant aroma that rises up before God. When we meet every week on the Lord's Day, part of our worship is to offer up to Him the systematic and proportionate giving of our money. So then, Jesus says to each of us: "From what you gain materially in this world, I want you to take a part of it and freely give it to Me, every Sunday, when you meet to celebrate My resurrection. I want your offering to be part of your acceptable worship of Me." Wow! That changes the offering of gifts to being as hallowed as the Lord's Supper, as hallowed as prayer, as hallowed as any other part of worship!

With all this in mind, let's now go back to 1 Corinthians 16 and put the pieces together. What Paul was saying is our giving should not be periodic or based on emotional appeals. Neither should it be related to when we get a bonus or unexpected check in the mail. No, it should be willing, regular, planned, and prompted weekly by the Holy Spirit. It should be a grateful commitment of our possessions to the Lord, to His people for His work.

The effect that has on our lives is it forces us to weekly consider ourselves stewards of what God gave us, and then freely sacrifice part to Jesus. Such giving raises our sensitivity to money, so giving is seen as our ongoing regular spiritual responsibility. Jesus said, "... *Where your treasure is, there your heart will be also*" (Luke 12:34). If we think weekly about our treasure being in heaven, and then materially place some treasure in Jesus' hands through His church for His glory, our hearts will be there in heaven and with His people.

Giving to the Lord is to be prepared and proportional.

Paul ordered the saints to ... *lay something aside, storing up as he may prosper* ... (1 Corinthians 16:2). A more literal translation would be "each one of you by himself lay up, or store." This speaks of maintaining a treasury where our valuables are stored, and conveys the idea of coming to church with our treasures already prepared for the Lord. Paul was saying, "I want you to prepare, to plan, and to reason before you come to church. Giving should never be humanly prompted. I never want to manipulate you. I want your giving to be from your heart, which has heard from God, and never as a result of high pressure fundraising."

This is so important. Paul says we should never make an emotionally based decision to give—one without a definite biblically directed focus. So much of modern-day giving is driven by the moment's impulse rather than the biblical plan. Giving is ordered to be regular, prepared, and proportional. Each should give as he is prospered, so we should give proportionately. Believers who have more should give more. If you once earned $100 and gave $10, when you earn $200 you should be giving more than when you only made $100. Grace giving is to always be proportional rather than according to income, and also be based on how much you need what you have. There is such graciousness about this. God says, "I am giving you this. Do what you need to do, and then freely give back to Me as I have freely given to you!"

A New Testament Example of Grace Giving—

> *Out of the most severe trial, their overflowing joy and their extreme poverty welled up in rich generosity. ... **They gave as much as they were able, and even beyond their ability.** ... And they did not do as we expected, but they gave themselves first to the Lord and then to us **in keeping with God's will.** So we urged Titus, since he had earlier made a beginning, to bring also to completion this act of grace on your part. ... I am not commanding you, but I want to test the sincerity of your love by comparing it with the earnestness of others. ... Now finish the work, so that your eager willingness to do it may be matched by your completion of it, according to your means. ... Our desire is not that others might be relieved while you are hard pressed, but that there might be equality (2 Corinthians 8:2-3, 5-6, 8, 11, 13-14 NIV, emphasis added).*

**Giving to the Lord is
to be an outcome of dedication to God.**

Examples of grace giving are found in giving according to ability, beyond that ability, and in a willing and devoted manner (2 Corinthians 8:3). Consider these insightful comments:

> Speaking of the churches of Macedonia, Paul wrote, "In a great ordeal of affliction their abundance of joy and their deep poverty overflowed in the wealth of their liberality" (2 Cor. 8:2). The

reason for their generosity was that "they first gave themselves to the Lord and to us by the will of God" (v. 5). They gave out of love for God and for His servants. Generosity is impossible apart from our love of God and of His people. But with such love, generosity not only is possible but inevitable.[47]

An acceptable spiritual sacrifice of giving comes as we first give ourselves to the Lord, and then generously give out of our financial resources. In such giving, the real issue isn't giving monetarily but in the giving of ourselves to Him. If we have really given ourselves totally to the Lord, the right kind of giving naturally follows.

Giving to the Lord is to be completed.

Regarding their giving, Paul told the Corinthians they must complete their ... *act of grace* ... (2 Corinthians 8:6). The Corinthian Christians may have intended to give. They may have thought about giving, or even been favorable to the idea. Yet all was useless unless they did, in fact, *complete this grace.* Intentions, vows, and resolutions are useless without action.

> The basic principle for voluntary giving in the Old Testament is reflected in Proverbs: "Honor the Lord from your wealth, and from the first of all your produce; so your barns will be filled with plenty, and your vats will overflow with new wine" (3:9–10). The idea was to give to the Lord generously and to give to the Lord first. Again we are told, "There is one who scatters, yet increases all the more, and there is one who withholds what is justly due, but it results only in want" (Prov. 11:24). In other words, if you want to increase your money, share it generously; if you want to lose your money, hoard it. To raise money to build the Tabernacle, the Lord told Moses, "Tell the sons of Israel to raise a contribution for Me; from every man whose heart moves him you shall raise My contribution" (Ex. 25:1–2; cf. 35:5, 21). The standard was heart-directed generosity, based on thankfulness to the Lord for what He had done and given. Based on that principle the gifts for the building of the Tabernacle were

[47] Ibid.

so great that Moses had to tell the people to stop giving (36:6)! Required giving was taxation; freewill giving was to be from the heart, with the amount left up to the worshiper. David had the key idea when he said that he would not give God that which cost him nothing (2 Sam. 24:24).[48]

48 Ibid.

Giving to the Lord is to be an act of grace, not by commandment.

Second Corinthians 8:8 shows no individual Christian can be commanded to give at any particular moment, even by the Apostle Paul. This is because commanded giving is not biblical giving; the illegal use of one's official position or powers to obtain property, funds, or patronage is called extortion.

No amount or percentage is ever required in the New Testament. Rather, each believer is to give from his heart. "Give," Jesus said, "and it will be given to you; good measure, pressed down, shaken together, running over, they will pour into your lap. For by your standard of measure it will be measured to you in return" (Luke 6:38). Paul expressed the same principle as, "He who sows sparingly shall also reap sparingly; and he who sows bountifully shall also reap bountifully" (2 Cor. 9:6). The benefits of our willing, cheerful giving to the Lord will produce both spiritual and material blessing. "And God is able to make all grace abound to you, that always having all sufficiency in everything, you may have an abundance for every good deed" (v. 8).[49]

49 Ibid.

Giving to the Lord is to be out of what we have.

Paul told the Corinthians to give out of what they had (see 2 Corinthians 8:11). We can't give what we lack. God judges our giving against what resources He has given. But the issue of what and how we spend is relevant to what we have. True giving is measured by obedience, proportion, and need—never by amount. When the issue of giving is brought up, many ask: "How much am I supposed to give?" Paul's principles throughout his letter to the Corinthians, and other letters, remind us there isn't one correct answer for every believer. In giving, many go back to the Old Testament Law of the tithe—the giving of 10 percent unto the Lord. This is a good principle for giving, and perhaps a broad benchmark. *Nowhere is tithing specifically commanded in the New Testament*, but it is certainly spoken of in a positive light and with a right heart (Luke 11:42).

Since giving is to be proportional, we should give some percentage, and ten percent is a good starting place. For some people, to give ten percent is nowhere near enough; for others, in their present situation or level of spiritual maturity, one percent may be a massive step of faith. But if our thinking is: *How little can I give and still be pleasing to God?*—our heart isn't in the right place. We ought to have the attitude of some of the first-century Christians who essentially said: We're no longer under the tithe—so we can give more!

Giving and money management are not only financial issues, but also spiritual ones (Luke 16:11). Some Christians have the idea God wants just ten percent, so they can do what they like with the rest. Such spirit is entirely contrary to the grace giving principle the New Testament teaches. No, as God richly blesses, we ought to increase the percentage of giving.

**Giving to the Lord is
to be enjoyed.**

The goal of giving is not to afflict or hurt the giver financially. For Paul wrote to the Corinthians: ... *I do not mean that others should be eased and you burdened* ... (2 Corinthians 8:13). The Corinthian Christians were not giving so the Jerusalem Christians could get rich and lazy at their expense. Paul was taking the collection so the Jerusalem Christians could merely survive, and both the recipients and the givers were benefactors of God's grace!

**Giving to the Lord is
to be viewed as investing money,
not as spending money.**

Paul compared giving to sowing seeds. A farmer sowing seed may feel he loses seed as it falls from his hand to the ground, and we may feel we lose monetarily when we give. But just as the sower gives the seed in anticipation of a future harvest, so we should give with the same heart. If a farmer sows only a few seeds because he wanted to "hold onto" as much as he can, he will only have "more seed" in his barn. But at the harvest, the one who sowed the most seed would have much more grain in his barn. No one should fear giving generously. Proverbs 11:24 is a great commentary on this concept: *There is one who scatters, yet increases more; and there is one who withholds more than is right, but it leads to poverty.*

No one thinks a farmer is "wasting" grain when he scatters it as seed; the more he plants, the more he will harvest. God promises the willing giver ... *will also reap bountifully* (2 Corinthians 9:6). Spiritually, we can trust God will reward the giving heart both now and in eternity. Jesus spoke of this in Matthew 19:29: ... *Everyone who has left houses or brothers or sisters or father or mother or wife or children or lands, for My name's sake, shall receive a hundredfold, and inherit eternal life.*

Giving to the Lord is
to be from a right heart—a cheerful heart.

Paul wrote: ... *Let each one give as he purposes in his heart* ... (2 Corinthians 9:7). Giving should be done ... *not grudgingly* [reluctantly, regretfully given with plenty of complaining] *or of necessity* [given because someone has made us or manipulated us into giving] ... (2 Corinthians 9:7). That is the spirit behind taxation, not biblical giving. Instead, ... *God loves a cheerful giver* (2 Corinthians 9:7). The Greek word for *"cheerful"* (hilaros, used only here in the New Testament) is the root for our English word "hilarious." God wants us to give happily, because that is how God Himself gives!

Giving should be motivated by the *purposes* of our *own* heart. It should never come through manipulation, intimidation, or domination. The way we spend our money shows the purposes of our own heart more accurately than our words, and bears witness to the truth of Jesus' simple statement: "... *Where your treasure is, there your heart will be also"* (Matthew 6:21).

Our giving should always include ministries that directly feed us spiritually. Paul, as one who fed the Corinthians spiritually, established he had the right to be supported by them materially (1 Corinthians 9:7-13). This idea is expressed in 1 Corinthians 9:11: *If we have sown spiritual things for you, is it a great thing if we reap your material things?* Paul draws on the principle of Deuteronomy 25:4 where God commanded, *"You shall not muzzle an ox while it treads out the grain."*

God was establishing the principle that a minister has the right to be supported by those he is ministering. This principle is also clearly expressed in 1 Timothy 5:17-18. Elders who govern and feed the church are to be given the double honor of office and a suitable salary comparable to other positions commensurate with their experience, maturity, and life. Those who preach and teach should be honored above those who serve only in administration.

Grace giving has many aspects. Sometimes Paul called giving a gift (1 Corinthians 16:3). At other times, he called giving a *diakonia*, meaning "a practical service or ministry" (2 Corinthians 8:4; 9:1, 12-13). I especially like how Paul literally called a "gift freely given" as "giving a grace." Our giving should be like God's giving of grace to us, which He gives freely and generously. We are to want to give a tangible demonstration of fellowship and participation with the body of Christ. For everywhere Paul went, wherever he founded a church, he taught them to give, because giving is an essential part of being a godly steward. If you want to experience the power of a Word filled life, know *giving* is never an option, but rather, something every Christian must do. If we do not give properly, we cannot worship properly.

Why Does God Give Wealth?

It is now time to honestly and prayerfully answer two important questions: (1) Do you think the Lord expects more or less from us who have His Holy Spirit dwelling within us as we live in comfort? and (2) Do you think He expects more or less from us than what He demanded from the poorest Israelite who worked fourteen hours a day, six days a week, just to live? God didn't give us wealth to become more and more comfortable and secure, but rather so we can grow in the grace of freely giving back to Him.

If you have not received anything from the Lord, if He has not given you salvation, if He has not given you His gracious mercy, forgiveness, and cleansing—please do not give Him *anything*. Keep your money, your resources, and your life to yourself. God does not want it; nor should any ministry if God has not moved into your life. But if Jesus has given much to you, you should be giving back to Him graciously and freely. Remember: you could not have bought your deliverance for any amount of money. So never forget the words of Jesus, "*… Freely you have received, freely give*" (Matthew 10:8, emphasis added).

My Prayer for You:
Father, thank You that You are a God of giving. You gave us the greatest gift possible when You gave us Your Son! And we so love You we want to give back to You the sacrifices and offerings that please You most. We do it not because we are trying to purchase Your love or trying to pay You back, but because we willingly, lovingly, and loyally rejoice to honor You. Truly, as David said, that which actually costs us something is what we want to give. We know You love our treasures, our sacrifices, and the systematic regular giving of Your people. The amount isn't as important to You as the heart attitude with which a gift is given. So I pray we would learn from cover to cover that Your Word is all about giving. For we are going to be giving to You throughout all eternity as a kingdom of priests and a holy nation offering spiritual sacrifices to You—as we did on this earth as living stones in Your house. And so we shall do forever around Your glorious throne! So teach us the joy, the wonder, and the duty we have to give to You. In Jesus precious name I pray. Amen.

11

... The twenty-four elders fall down before Him who sits on the throne and worship Him who lives forever and ever, and cast their crowns before the throne, saying: "You are worthy, O Lord, to receive glory and honor and power; for You created all things, and by Your will they exist and were created."

— **Revelation 4:10-11**

Stewardship: Giving Worshipfully for Eternity

WHAT IS GOING ON THIS very instant around God's throne? Saints and angels are giving Him their worship—and we can join them! Not only are we to freely give our hearts to God in devotion, our prayers as a fragrant sacrifice, and our lips in praise to God, but we are to also give tangibly of our treasures to God.[50] The glimpse into our future we see in the Book of Revelation shows we are going to be offering such loving worship to the most High God forever. So, in that sense, we could say "the discipline of stewardship" is actually all about giving worshipfully for eternity! Giving of ourselves in every possible way requires we walk with God day by day, hour by hour, moment by moment.

Matching God stride for stride along the path of life, while headed for the City of God, is what enabled Enoch to walk in profound righteousness and experience deep fellowship with God. Thus, he pleased God long before the Apostle Paul wrote these words: *... Seek those things which are above, where Christ is, sitting at the right hand of God.*

[50] MP3 CD Audio DYG-07:030216AM, MP3 CD Audio DYG-08 – 030223AM

Set your mind on things above, not on things on the earth (Colossians 3:1-2). In fact, Enoch had been exercising himself toward godliness for so long "his transfer to heaven was not even an interruption."[51]

[51] Warren Wiersbe, Running with the Winners: A Study of the Champions of Hebrews 11 (Wheaton: Tyndale House, 1985), p. 44.

How can we learn to walk with God in this manner? We begin by setting our minds on things in heaven rather than on earth. Often we think of heaven in the past, as when Christ left earth and the angels came, or in the future when Jesus returns as King of Kings. However, we often forget at any moment the epicenter of the universe, the throne room of God, is very active—and you and I are participants in activity! How can that be? To address this question, set aside all earthly cares and busyness, and quietly let your heart, mind, and spirit soar heavenward! Let God's Word take you by angel wings to the worship center of the universe!

The Sights of Heaven's Glory

This very moment, stand with me in the vestibule and peer through the door into the chambers of the Most High God! By faith's eye, gaze at the One seated on the eternal throne. Exalt God in your spirit for the endless praise ascending around His throne. Be still and know before whom you stand, adore the loveliness of Jesus as the center and focus of your worship. See Christ in all His resplendent beauty—the One who alone is worthy of all your worship and praise!

Listen to choirs of angels in numberless circles about the glassy sea and its throne as they say His worthy praises. Listen to those eternal creatures chant ... *"Holy, holy, holy, Lord God Almighty, Who was and is and is to come!"* (Revelation 4:8). See, with the Apostle John, the band no man could number and listen to their songs of adoration. Do you know Him, Christ the Lord? See Him now as the slain Lamb! For He is to be praised by us who owe Him our all!

Watch with me as God pulls back the veil further. Through John's eyes, his inspired words portray the Revelation 5 scene of hundreds of millions of *angels—ten thousand times ten thousand*—all clustered about the smooth crystal sea reflecting awesome images from its surface. Our senses are besieged by endless sensations, and the colors surrounding God's throne are beyond human description.

A cool, emerald-green hue dominates the color rainbow surrounding God's throne. The city surrounds us with thick walls of sparkling diamonds. To get the full sensation, hold a diamond ring to a light, look through the stone, and see dazzling flashes of light. Multiply that by diamonds large enough to build walls, plus an entire city over 1,500 miles high! Looking down beneath your feet, you see gold, transparent so the overpowering radiance of God's glory can refract and glisten through the city where everything is made of beautifully colored gems reflecting His glorious light!

These are the colors of heaven, the colors God chose to surround Himself and reflect His glory in all the hues: sky-blue stones with translucent, colored stripes; parallel layers of red and white; orange-red to brownish-red to blood-red; a transparent, yellowish gold; light blue aquamarine; yellowish-green; apple-green and gold-tinted green; deep blue; shining violet; and intense purple.

All the sights of heaven's glory—their beauty, color, and brilliance—are hard to take in! But our sight is soon riveted on the celestial scene before us. First, ANGELS capture our attention. Countless white-robed angels stand like living walls of purity, rising in circular rings and reflecting the light of God. They rise and fall to the sounds of four creatures crisscrossing the expanse of the throne's corners. They move as one, falling down on their faces as they speak the wonders of God's glory.

Next, the FLOOR is an ocean of completely clear and reflective glass. In this crystal sea we can see all colors, lights, and objects reflected and amplified. But central to heaven is the THRONE of God. Completely encircled by the emerald green rainbow that is over, around, and beneath the throne, we are overcome with awe by the massive rumble of power, as endless peals of thunder and lightning flashes seem to radiate outward from within. Listen carefully as we hear, with John, the loud voices like roaring waterfalls rolling past the seven blazing pillars of flame that burn in a circle around God's throne.

Our focus is then captured by the BURNING ONES (the meaning of seraphim). As our eyes turn to follow the four glistening, living beings, each with four distinct faces (lion, calf, man, eagle) and completely covered with eyes. They move like flashes of light with fire passing between them, gliding through the expanse around the Ancient of Days in theocentric orbit—always facing the Almighty One.

The twenty-four ELDERS rise and fall under the breathtaking expanse of space over the throne that sparkles like pure crystal on the sparkling blue pavement (as it is called in Exodus). We see a circle just beyond the burning pillars and the four living creatures surrounding God's throne. That circle, made up of twenty-four small thrones, seats white-robed celestial men who each holds a harp and a golden bowl, and wears a crown. These golden bowls contain the worship offered by God's saints on earth, and repeatedly, we see those twenty-four elders fall on their faces pouring out to the Lord the collected *worship* of the saints as the hosts of heaven loudly chant God's glory. With the mighty sound of seraph wings we hear the voices, thunders, and sounds of the entire universe blending into Revelation 4:8's crystal clear affirmation:

> *"Holy, holy, holy,*
> *Lord God Almighty,*
> *Who was and is and is to come!"*

Finally, at a special moment, every angel, elder, and saint falls prostrate before Him—those four great angels, those twenty-four elders, the hundreds of millions of worshipers around the sea—and most of all, us! And, in Revelation 5:12, we all gloriously and exuberantly join together to sing with them:

> *"Worthy is the Lamb who was slain*
> *To receive power and riches and*
> *wisdom,*
> *And strength and honor and glory*
> *and blessing!"*

Wow! Do you feel as I do? It's hard to come back down to planet Earth. Why is that? To worship is not just our duty—*it is our purpose for existence,* and nothing less can ever satisfy! True worship is to ascribe to Jesus Christ the honor, praise, glory, and majesty He so rightly deserves. And the great news is you and I can participate in such worship in heaven even while we are still here on earth! The sights of heaven's glory, just described, takes place as God prepares to unfurl His judgment on this unrepentant earth.[52] But right now, in the twenty-first century, heaven's activity centers around the worship offered up to God by His devoted children. As a holy priesthood, everything we worshipfully do, say, think, pray, and give to Jesus rises above as a sweet-smelling fragrance and enters into God's very presence! What an awesome thought!

[52] For a full exposition of Christ's Second Coming, and the judgment to come, see my daily devotional book entitled Living Hope for the End of Days, available at www.discoverthebook.org.

Seven Priestly Spiritual Sacrifices to God

In the Old Testament, God said He had a selective family—the Levitical family of priests that represented the whole nation of Israel. But in the New Covenant, when we were saved, we became part of the body of Christ, and thus a member of a kingdom of priests; we became a holy nation like Israel, so each of us can … *offer up spiritual sacrifices acceptable to God through Jesus Christ* (see 1 Peter 2:4-5). And what God wants from us most is clearly identified in Mark 12:33. We were created:

> "… To love Him with all the heart, with all the understanding, with all the soul, and with all the strength, and to love one's neighbor as oneself, [which] is more than all the whole burnt offerings and sacrifices."

There are seven types of spiritual sacrifices we are to freely offer up to Jesus in worship: (Emphasis added to the verses below.)

1. **Our devotion—a burnt offering:** As referenced in Mark 12:33 above, to God, devotion to Christ is like the smoke rising from a burning offering on an altar. As His priests, the devotion of our heart, our understanding, our emotions, our soul, our strength, and our loving others mean more to Him than all the burnt offerings of animal sacrifices throughout history.

As you wake every morning, I hope this is your first thought: *When morning gilds the skies, My heart awaking cries, May Jesus*

Christ be praised! As each new day begins, offer your devotion and love to the Lord. Allow God to fill your thoughts, and say, "Holy Spirit, this is Your day, not mine. Use it as You see fit; continue to keep me from sin, direct my choices and my decisions. Use me to glorify Jesus Christ!" Devotedly giving yourself to the Lord will fill one of the bowls of the worship leaders in heaven. When the bowls are poured out, you immediately become a part of the worship activity in heaven. *Have you offered your devotion up to Him irretrievably, completely, and lovingly?*

2. **Our lives—a living sacrifice:** *I beseech you, therefore, brethren, by the mercies of God, to* **present your bodies a living sacrifice,** *holy, acceptable to God, which is your reasonable service* (Romans 12:1). Think about what God required of the Jews to worship Him: they first very carefully picked a sacrifice—their best, unblemished animal— then led the sacrifice by hand to be offered up in the temple area. In verse 1, the Lord says, "I want you to do the same as I instructed My people, Israel. I want you to give Me the best and greatest you have— your body. I want you to be My living sacrifice, for that is your true spiritual worship."

"True spiritual worship" is what *reasonable service* means. It is a word from the temple that speaks of temple worship. God is saying, "I want you to keep giving yourself to Me, and regularly renew commitment by saying, 'As Your living sacrifice, what do You want to do with my life today? I am Yours to use as You wish, Lord, because I *love* You!'"

Paul also talks about this stewardship principle in Romans 15. When he went out soul winning and preaching, he viewed people as coming to Christ, getting saved, and joining this ascent of smoke from the altars of their hearts while offering their lives back to Him daily. Paul himself offered that great sacrifice to God as ... *a minister of Jesus Christ to the Gentiles, ministering the gospel of God, so the offering of the Gentiles might be acceptable, sanctified by the Holy Spirit* (Romans 15:16).

"When these pagans are redeemed," said Paul, "the Holy Spirit energizes them to give their lives back to God because He bought them with the price of Christ's shed blood. They acknowledge His ownership by saying, 'I am Yours!' Offering themselves to the Lord is as the smoke of a sacrificial offering rising before God in heaven!"

All the way through the Old Testament Scriptures, the sacrifices of Abel, Noah, Abraham, Isaac, Jacob—and all the other myriad of offerings from the children of Israel—were received as a sweet-smelling aroma because they represented God's only Son's sacrifice on the cross for sin. So what they did on earth rose before His presence in heaven, and He was pleased. It is also like a flaming sacrifice sweetly rising before God, when you freely and lovingly acknowledge His ownership of you by regularly reaffirming total commitment to Him, as in these words written by Fanny Crosby:

I am Thine, O Lord—I have heard Thy voice,
And it told Thy love to me;
But I long to rise in the arms of faith
And be closer drawn to Thee.

Consecrate me now to Thy service, Lord,
By the power of grace divine;
Let my soul look up with a steadfast hope
And my will be lost in Thine.

You can make such an affirmation any time, no matter what you are doing. This will be a precious spiritual sacrifice, acceptable to the Lord. *Have you recently reaffirmed your total commitment to Jesus?*

3. **Our acts of service—a drink offering:** … *If I [Paul] am being poured out as a drink offering on the sacrifice and service of your faith, I am glad and rejoice with you all* (Philippians 2:17). A lot entails service for the Lord, and Paul did all he could as a ministering servant to the saints. There are so many things that can be done in your local church. If you pay close attention, you'll see saints constantly ministering there. A few arrive early to set up, move things around as needed, or do a quick repair. During the week, some stand at the copy machine, reproducing papers or prayer lists for Sunday school. Still others love to cook or prepare refreshments, and make sure everything is ready in time. Such serving, and much more than you probably will ever know, goes on all through the week.

All those little acts of service are like drink offerings. Do you know what a drink offering is? It is like taking a glass of water and pouring it on sand. When you pour the water out, you can't get it back because it gets absorbed—it's gone. The Lord says, "When you freely and lovingly give your strength, energy, time, and devotion in working in service for My church, it is as if you poured out part of your life, and can never get it back. But that drink offering is an investment in eternity because it rises before Me as a beautiful act of worship!"

Remember this truth when nobody knows about or acknowledges what you do. Remind yourself about the "compound interest" you receive from the Lord by investing in the treasury of heaven. Acts of service done secretly for the Lord become a complete offering of worship. For that reason, if you have a ministry in the public eye (teaching, singing, and so forth), be extra alert to Satan's attempts to entice you to accept the credit God rightfully deserves. Some of your reward can be lost because those acts of service don't all rise and ascend before His throne. They become stunted and stilted because of pride, which always competes with God for control and glory. (That was Satan's downfall!)

From Philippians 2:17 we learn how Paul lives life in this spirit. Even in his last days he says: "... I am already being **poured out as a drink offering**, *and the time of my departure is at hand. I have fought the good fight, I have finished the race, I have kept the faith. ... [And] there is laid up for me the crown of righteousness ...* (2 Timothy 4:6-8, emphasis added). Paul's whole life as a believer was an act of worship which he lovingly poured out to the Lord. As God's priests, we are also expected to pour out our whole lives as a drink offering in the name of Christ, which is our *"reasonable service"* (Romans 12:1).

4. **Our gifts—a fragrant freewill offering:** *... I [Paul] have all and abound. I am full, having received from ... you,* **a sweet-smelling aroma, an acceptable sacrifice,** *well pleasing to God* (Philippians 4:18). This is a very dollars-and-cents kind of thing, an offering verse; a money gift was a spiritual sacrifice. In the book of Acts, reports of Paul's missionary journeys reveal he was financially supported by this wonderful church in Philippi so far away.

That the church in Philippi contributed heavily to Paul's ministry is interesting because many of those Philippians were slaves who had to work very hard. But when they found something that was their possession, they placed it in the hands of the church leaders to send to Paul. Instantly, their offering rose up to God's throne as a sweet-smelling and pleasing sacrifice. Every gift you, too, have prayerfully prepared to give to Jesus out of the devotion of your heart goes up in a puff of smoke the minute you offer it to Him on the Lord's Day. You won't see it, but it rises like a fragrant burnt offering to Jesus—and is poured out before God's throne. Every gift we give in this spirit will be received as a fragrant, freewill offering for eternity. *What aroma is ascending from your living before Christ's eyes today?*

5. **Our worship—a praise offering:** ... *By Him let us continually offer the sacrifice of praise to God, that is, the fruit of our lips, giving thanks to His name* (Hebrews 13:15). Here again is another priestly offering scenario. As Christ's priests, we are to regularly worship Him through the sacrifice of praise.

Every time I read verse 15 it brings up vivid memories of when I was a thirty-year-old senior pastor just starting out in a New England church. One of the first times I preached, as I went to the pulpit, the back door opened and a Paul Bunyan sort of man entered. He took a folding chair, popped it open, sat in back, right down in the middle of the center aisle, looked up at me—and pulled out a great big hunting knife. I thought: *Wow! Lord,* what are we going to do about this? As I preached, I kept an eye on HIM, and he kept an eye on ME—while he cleaned his fingernails with his long knife.

The next week, "Mr. He-Man" moved from the back row to the front row and, while listening intently to the sermon, once again cleaned his fingernails with that huge knife. But, unusual as it was, what especially struck me about him was he couldn't carry a tune. He would sit right in front of me and bellow out the words whenever we had chorus time. So we would hear: "WORTHY IS THE LAMB ... WORTHY IS THE LAMB ..." His singing was SO bad the whole congregation was soon off-key with him! But do you know what? His singing was definitely in keeping with: Make a joyful noise unto the LORD .... *Serve the LORD with gladness: come before his presence with singing* (Psalm 100:1-2 KJV). So, even though this man, who later became a dear friend, was so loud and badly off-key, his offering of praise was received by God as a spiritual sacrifice, a wonderful act of worship. For true worship is a matter of the heart.

Now let's look at Hebrews 13:15 again to see what the writer was saying: "Any time it is possible, I want to continuously offer up the sacrifice of praise to God! I want my lips to bear fruit as I give thanks to His name!" As priests we can use our mouths to offer a praise offering as an acceptable spiritual sacrifice. This is the same spirit seen in Psalm 19:14: *Let the words of my mouth and the meditation of my heart be acceptable in Your sight, O LORD, my strength and my Redeemer.* We should use our mouths primarily to express what will last for eternity. Our worship is a praise offering. *When did you last stop and launch a wave of praise-filled worship toward God's throne?*

6. Our deeds of kindness—spiritual sacrifices: ... *Do not forget to do good and share, for* **with such sacrifices** *God is well pleased* (Hebrews 13:16). When we live out the kindness and love of Jesus Christ those deeds are spiritual sacrifices to God, and thus acts of worship. Jesus, Himself, always went about doing good—even to those who hated and refused to receive Him. He also did good to those He knew would neglect to acknowledge His kindness, like the nine lepers; only one of the ten lepers He healed ever returned to thank Him and glorify God (see Luke 17:11-15). On the basis of how much God has done for us, He wants us to pass on His love to others by doing good deeds and kindnesses. Such deeds are sacrifices that will rise up in eternal worship.

God's people in the twenty-first century should be as well known for their loving acts of service as were first century Christians. Those martyred saints had been the best citizens, workers, neighbors, and the best friends of the time. They were honest, not greedy, and always ready to share with those in need. If you wanted something, and compelled them to go one mile, they would go two instead. If asked for their coats, they would also give their shirts. So what was the outcome of these spiritual sacrifices? Because they were characterized by giving, their lives were used by God to help revolutionize the whole world through the love of Christ!

In John 3:16, God so loved He did what? He gave. Therefore, God wants our lives to be characterized by giving as well. In Matthew 25:34-36, Jesus gave a wonderful example of this spirit: "... *'Come, you blessed of My Father, inherit the kingdom prepared for you from the foundation of the world: for I was hungry and you gave Me food; I* was thirsty and you gave Me drink; I was a stranger and you took Me in; I was naked and you clothed Me; I was sick and you visited Me; I was in prison and you came to Me.'" When the righteous were surprised at His comments, asking when they did all that for Him, Jesus responded: "... 'Assuredly, I say to you, inasmuch as you did it to one of the least of these My brethren, you did it to Me'." (Matthew 25:40).

The little things in life count to the Lord—like the opportunity He gave me to sacrificially fulfill the request of a sick, lonely soul in the hospital who craved a three-quarter pound cheeseburger for his Thanksgiving meal. Or, if someone is stuck somewhere, and in spite of being in a hurry, you offer aid. An act of kindness can even be as simple as stepping aside to let someone get in line ahead of you at a busy checkout. Any kindness, no matter how small, if done in the power of the Holy Spirit becomes a gift of worship to the Lord.

Because of the sacrifice of Christ, those offerings immediately go into the presence of God. As He sits upon His throne, because of the redemption of Jesus Christ and His salvation to us, all our kindnesses, words, gifts, devotion, and worship-filled praise offerings are collected in the worship leaders' bowls. And they will be poured out in worship before Him—even though we are frail, even though we fail, even though we are sinners—because the blood of Jesus Christ has cleansed us. Since we are ... *accepted in the Beloved* (Ephesians 1:6), our offerings go straight through to heaven and are graciously received by God. *What acts of kindness and good deeds have you carried out this week for Jesus?*

7. **Our prayers—an incense offering:** *Then another angel, having a golden censer, came and stood at the altar. He was given much incense, so he should offer it with the prayers of all the saints upon the golden altar which stood before the throne. And the smoke of the incense, with* **the prayers of the saints, ascended before God** *from the angel's hand* (Revelation 8:3-4).

From Revelation 4 to the end of the book, the language is very Old Testament. Therefore, if you don't understand Israel and the sacrificial system, the tabernacle and the temple, and the whole routine of what is going on, you can feel lost. In verses 3-4 above, John is talking about the tabernacle and the angel standing at the golden altar. And where is that altar? If you think back to all the flashes and lightning and thunder and glass sea and towers of flames, and four angels flying around the twenty-four elders, what is right in front of God Himself? That altar made of gold with incense on it—a picture of the prayers of God's children rising before Him. So if you want to draw closer to God today, stop, tune in, and talk to Him. When you pray, those prayers, like a puff of smoke, reach the worship center of the universe, get poured on that golden altar, and rise up into the very face of the Almighty God of the universe!

Our prayers are as an incense offering to God. He collects them, treasures, wants, seeks, and responds to them. How God operates in our world is in response to the prayers of His people. He wants you to worship Him through prayer, calling upon Him to do great and mighty things. He then answers those prayers in a way He is glorified through you and me as we pray. Since God loves our prayers so much He collects them all, we need to send Him even more! *What do you have in the bowl of your collected prayers?*

In closing, you may have noticed only one of the seven priestly spiritual sacrifices of worship involves the giving of our finances. The reason is "the discipline of stewardship" is not about money—but life itself. Time and life are far greater treasures than money and possessions. First and foremost, God wants you follow Mark 12:33.

You prove love for Jesus by worshiping Him through your devotion, good deeds and acts of service, words of praise, prayers, and giving your treasures. When the four angel worship leaders say, "It is time!"—and the hundreds of millions of angels fall on their faces, and the twenty-four elders representing the redeemed get off their thrones and fall on their faces—at that moment, your worship and mine is poured out before God! So I ask you: Is your entire life a love offering to worship God? For that is what He most wants from you!

Missionary C.T. Studd captured the essence of "the discipline of stewardship" when he said, "Only one life, 'twill soon be past; only what's done for Christ will last." On his deathbed, his children gathered around and heard him say, "I wish I had something to give you … I am sorry, but I gave it all to the Lord a long time ago." All of his children served the Lord to their last days. They saw the example of his great beneficence to God—a sweet-smelling fragrance of a life totally given over to Jesus as a spiritual sacrifice for eternity! Will your loved ones be able to say the same about you after your homegoing to heaven? They *will*—if you choose by the power of the Holy Spirit to live a Word filled life!

My Prayer for You:
Thank you, oh Father, for worship we can offer that is well pleasing to You. We want to give You the worship of our words, the fruit of our lips praising Your name. We want to offer the worship of our spirits as they ascend like a fragrant aroma to You. We freely and cheerfully want to give back to You our material resources, treasures, and money. From what You have given us, we want to use what we need for our everyday life and then worshipfully offer up to what we have prayerfully chosen and carefully planned in our hearts to give as an expression of our love. Thank You that our giving is not bound by the Law, for You demand no specific percentage. But our gifts are a reflection of hearts of love, and a desire to abound in the grace of giving. I pray You would touch our hearts. On the Lord's Day, may each offering be an act of worship from every one of Your saints. May it be prayed over, thought over, planned and prepared, then wrapped as lovingly as possible to be offered willingly into Your hands because we love You. And then, Father, I pray as we look into Your Word, it will change our lives more and more into being a pleasing kingdom of priests that offers acceptable spiritual sacrifices in every part of our lives—for eternity. In the name of Jesus I pray. Amen.

12

Brethren, I do not count myself to have apprehended; but one thing I do, forgetting those things which are behind and reaching forward to those things which are ahead, I press toward the goal for the prize of the upward call of God in Christ Jesus.

— **Philippians 3:13-14**

Discipline Five—Simplicity:
Reordering to God's Priorities

Has life become a blur for you?[53] Have you reached the point where you wish there were more hours each day? Have the lists and piles of unfinished tasks started to bury you? Are your quiet moments often haunted by thoughts of unreturned calls, unanswered letters, unfixed problems, and undone deeds? Has the immensity of life started to make you feel helpless? All of these may be indicators of the lack of biblical simplicity. Simplicity means "something that is simple, easy to grasp and do, non-complex."

Biblical simplicity is reordering our priorities back to what God has asked us to do.

Listen to what one gifted writer has written about the general lack of simplicity in today's society:

When we stop to evaluate, we realize our dilemma goes deeper

[53] MP3 CD Audio DYG-15:030504AM, MP3 CD Audio DYG-16:030518AM, MP3 CD Audio DYG-17:030525AM, MP3 CD Audio DYG-18:030601AM, MP3 CD Audio DYG-19:030608AM

than shortage of time; it is basically the problem of priorities. Hard work does not hurt us. We all know what it is to go full speed for long hours, totally involved in an important task. The resulting weariness is matched by a sense of achievement and joy.

Not hard work, but doubt and misgiving produce anxiety as we review a month or year and become oppressed by the pile of unfinished tasks. We sense uneasily that we may have failed to do the important.

The winds of other people's demands have driven us onto a reef of frustration.

We confess, quite apart from our sins, "We have left undone those things which we ought to have done; and we have done those things which we ought not to have done."

Over the years the greatest continuing struggle in the Christian life is the effort to make adequate time for daily waiting on God, weekly inventory, and monthly planning. Since this time for receiving marching orders is so important, Satan will do everything he can to squeeze it out. Yet we know from experience that only by this means can we escape the tyranny of the urgent. This is how Jesus succeeded.

Jesus did not finish all the urgent tasks in Israel or all the things He would have liked to do, but He did finish the work which God gave Him to do.

The only alternative to frustration is to be sure that we are doing what God wants. Nothing substitutes for knowing that this day, this hour, in this place we are doing the will of the Father.[54]

What is the answer to the anxiety of the unfinished life? "The discipline of simplicity"—*or the practice of reordering our priorities back to what God has asked us to do according to the Scriptures.*

---

[54] From Charles E. Hummel's booklet entitled The Tyranny of the Urgent! (Downers Grove, IL: InterVarsity Press, 1997).

The Simplicity of Christ Alone

How can we begin to practice "the discipline of simplicity?" We simply ask the Holy Spirit to speak through His Word to keep us constantly mindful of our highest priority: "… *Seek first the kingdom of God and His righteousness, and all these things shall be added to you*" (Matthew 6:33).

Matthew 6:33 summarizes the biblical discipline of simplicity. In the Sermon on the Mount, Jesus commanded us to first seek the kingdom of God by letting His kingdom rule in our lives. With simple words, as clearly as possible, Jesus stated: "This is what I want you to do …" When He said it, those who were sitting there, listening to His words in the first century, heard Him use a very powerful form of speech. The word "*seek*" is a present active imperative command. "Present" means "do it now"; "active" means "YOU do it now"; "imperative" means "you do it NOW." It is an emphasis on the imperative nature—the command mode. That sounds simple and clear to me, doesn't it to you?

The word "*seek*" is a very graphic word in the Greek language. The word is *zeteo*, which means "to seek in order to find; to seek a thing; to seek [in order to find out] by thinking, meditating, reasoning, to enquire into; to seek after, seek for, aim at, strive after; to seek by requiring or demanding; to crave, demand something from someone. Use all available means to get that which I seek for." That is the first thing Jesus commanded: "I want you to be seeking, craving, demanding, striving to get …"

The next word Jesus used was "first." The English word comes from the Greek word which you probably know—proton, as in the physics of the anatomy of the atom. The word "*proton*" means "first in time or place in any succession of things or persons; first in rank, influence, honor; chief; principal; first, at the first." In essence, Jesus was commanding: "I want you to crave, desire, long for, and aggressively, in any manner, seek at the front of everything else, My rule in your life. My righteousness is to be in your daily walk!"

All of us at one time or another have heard the Great Commission: … "*All authority has been given to Me in heaven and on earth. Go therefore and make disciples of all the nations … teaching them to observe all things that I have commanded you ...*" (Matthew 28:18-20). At any evangelistic or missionary conference someone will state this commission represents Jesus' marching orders for us, which is true. You and I need to ask ourselves daily: *What has Jesus "commanded" me to do?*

Our Commander-in-Chief, the Lord Jesus Christ, could not give us an order more clearly than He has in Matthew 6:33. His true children heard Him then, and responded, just as those who belong to Him by faith do today. Jesus is calling us, His army on earth, to order our lives with Him as our FIRST priority: He is to be FIRST in our time, FIRST in rank of who can tell us what to do, and FIRST in place of what we are seeking. Just as members of the military are expected to obey their superior officers or suffer the consequences, so it is with us who have a far greater Commander than any president, general, or chief of staff.

In any areas where you and I are not following our Commander-in-Chief's orders, we need to ask the Holy Spirit to help us reorder our priorities. First and foremost, we need to let Him rule in our lives so Christ's righteousness reigns in us. Whenever anything is out of control in our lives, it means we are not totally under Christ's control. In that case, we need to promptly get back to faith's basics.

The Apostle Paul, a complex, brilliant, gifted, highly successful and well-known man, knew how to simplify his life. Look again at what he said in Philippians 3:13-14. In that verse, Paul said, "I haven't made it. I am not the ultimate, the pinnacle, or the paragon of perfection. But this is why my life is so powerful." Note he didn't say he had *many* goals; Paul simply had the one goal of keeping his eye on the finish line. Paul had a driving purpose in life and we can see it all the way to the end of his life.

How well did he do? The answer is in 2 Timothy 4:7. Did you know when Paul wrote that verse he was in a subterranean maximum-security dungeon called the Mamertine Prison? This same prison still exists today, right next to the Roman Forum in the city of Rome. Every time I read 2 Timothy 4:7, I am reminded of the time I took a tour group down into that dungeon, which is now a little chapel. After packing everybody into a cramped cell, I had them look up to see a tiny grill, a grate at the top of the dungeon, and the only place light and air comes in. On the dungeon wall we saw a pillar with metal, which is probably where Paul's chains were attached. Seeing the place makes 2 Timothy 4:7 all the more special from knowing Paul was an overcomer through Christ—even while living in a dungeon!

In that verse Paul included his entire life as a believer under the heading of *"the good fight"*—not *"fights."* He had one focus, one simple direction: Paul wanted to run a good race on his God-assigned track. So every day he would check to make sure he was running in the right lane to reaffirm: "Am I accomplishing the will of my Father in heaven?" Thus he could rightfully say: ... *I have kept the faith.*

Paul's life modeled how to reorder personal priorities back to God's. If we don't do so, the sheer weight, gravity, force, and pressure of the world will conform us into a set of priorities other than God's. When that happens we expend energy haphazardly, and end up failing to accomplish what God has planned for us. Do you see why we need to maintain constant vigilance? Satan loves it when we miss out on God's best for us! Thus we are warned: *Be sober, be vigilant; because your adversary the devil walks about like a roaring lion, seeking whom he may devour. Resist him, steadfast in the faith ...* (1 Peter 5:8-9). God says, "Resist! Stop, reorder your priorities to become Mine!"

If you want God's best for your life, you must always put Him first by disciplining yourself daily to spend time alone reading the Scriptures, memorizing, and meditating. During these times of solitude with the Lord, the Holy Spirit will teach you how to cultivate simplicity in your life by totally surrendering to Jesus and completely trusting Him.

Whenever you even begin to sense you're losing touch with God's priorities, and are starting to feel frustrated and anxious about the unfinished tasks in your life, meditate on Psalm 46:10: *Be still, and know I am God ....* For greater impact, look at how this verse reads in other versions of the Bible:

- *Cease striving and know that I am God. Stand silent! Know that I am God! [TLB]*
- *Let be and be still, and know (recognize and understand) that I am God. [AMP]*
- *"Give in", he cries, "admit that I am God." [Moffat]*

- "Stop fighting," he says, "and know that I am God." [TEV]
- ... "Step out of the traffic! Take a long, loving look at me, your High God, above politics, above everything." [The Message]

However we may prefer to read it, this is an emphatic imperative addressed to God's own people. People of every race, color, culture, and era ... people of any level of maturity and age ... people who are employed or unemployed, single or married, with or without children, all people whose God is the Lord. We are commanded to stop (literally) ... rest, relax, let go, and make time for Him. The scene is one of stillness and quietness, listening and waiting before Him. Such foreign experiences in these busy times! Nevertheless, knowing God deeply and intimately requires such discipline. Silence is indispensable if we hope to add depth to our spiritual life.[55]

Solitude, time alone with God in His Word, is the great necessity of our spiritual lives. We need to find times to get alone with God. Few are called to spend many hours in daily prayer, but *all* must spend *some* time. If it is impossible when the family is awake, pray before they get up and after they've gone to bed. If you have no place you can do this at home, find a place to park your car on the way to work and pray in the anonymity of the passing traffic of a busy world. Jesus made time in His ultra busy life, and we can learn much from His perfect example.

55 Charles Swindoll, Intimacy with the Almighty (Dallas: Word Publishing, Inc., 1996), pp. 37-38.

Jesus Modeled the Discipline of Simplicity

Jesus led an incredibly full life. Mark 1:21-34 represents just one day for Christ. Life was filled to the brim with His ministry on that Saturday in Capernaum. Jesus had gone from morning to night giving of Himself to all who came. They came on donkeys, in carts, carried by family, surrounded by crowds; multitudes flocked to the Messiah, the Healer, and the Friend of Sinners.

The truth of this statement appears in Mark 1:32-34 in which Mark recalled Peter's account of the works done by Jesus at the close of a busy day:

At evening, when the sun had set, they brought to Him all who were sick and those who were demon-possessed. And the whole city was gathered together at the door. Then He healed many who were sick with various diseases, and cast out many demons; and He did not allow the demons to speak, because they knew Him.

Capernaum was witness to more of Christ's miracles than any other spot on earth. He preached more sermons in and around Capernaum than at anywhere else during His entire ministry. It is also just outside of Capernaum we discover the habit that gave Jesus the power and strength to live a life focused on giving—He cultivated the discipline of simplicity.

Jesus perfected the art of getting alone with God, always choosing His Father's priorities, because He had learned the secret of waiting on God. Was this practice a regular habit in Christ's life? Yes, from start to finish. Notice these verses: (Emphasis added to the verses below.)

- *… When He had sent the multitudes away, He went up on the mountain by Himself to pray. Now when evening came,* **He was alone there** *(Matthew 14:23).*

- *… When He had sent them away,* **He departed to the mountain to pray** *(Mark 6:46).*

- *… When it was day,* **He departed and went into a deserted place.** *And the crowd sought Him and came to Him, and tried to keep Him from leaving them … (Luke 4:42).*

- *… It came to pass in those days that* **He went out to the mountain** *to pray, and continued all night in prayer to God (Luke 6:12).*

- *Coming out,* **He went to the Mount of Olives**, *as He was accustomed, and His disciples also followed Him. When He came to the place, He said to them, "Pray that you may not enter into temptation." And* **He was withdrawn from them** *about a stone's throw, and He knelt down and prayed, saying, "Father, if it is Your will,* take this cup away from Me; nevertheless not My will, but Yours, be done." Then an angel appeared to Him from heaven, strengthening Him. And being in agony, He prayed more earnestly. Then His sweat became like great drops of blood falling down to the ground. When He rose up from prayer, and had come to His disciples, He found them sleeping from sorrow. Then He said to them, "Why do you sleep? Rise and pray, lest you enter into temptation" (Luke 22:39-46).

- ... *When Jesus perceived that they were about to come and take Him by force to make Him king,* **He departed again to the mountain by Himself alone** *(John 6:15).*

Mark 1:35 reveals this passion of Jesus is seen in His pre-dawn solitude with God. Why do I say that? Because the story of Saturday's river of miracles continued with a wonderful Sunday morning: V*ery early in the morning, while it was still dark, Jesus got up, left the house, and* **went off to a solitary place**, *where he prayed* (NIV, emphasis added).

Jesus had gotten as much sleep as He desired, and then He awoke. It was dark, and everyone was asleep. He noiselessly stole out of the room and found His way to the street. Soon He was out of town and climbing a hillside to some remote spot, possibly a hidden hollow, where He lifted up His soul in ecstasy to the Father.

Jesus exposed His humanity to God as our Perfect Example. As God the Son, Jesus needed no more of the fullness of God (Colossians 2:8-9). Jesus is the exact representation of God's nature (Hebrews 1:3). But the reason Jesus prayed was to show He did not live His life as God the Son apart from God the Father, but rather as a man dependent upon God. Jesus thus stated: "... *The Son can do nothing by himself*..." (John 5:19, NIV) and "... *The words I say to you are not just my own. Rather, it is the Father, living in me, who is doing his work*" (John 14:10, NIV).

Just as Jesus came, lived, and died constantly doing the will of God His Father, so we should seek to live our lives in step and under the control of God's Spirit.[56]

---

[56] These ideas drawn from R. Kent Hughes; Mark 1:35-39

The Joy of Oasis Living—Seeking God First

If you choose to discipline yourself to seek God first, and long to walk as Jesus walked through the power of the Holy Spirit, you will experience the joy I call "oasis living." Having toured the Holy Land many times, I'll now be your guide to the En Gedi oasis. Visiting the oasis has been one of the most enduring experiences for me from the area.

When you get to the lowest spot on the face of the earth, the shores of the Dead Sea, you immediately notice it is hot most of the time. It is also dry, sunbaked, and salted with minerals and chemicals that combine to make the place quite inhospitable for most life forms, other than bacteria. In every direction but one there is lifelessness, death, and scorched rocks. But sprouting from the rocks like a modern-day Garden of Eden is a Dead Sea oasis called En Gedi.

From the earliest times En Gedi has been known and inhabited by desert travelers. From the rocks flow the coolest, sweetest, and freshest waters imaginable. The contrast between the lush green gardens of En Gedi and the stark, barren, lifeless shores of the Dead Sea and the sun-baked mountains ringing it are almost beyond words. Most people have to experience it to fully feel the side-by-side contrast of life and death.

It is to this spot in the wilderness David and his men ran for their lives from King Saul. Hungry, exhausted, hot, and thirsty, they stayed there to refresh and renew their bodies and souls before marching on. And it was this … dry and thirsty land … that prompted David's mighty 63rd Psalm. For David, meditation was taking the God he longed for along with him—no matter what was going on:

> O God, You are my God; **early will I seek You**; my soul thirsts for You; my flesh longs for You in a dry and thirsty land where there is no water. So I have looked for You in the sanctuary, to see Your power and Your glory (Psalm 63:1-2, emphasis added).

The Hebrew word for "seek" means "to seek early or earnestly, look early or diligently for." The word "longs" means "to long for, faint, faint with longing; the word seems to mean "has gone blind," or "gone dark." So Psalm 63:1 means David longingly sought after the Lord so greatly he could hardly wait until the first light of the dawn to spend time alone with Him! Why? Because David sought God *first*, he had found the joy of an ever-present oasis through communing with God in His Word!

With that framework in mind, let's review what I said earlier about meditation: At salvation we became a soul who thirsts for God and longs to "drink in" His Word; a soul longing for the "water of life" (the continual flow of eternal life) to "drink in" freely from God in His Word. Amidst life's arid, sunbaked, lifeless deserts we will find a beautiful, ever-present oasis through communing with God in His Word. In light of this, can you see how beautifully the description fits the depth and joy of David's oasis meditation?

There is simply no better way to bring cool rivers of refreshing water into the driest of times than by a daily En Gedi oasis of meditating upon God through His Word. As one veteran guide expresses it:

> Where can you find an "En Gedi," a place where you can become restored with God's shade and living water, in the midst of your busy days? Just as David and his men needed the life-giving, living water of En Gedi in order to survive their time in the wilderness, God's people today need God's life-giving, living water in order to serve Him in the wilderness of life.
>
> When we are nourished and filled with His living water, we will overflow with streams of living water that we can share with thirsty, needy people who live in a spiritually barren world (John 7:38). But in order to have anything to give, we need to have an En Gedi times of devotion, Bible study, prayer, retreat, meditation where we can meet with God to satisfy our own spiritual thirst. What will you do this coming week to guarantee that you will have time with God your "oasis" who will give you what you need in order to flourish? Accept no substitutes for living water! Although many things in our culture may look like living water, they all fail to give us life, to satisfy our thirst for God.[57]

If we fail to let the Holy Spirit's *"rivers of living water"* flow out of

---

57 Ray Vander Laan, 4-L 314 Faith Lessons On The Life & Ministry Of The Messiah. Leader's Guide (Grand Rapids: Zondervan Publishing House, 1999), p. 314.

our lives, we will not hear the Lord's voice in His Word. Not seeking God first and reordering our priorities to what He would have us do will dry up the wells of our oasis living. As a result, the invisible killer "overload" will soon steal our peace. When our lives become too full and too complex, we're likely to fall prey to letting in influences that distract our minds, crowd our hearts, or blur our perceptions. How can we get back on our God-assigned track so we're once again running in the right lane—God's?

Spiritual Fasting Can Restore Oasis Living

Practicing a spiritual fast is one of the best ways to reorder our priorities, and experience the immense rewards it will bring to our lives. Fasting in the Bible is always described as withholding something that is a proper part of daily life. The saints sometimes fasted from "pleasant foods" or from "the king's wine and meat." Each fast was for focusing intently upon the Lord. But what is a spiritual fast? It is fasting from non-material things which affect, distract, and touch our spiritual lives. This type of fast is the most powerful way to deeply impact your spiritual life because fasting will discipline and focus you.

Here are some ways to help to fast from influences that can distract your mind, crowd your heart, and blur your perceptions as you seek to walk with the Lord:

- **Television:** TV is predictable, available, and captivating. We can be at the cutting edge of events, weather, finances, culture, products, and the pleasures of the entire world. Just as a window opens up a wall so we can see things outside, television is a window that opens our sight to the WHOLE WORLD. Through this window we can see the good and the evil, the profitable and the unprofitable, the useful and the useless. Try a week without any television and invest the same time slots in reading, learning, and meditating upon God's Word. If you can make it for a week, and actually devote equivalent time, your entire life will be impacted by God!

- **News:** Try to go a day with no news of the outside world. Spend the same time in the Word you would spend online, reading the newspaper, skimming articles in magazines, or listening to news on the radio. The Bible is so current it accurately describes the future. The Bible is the ultimate news source. Remember: ... *There is nothing new under the sun* (Ecclesiastes 1:9). If you meditate on the Scriptures, you will be far ahead of those who neglect this discipline. In Psalm 119:97-104, God says you will be much wiser, smarter, and skillful than others in any field because of time spent meditating upon His Word!

- **Radio:** Now we are getting revolutionary. Try a week where, instead of having the radio on in the car, you pray. Pray aloud for each request God brings to mind, for every missionary your local church supports. Then pray for your elders, deacons, music ministry, teachers, and so forth. If you run out of requests, do what I do—pray for every family in the church directory. Ask God to make them grow in Christ, to stir their hearts to turn from evil, and cause them to hunger for the Word.

- **Music:** Fast from all secular, non-Christian music for a day or a week. Substitute only soothing, heart-quieting music that reflects God's character, draws you to worship Him, and mirrors His Word. Especially seek to listen to music based on Scripture, sound doctrine, worship, the Psalms, and all putting God *first*. With the proper music, your heart and mind will be flooded with peace and focused upon the Lord.

- **Magazines:** Try fasting for a month from *all* magazines. Substitute equivalent time and attention to God's Word and see what happens!

- **Videos:** Try a whole month without watching any videos, DVDs, or movies.

To live a powerful Word filled life, be vigilant to discipline yourself to continually rid life of influences leading you astray from your *first* priority of ordering your life with Jesus. He is to be *first* in your time, *first* in rank of who can tell you what to do, and *first* in place of what you are to seek. Ephesians 5:15-16 tells us to … *walk circumspectly [accurately or precisely with great care[58]], not as fools but as wise, redeeming the time, because the days are evil.*

[58] The MacArthur Study Bible, p. 1812.

Some Byproducts of a Spiritual Fast

If you practice substituting scriptural meditation on God in His Word for wasted time, you will experience His blessings through fifteen signs of spiritual maturity that will appear in your life:

1. You will experience a growing hunger and desire for God Himself, His Word, and His Way.
2. You will learn the difference between walking in the flesh and walking in the Spirit on a daily basis.
3. You will show a growing ability to apply God's Word.
4. You will show obvious "works of faith" such as serving others and giving.
5. You will become firmly grounded in Truth and no longer be swayed or deceived by false doctrines.
6. You will exhibit a great desire for fellowship with other believers, and your life will evidence the fruit of the Holy Spirit.
7. Your desire for worldly possessions will diminish, but unselfish motives and a spirit of cooperation will increase.
8. You will be quick to repent of your sins, and readily forgive others.
9. You will experience a growing compassion for the lost, and among believers be actively assisting in the spiritual development of others.
10. You will live with a continuous sense of God, knowledge of His character, and His will.
11. You will live a life characterized by peace.
12. You will have a growing attitude of meekness and humility.
13. Your will have an orderly life at home, and you will set your life after seeking God's purpose for your family rather than just your own.
14. You will see the marks of "the disciplines of a godly life" in each area of your life (physical, mental, spiritual) as you grow in the ability to put to death any ungodliness that rears its ugly head.

15. You will mature into having an increasingly powerful prayer life, coupled with a dynamic lifestyle of worship![59]

God wants us to be godly stewards of the time He gives us! We are each allotted the same amount of time daily, and we can put God first by making it count for Christ. Even incremental moments can result in huge blocks of time. Remember, just twelve minutes per day equals seventy-three hours per year, or once through God's Word; twenty-four minutes per day equals 146 hours per year, or twice through God's Word; and thirty-six minutes per day equals 219 hours—enough time to thoughtfully read God's Word through three times!

If you aren't using your time wisely, perhaps you have a wrong perspective of time. Poor time management can make you an easy target for "overload" and its ever-mounting pile of "unfinished tasks." So ask the Holy Spirit to reveal where you're falling short and then give you the empowerment to reorder your life according to God's priorities. Oh, how we should pray: *"Precious Holy Spirit, … teach us to number our days, that we may gain a heart of wisdom* (Psalm 90:12)!"

[59] Adapted from Doug Morrell's Disciples Corner e-mail newsletter, October 11, 2003.

Reordering to God's Priorities: Getting Started

Perhaps the Holy Spirit has stirred your heart in this chapter, but you are young in the faith and need a little more direction on how to form a meditation habit. Here are some simple but important principles I use to deepen and enrich my own meditation in God's Word:

- **PRAY FIRST: Ask God for the Spirit of wisdom and revelation into God's Word** (Ephesians 1:17). God wants to give you His insights through your meditation! It's very important you understand this, and keep from letting feelings and emotions stand in the way of time with the Lord. You may have to occasionally fight through a case of the "blahs," but God never does!

- **GRAB SOMETHING: Write the Scripture down in your notebook or journal.** Writing down the Scripture takes disciplined effort, but the more disciplined you are, the more opportunity you give the Holy Spirit to speak. Write something down, and you will tend to think about it in a deeper way because you'll analyze it more carefully, and your thoughts will then be more penetrating.

- **STOP FOR A MOMENT: Write down what you understand from a particular Scripture.** Initially you might think: *This thought is nothing new—nothing unusual. Why bother writing it down? I'll wait until I think of something really profound.* But if you do that, your mind is going to start floating away to another subject. So write down your thoughts, even though they might not seem very insightful at the time.

- **LISTEN TO GOD: Apply the understanding to your life.** As you continue to meditate, the Lord will probably begin to fill you with incredible insight concerning His character and love. When you receive these "nuggets of gold" in your heart, don't just relax and be content to store them away for safekeeping—apply them to your life.

- **ANSWER HIM: Respond to God.** Meditation will bring you to a point where you're bursting with a new response to God. Don't lose the moment by hesitating to apply what you've just learned. Seize this wonderful opportunity to obediently respond to the living God.

- **START A NEW HABIT: Seek wisdom.** Meditating and receiving understanding from the Lord is not just a quiet and passive activity. The Lord won't fill you to the brim while you sit with an open Bible. Instead, He requires you take an active stance in meditation. As the truth of God penetrates your mind it will attack and demolish the sin it confronts. John 17:17 was what Jesus told us: *"Sanctify them by Your truth. Your word is truth."* In Matthew 4:1-11 (the three wilderness temptations) He demonstrated it! Jesus said the way we become holy is through the Word. Always remember this principle:

God's Word will keep you from sin—and sin will keep you from God's Word!

Why have I been emphasizing meditation so much? Because meditation is a simple key of being empowered by the Holy Spirit to live a Word filled life! If you long for the joy and simplicity of an ever-present oasis through communing with God in His Word, then seek Him first, and continually reorder your priorities back to what God wants you to do!

My Prayer for You:
Father in Heaven, I pray simple words and thoughts, a simple message, and a simple yet powerful truth will grip all of our lives; that not one of us who has ears to hear will miss what You want to say to us. We need to reorder the priorities we live by—the marching orders we march to every day—we need to reorder them on a regular basis back to Yours. We slip, we slide, we slowly move off course. We are pushed by the winds of our own and other people's desires. When we find ourselves on the reefs of anxiety and feel unfinished in every part of our lives, it's time to look at how we got off-course. I pray we would do that today and make some simple choices to reorder our lives to follow Your priorities. Open our eyes to see Your truth. Touch our wills and stir our hearts to obey them. In Jesus precious name I pray. Amen.

13

> " 'Call to Me, and I will answer you, and show you great and mighty things, which you do not know.' "
> —**Jeremiah 33:3**

Discipline Six—Supplication:
Prayer Is the Power of a Word Filled Life

D**ID YOU KNOW COMMUNICATION IS** the largest single global business? From cell phones to e-mail, instant messaging to vast online communities like MySpace and FaceBook, humans have a great desire and capacity to communicate with those they need and love.

If you love someone, don't you just naturally want to communicate with them?[60] Communication, because it is love's nourishment, is a foundation key in any healthy relationship.

60 MP3 CD AudioDYG-22:030713AM, MP3 CD Audio DYG -09:030302AM

God blessed Bonnie and me with eight dear children to love and train for Him. As newborns, it was so sweet to watch their little eyes adjust and start following objects. When we could tell we had their attention, we put our faces up close so they knew we were there for them. We communicated our love during their infancy through smiles, the way hands gently bathed, dressed, and cradled them, through soft voices and songs we sang about Jesus. It was precious to teach them words like "Mama," "Daddy," "Thank you," and "Jesus." As they grew in their relationship with us, we delighted more and more in conversations with them—and received love back!

It's the same in our relationship with God. Have you ever considered that the Bible is a "love letter" from an infinite, eternal heavenly Father? Look at how He so clearly revealed His love for us in John 3:16: *"For God so loved the world that He gave His only begotten Son, that whoever believes in Him should not perish but have everlasting life." In return, we love Him because He first loved us* (1 John 4:19). All who enter into God's family by faith in Jesus should want to communicate love back to Him.

Throughout the Bible, God communicates how greatly He loves us and longs to enjoy the delight of whole conversations with us—and receive love back from us. Prayer is talking to the God we love. Just as we parents find it precious to teach our little ones to talk, God finds it precious to teach His children "How to Talk to Me" lessons, or what the Bible teaches on prayer. If you have never done a word study on prayer, you would be enriched beyond measure to go from cover to cover in His Word and find out what your heavenly Father wants you to know on this subject.

Many years ago someone challenged me to do exactly that. I was to take as long as necessary to listen to everything the One I pray to has to say about how, when, where, and *why we should pray to Him*. That made sense, so I took my Bible, a blue highlighter, and underlined every passage that deals with prayer: every prayer, every person who prayed, what they said, and what God instructed about prayer. I avidly read each of the 31,102 verses of God's Word and found there are many different references to this vital topic. In the process, I also discovered there were a lot of truths I didn't know about prayer.

Did you know everything we need to know about communicating with God, is mentioned in the Word about 350 times? The words "pray" and "prayer" are actually translations of ten different Hebrew words and seven different Greek words, providing a multitude of personalized options in our approach to Him. In each of those seventeen words the Almighty portrays the attitudes and approaches He wants us to use when we communicate with Him. As He catches our attention, and our eyes start following Him, He wants to teach us how to talk to Him. So we need to go to His "love letter"—God's Word—and ask: "Lord, would you teach me how to talk to You in a way that pleases You?" This is a fundamental and foundational study, and the sixth of the godly disciplines we'll be studying for the next three chapters—"the discipline of supplication."

What Is Biblical Prayer?

To practice biblical prayer, it is essential to grasp the richness of key prayer words. Do a personal word study on prayer (Strong's Exhaustive Concordance of the Bible is an excellent study tool), and feel the depth of the heart's desire for the Lord as reflected in these special God-inspired words to us. For example, look at this wonderful passage Jesus spoke about prayer:

> "**Ask**, and it will be given to you; **seek**, and you will find; knock, and it will be opened to you. For everyone who asks **receives**, and he who seeks **finds**, and to him who knocks it **will be opened**" (Matthew 7:7-8, emphasis added).

Do you really believe everyone who asks actually receives? Perhaps you've asked God for something and concluded He didn't hear you because whatever you asked didn't happen. Maybe you prayed He would heal a loved one, but the person died. Or you asked Him for a particular job but didn't get it. So you thought: God didn't answer me! Oh, but He DID. Don't forget that God gives three answers to prayer: "Yes," "No," and "Wait." This last option can be the worst answer because it's so hard to wait.[61]

God's promises can never fail because He is GOD. Therefore, if you seek from Him you will find what you are seeking for—God's will for your life, a life partner, your mission in life, the right career, and so forth—all in His perfect timing. In response to your prayers, He might say: "Yes, I agree that is best for you"; "No, that is not good for you"; or "Wait, because I am going to show you something better." We have to accept such truth about prayer. And Matthew 7:8 says everyone who communicates with God properly *will* get an answer!

Not only are we to exercise "the discipline of supplication," but we are also to pray unceasingly (1 Thessalonians 5:17). As Jesus told His disciples in Mark 9, there is territory we will never enter for Him

---

[61] There are ten different Hebrew words on how to wait. If you want to do another highly profitable study, get out a highlighter and look for the "waits" of the Bible.

without learning the secret of supplication, which is fasting (denying ourselves) and praying for God's intervention. So we should make it a top priority to discipline ourselves for the purpose of prayer—like the following Old Testament warriors of the faith from whom we can learn a lot.

Prayer: The Pathway to God's Power

Wouldn't you like to learn to pray powerfully like saints in the Scriptures? They understood the key to unleashing prayers God always answers is to have them flowing from a Word filled life. If we considered just Old Testament saints alone, there is a whole host who led Word filled lives because they formed a lifelong habit of prayer. Among those saints are Hannah, Daniel, Samuel, David, Solomon, Hezekiah, Abraham, Ezra, Nehemiah, Job, and Jonah. All had two special traits in common: (1) they judged themselves, and (2) they prayed habitually. Because their lives were open before God, He could cleanse and commune with them at all times. This is vital in enabling us to be in touch with our God. Consider these prayer examples:

- **Hannah** prayed in 1 Samuel 1:10, 12, 26-27 and 2:1. Her times of bitter suffering drove her to prayer.

- **Solomon** prayed as he dedicated the temple in 1 Kings 8:23-53. In the prayer he referred to conscious needs of his people, who were God's people, and how they pleaded for help (vv. 33-36, 38-39, 44-45, and 48-49). He directed prayer toward the great name of God.

- **Hezekiah** prayed in 2 Chronicles 30:18-20. There was sin in the nation he dealt with as king; he prayed, and God answered him.

- **Nehemiah** prayed in Nehemiah 1:4-11 after receiving the report about the condition of Jerusalem. It was always a part of his daily life to pray.

67 Dr. James Strong (1822-1894) labored along with 100 colleagues to produce one of the most widely used reference works to catalogue the Greek and Hebrew words of the Bible. In 1890 Strong's Concordance listed 8,674 different Hebrew root words and 5,523 Greek root words. These are used to help those who do not understand Greek and Hebrew to find the original inspired words that underlie the translation of the Bible into English.

- **Job** prayed in Job 42:10 for his friends and God heard him. It is important to note he first came to a proper view of himself before he could properly intercede for others.

- **Daniel** prayed one of the great prayers of the Bible in Daniel 9:4-19 where he first identified with the sin problems of the people as an intercessor.

Let's now turn our attention to that giant of faith—Ezra—and his exciting prayers in Psalm 119. The priority of prayer in a Word filled life is seen in Ezra's extensive use of the imperative class[62] of verbs in the Hebrew language. There are also, in the beauty of Hebrew language, three different verb forms used in the imperatives of the 119th Psalm: Piel,[63] Hiphil,[64] and Qal.[65]

Forty-eight times, with twenty-three phrases, Ezra cried to the Lord. The secret of his fruitful life was his choice to invite the Lord into every part of his life, every day. Now let us examine these in the order of Ezra's use, beginning with his top three prayers: **1.** revive (quicken) me, **2.** teach me, and **3.** give me understanding. Let us meditate on his prayers to learn the power and joys of a Word filled life![66]

Prayer One—Revive me (Strong's[67] #2421, *chayah*: to preserve alive, let live; to give life; to quicken, revive, refresh; to restore to life; to cause to grow). *"Revive me"* was what Ezra prayed for most. In fact, he prayed for that sixteen times, which amounts to one-third of the prayers recorded in Psalm 119. He was saying to the Lord, "Refill me with Your life. Cause me to grow in Your fullness of life. Quicken me." "Quicken me" is an old-fashioned way of saying "Fill me with life!" (Emphasis added in the verses below.)

- *My soul clings to the dust;* **revive me according to Your word** (v. 25). This, Ezra's first Word filled prayer, is the best of all the revival verses. He was saying, "Revive me; cause me to grow through my afflictions; cause me to grow through my discouragements; cause me to grow and be filled with life when my soul is face down in the dust."

---

[62] This verb class indicates an order or a command.

[63] PIEL usually expresses an "intensive" or "intentional" action. Qal: "he broke" vs. Piel "he broke to pieces, he smashed." Also the Piel can express a "repeated" or "extended" action. Qal: "he jumped" vs. Piel "he skipped, he hopped." And finally, some intransitive verbs in Qal: "to be strong/to become great" become transitive in Piel "to strengthen, to fortify/to make great." This verb form is found 18 times in the imperatives of Psalm 119 verses – 27; 29; 33-39; 73; 94; 125; 133; 135; 144; 146; 169-170.

[64] HIPHIL usually expresses the "causative" action of Qal. Qal: "he ate, he came, he reigned" vs. Hiphil: "he caused to eat, he fed," "he caused to come, he brought," "he made king, he crowned." Hiphil is also often used to form verbs from nouns and adjectives. Noun or Adjective: "ear/far" in the Hiphil: "to listen (lend an ear)/to remove oneself, put far away." The form accounts for 13.3% of the verbs parsed. While Qal accounts for 66.7% of all verbs in the Old Testament. This verb form is found 21 times in the imperatives of Psalm 119 verses – 12; 18; 25-26; 28; 37; 40; 64; 66; 88; 107-108; 124; 135; 149; 153-154; 156; 159; 176.

[65] QAL is the most frequently used verb pattern. It expresses the "simple" or "casual" action of the root in the active voice. Examples: he sat, he ate, he went, he said, he rose, he bought. This form accounts for 66.7% of the verbs parsed. This verb form is found 19 times in the imperatives of Psalm 119 verses – 17; 22; 29; 49; 58; 86; 108; 115-117; 122; 124; 132; 145; 149; 153-154; 159.

[66] The following definitions were taken from Strong's Exhaustive Concordance of the Bible.

When I pastored in Georgia for a couple of years, it was quite an experience to be in the Old South. When I went for a haircut in the local barbershop, I enjoyed listening to the men talk while the barber worked. Once I heard, "Man, I am feeling lower than a snake's belly!" He meant life was hard, and that is what I think of in verse 25. Ezra—the man who copied the whole Bible, the man who started the synagogues, the most revered Jewish spiritual leader, except for Moses—had hard, discouraging, depressing times in his life. So much so he said, "It's like I am face down in the dust!" If an Old Testament giant of meditation could feel like that, anybody can.

The true character of a person is revealed by how he or she responds to trials and afflictions. How do you get out of the position of feeling "lower than a snake's belly", and cope with times of struggle, loneliness, or depression? There is only one method of getting quickened; become immersed in God and His Word.

- *Turn away my eyes from looking at worthless things, and **revive me in Your way*** (v. 37). This was Ezra's greatest prayer: "I have choices to make as I am going through life," he said, "so I ask You, Lord, to turn my eyes away from looking at worthless things." He is so practical. Whenever I notice someone not growing spiritually—not being alive and flourishing and bearing fruit—I surmise it is because they are spending their time looking at and investing in worthless things. To avoid that in his own life, Ezra prayed: *"Revive me in Your way."* God does this by turning away our eyes from looking on what displeases Him.
- *Behold, I long for Your precepts;* **revive me in Your righteousness** (v. 40). You grow in righteousness by longing for God's precepts—His divine directions for life that are right, and cause great rejoicing!
- **Revive me according to Your lovingkindness,** *so I may keep the testimony of Your mouth* (v. 88). What is *"lovingkindness"*? The Hebrew word, chesed, means "loyalty to us." God is loyal to us. He says, "I call you by name. I purchased you; you are My very own, and belong to Me." In light of verse 88, we can have confidence in God's lovingkindness; He will keep His Word, take care of us, and save us to the uttermost!
- *I am afflicted very much;* **Revive me, O LORD, according to**

Your word (v. 107). Did you know Ezra talked about affliction seven times? "Whenever things don't turn out as I'd hoped, and I am afflicted with trouble," he said, "I am driven to God to find strength and renewal!" The Lord wants us to turn to Him and His Word in troublesome times.

A dear friend of mine, having just lost a family member, shared in a Bible study that when he went through the dead person's effects he found seventy unopened boxes of shoes. Apparently, whenever that family member became discouraged, a buying trip to the shopping mall was a typical coping method. This is a common scenario in America. To forget all their troubles, many shop for things they don't even need, see a movie, attend a special event, go to a party, or eat comfort foods. But that is not God's way. What does His Word say to do when we are feeling down, or suffering afflictions? Like Ezra, we are to turn to the Bible and be revived by the Word.

If you read these verses carefully, you can almost hear Ezra's aching heart beating as he cried out to the Lord: Hear my voice according to Your loving-kindness; O LORD, revive me according to Your justice. ... *Plead my cause and redeem me; revive me according to Your word. ... Great are Your tender mercies, O LORD; revive me according to Your judgments* (vv. 149, 154, 156).

- Consider how I love Your precepts; **revive me, O LORD, according to Your lovingkindness** (v. 159). This was Ezra's frequent prayer. He was saying, "I am deflated, afflicted, and troubled. My life is bent out of shape!"

Second Prayer—Teach me (Strong's #3925, lamad: teach, help me to learn, help me become skillful, help me to become instructed in, diligently, expert, skillful, teachers). Ezra's second Word filled prayer, prayed thirteen times, was: *"Teach me!"* He didn't go through life trying to find out everything he could. Instead, his focus was: "I want to know all there is to know about You, God"; usually something that happens from love. For example, I am a lifelong student of my wife, Bonnie. I want to know everything I can about her. When we visit where she used to live in New York, I want to learn all about her life back then. Am I an observer of her because I am paid, and have to do so? No, I simply love her.

Ezra likewise wanted to know all about the Lord because he loved Him. His continual exposure to God's Word, his love for Him became insatiable: the more he learned, the more his love grew; the more his love grew, the more he wanted to know about God and His ways. Remember these prayers are imperatives: Ezra was crying out to God saying, "Teach me!" What did Ezra so fervently ask God to teach him? Repeatedly, Ezra wanted God to teach His statutes, so he might have good judgment and knowledge. (Emphasis added in the verses below.)

- Blessed are You, O LORD! **Teach me Your statutes** (v. 12).
- I have declared my ways, and You answered me; **teach me Your statutes** (v. 26).
- **Teach me**, O LORD, the way of Your statutes, and I shall keep it to the end (v. 33).
- The earth, O LORD, is full of Your mercy; **teach me Your statutes** (v. 64).
- **Teach me good judgment and knowledge,** for I believe Your commandments (v. 66).
- You are good, and do good; **teach me Your statutes** (v. 68).
- Accept, I pray, the freewill offerings of my mouth, O LORD, and **teach me Your judgments** (v. 108).
- Deal with Your servant according to Your mercy, and **teach me Your statutes** (v. 124).
- Make Your face shine upon Your servant, and **teach me Your statutes** (v. 135).

Ezra said, "I want to know You are smiling upon me, and approve of what I am doing! I want it so much I want You to teach me—to show me what You want me to do." Wouldn't you like a child or employee like that? To be involved in a relationship where the person says, "I just want to please you, so tell me what you want me to do and I'll do it!" Can you imagine what God will do with a life presented to Him, and the person says, "Lord, revive me! I want my life to be quickened, and brought to fullness by You—not by substances or experiences, not by media or shopping, not by music or comfort foods, or anything else in this world. I don't need any of these to cheer me because I am going to be revived by You." What a relationship of dependence! And when we get into a Word filled living, depending on Him, then He lays His desires upon us so they become ours—desires we long for, and pray for, and God accomplishes supernaturally through our lives. Oh, the wonder of a Word filled life!

Third Prayer—Make me understand (Strong's #995, biyn: cause me to—understand, consider, be prudent, perceive, regard, discern, be instructed). Ezra always wanted to see things God's way. He didn't just say, "Tell me what You think." He said, "I want to know what Your will is so I can do it, so help me understand it." This is the heart of a willing servant. This is an attitude God can't resist. He pours His blessings and power into and through a life. As you can see from the following verses, Ezra longed for God to give the understanding needed to please Him. (Emphasis added to the verses below.)

- **Make me understand** the way of Your precepts; so shall I meditate on Your wonderful works (v. 27).
- **Give me understanding,** and I shall keep Your law; indeed, I shall observe it with my whole heart (v. 34).
- Your hands have made me and fashioned me; **give me understanding,** that I may learn Your commandments (v. 73).
- I am Your servant; **give me understanding,** that I may know Your testimonies (v. 125).
- The righteousness of Your testimonies is everlasting; **give me understanding,** and I shall live (v. 144).
- Let my cry come before You, O LORD; **give me understanding** according to Your word (v. 169).

Prayer: The Pathway to God's Blessings

Now feast upon the beauty of these remaining prayer phrases that flowed from Ezra's insatiable Word filled heart. (Emphasis added to the verses below.)

- **Strengthen me** (Strong's #6965, quwm). *My soul melts from heaviness; strengthen me according to Your word. … Establish Your word to Your servant, who is devoted to fearing You* (vv. 28, 38).

- **Incline me** (Strong's #5186, natah). *Incline my heart to Your testimonies, and not to covetousness* (v. 36).

- **Help me** (Strong's #5826, azar). *All Your commandments are faithful; they persecute me wrongfully; help me!* (v. 86).

- **Save me** (Strong's #3467, yasha). *I am Yours, save me; for I have sought Your precepts. ... I cry out to You; save me, and I will keep Your testimonies* (vv. 94, 146).

- **Grant me graciously** (Strong's #2623, chanan). *Remove from me the way of lying, and grant me Your law graciously. ... I entreated Your favor with my whole heart; be merciful to me according to Your word. ... Look upon me and be merciful to me, as Your custom is toward those who love Your name* (vv. 29, 58, 132).

- **Remove from me** (Strong's #1556, galal). *Remove from me reproach and contempt, for I have kept Your testimonies* (v. 22).

- **Take away from me** (Strong's #5493, suwr). *Remove from me the way of lying, and grant me Your law graciously* (v. 29).

- **Come upon me** (Strong's #935, bow). *Let Your mercies come also to me, O LORD—Your salvation according to Your word. ... Let Your tender mercies come to me, that I may live; for Your law is my delight. ... Let my supplication come before You; deliver me according to Your word* (vv. 41, 77, 170).

- **Consider me** (Strong's #7200, rawah). *Consider my affliction and deliver me, for I do not forget Your law. ... Consider how I love Your precepts; revive me, O LORD, according to Your lovingkindness* (vv. 153, 159).

- **Shine on me** (Strong's #215, owr). *Make Your face shine upon Your servant, and teach me Your statutes* (v. 135).

- **Make me go** (Strong's #1869, darak). *Make me walk in the path of Your commandments, for I delight in it* (v. 35).

- **Turn me away** (Strong's #5674, abar). *Turn away my eyes from looking at worthless things, and revive me in Your way. ... Turn away my reproach which I dread, for Your judgments are good* (vv. 37, 39).

- **Uphold me** (Strong's #5564, sawmak). *Uphold me according to Your word, that I may live; and do not let me be ashamed of my hope* (v. 116).

- **Hold me up** (Strong's #5582, sawad). *Hold me up, and I shall be safe, and I shall observe Your statutes continually* (v. 117).

- **Redeem me** (Strong's #6299, padah). *Redeem me from the oppression of man, that I may keep Your precepts* (v. 134). (Strong's #1350, ga'al: to redeem, deliver, avenge, act as a kinsman). *Plead my cause and redeem me; revive me according to Your word* (v. 154).

- **Deliver me** (Strong's #2502, chalats). *Consider my affliction and deliver me, for I do not forget Your law* (v. 153).

- **Hear me** (Strong's #6030, anah). *I cry out with my whole heart; hear me, O LORD! I will keep Your statutes* (v. 145).

- **Seek me** (Strong's #1245, baqah). *I have gone astray like a lost sheep; seek Your servant, for I do not forget Your commandments* (v. 176).

- **Let me not wander** (Strong's #7886, shagah). *With my whole heart I have sought You; oh, let me not wander from Your commandments!* (v. 10).

- **Open me** (Strong's #1540, galah). *Open my eyes, that I may see wondrous things from Your law* (v. 18).

I pray you, like Ezra, long to experience the wonders of a Word filled life through the power of prayer. Ask the Holy Spirit to give you an insatiable desire to know and love Jesus Christ with all your heart, soul, mind, and strength—and He will. Make God's Word your top priority: obey what He tells you to do, which also means making prayer an absolute must in your life. Practice God-consciousness throughout each day by sweetly communing with Him about anything and everything. Nothing is too large or too small to discuss with the Lord!

As we close this introductory chapter on prayer, it is *my* prayer God will give you a personal vision for how to pray more effectively. For, as we saw in chapter 12, our prayers are as an incense offering to God! He collects them, treasures them, wants them, seeks them, and responds to them. It glorifies Him when we call upon the Lord to do great and mighty things!

My Prayer for You:

Father in Heaven, I thank You for the privilege of sharing the truths of Your Word with those who are hungering to know You better! I pray we hear Your voice calling us to make whatever choices necessary to have a life filled with Your Word. As a by-product, may our prayers flow from a Word filled life so You will hear them and respond. I ask You to stir our hearts toward that end. Oh, what power, what joy, what fruitfulness flows out of a Word filled life! In the name of Jesus I pray. Amen.

14

Now in the morning, having risen a long while before daylight, He went out and departed to a solitary place; and there He prayed.
—**Mark 1:35**

Supplication:
With Jesus in the School of Prayer

JESUS NEVER TAUGHT HIS DISCIPLES how to preach—He only taught them how to pray.

Although we don't know much about Christ's life before His public ministry started, we do know this: He was the perfect son, brother, worker, neighbor, and student.[68] The next era was His three years of perfect serving and teaching, when Jesus operated His School of Prayer, with twelve students who followed Him everywhere. They learned to pray by listening and watching Jesus. Their textbook was God's Word. Through the eyes of those inspired writers and the quickening of God's Holy Spirit we, too, can learn how to pray like Jesus.

Have you ever caught the connection that Jesus was perfect all the time because He prayed all the time? And twenty-plus centuries later, He is *still* praying; He has never stopped! In fact, Hebrews 7:25 tells us Jesus, our High Priest, … *always lives to make intercession for* [us]. If you stop and think long enough about this verse, you'll see what a

68 MP3 CD Audio DYG-22:030713AM, MP3 CD Audio DYG-09:030302AM

tremendously great emphasis on the power of prayer it is! Don't you find it absolutely *amazing* the Lord God of the Universe continually prays for you? What a comfort!

Look at the beauty of Christ's longest recorded prayer in John 17, which is probably what was often on His lips as He spoke to His Father. Note He also prayed for all who would ever believe in Him by faith—including you and me.

> **Christ prayed for Himself (see John 17:1-5):** *Jesus spoke these words, lifted up His eyes to heaven, and said: "Father, the hour has come. Glorify Your Son, that Your Son also may glorify You ..." (v. 1).*

> **Christ prayed for His disciples (see John 17:6-19):** *"I have manifested Your name to the men whom You have given Me out of the world. They were Yours, You gave them to Me, and they have kept Your word" (v. 6).*

> **Christ prayed for all believers to the end of the age (see John 17:20-26):** *"I do not pray for these alone, but also for those who will believe in Me through their word ..." (v. 20).*

No matter what was going on, or where He was, Jesus found a way to be alone with God. He needed and wanted to find **places** where He was away from everything and everyone else so He could uninterruptedly delight in prayer as He communed with His Father. Even in Jesus' incredibly perfect moment of death, the last words on His lips are a prayer to His Father as He gave up His Spirit!

Six Lessons in the School of Prayer

Although prayer is mentioned by Christ, we don't find an actual record of Him praying in the Gospels until Matthew 11. Therefore, we will start His "How to Talk to Me" lessons in Matthew 11.

Lesson 1—
Prayer should be natural.

In the verses below, Jesus was upbraiding and berating the cities around Chorazin, Bethsaida, and others. These cities were in the golden triangle where about 60 percent of His ministry took place, but their citizens did not respond to what they heard.

> *Then He began to rebuke the cities in which most of His mighty works had been done, because they did not repent: "Woe to you, Chorazin! Woe to you, Bethsaida! For if the mighty works which were done in you had been done in Tyre and Sidon, they would have repented long ago in sackcloth and ashes. But I say to you, it will be more tolerable for Tyre and Sidon in the day of judgment than for you. And you, Capernaum, who are exalted to heaven, will be brought down to Hades; for if the mighty works which were done in you had been done in Sodom, it would have remained until this day. But I say to you that it shall be more tolerable for the land of Sodom in the day of judgment than for you"* (Matthew 11:20-24).

Right in the middle of going through that indictment of the cities (and most likely dealing with questions from His disciples as well) Jesus prayed: … *"I thank You, Father, Lord of heaven and earth, that You have hidden these things from the wise and prudent and have revealed them to babes. Even so, Father, for so it seemed good in Your sight"* (Matthew 11:25-26).

Did you catch what was happening there? Jesus explained to His disciples the hardness of the human heart, and how those people were rejecting the gospel. Then, right in the middle of it, while still looking at them, He prayed to His Father. Do you see how natural prayer was for Jesus? He talked to God all the time. He could be going through everyday life and suddenly continue the conversation He had all the time with His Father. Prayer was just like every other part of His natural life, and is how He wants prayer to be to us.

Did you know the way people respond when asked to lead in prayer is a good indicator of where they are spiritually? If they seem "caught off guard," and must think for a while before coughing out a prayer, it is a sign prayer is not natural for them. If someone asked you to introduce your spouse, would you hesitate or use flowery, lofty language? Of course not. You know your spouse so well it would be easy to respond immediately to such a request. That is simply what prayer is. If asked to lead in prayer today, how would you respond? Hesitantly or naturally?

Lesson 2—
Always give thanks for God's provisions.

This is the second time Jesus prayed in Matthew. It took place on the grassy slopes going down to the Sea of Galilee, and Jesus is about to feed the 5,000: ... *He commanded the multitudes to sit down on the grass. And He took the five loaves and the two fish [the little boy's bag lunch], and looking up to heaven, He blessed and broke and gave the loaves to the disciples; and the disciples gave to the multitudes* (Matthew 14:19).

I love Israel! Having been there many times, I can easily envision the Sea of Galilee, the thousands of hungry people milling around on those luscious, green, grassy hillsides, the looks on their faces as they all pondered what was going to happen, the disciples walking through the crowd, urging them to sit, and all eyes intently focused on Jesus as He held the only food in the place—and looked up to give thanks to His heavenly Father for His provision! What is the lesson? Jesus didn't need that little boy's lunch; nor did He need His disciples. He could have had angels come and hand out personal pizzas to everyone. But everything Jesus did had a lesson behind it. In this case, He was stopping to focus on the One whom He taught about in the Lord's Prayer: *"Give us this day our daily bread"* (Matthew 6:11). Jesus acknowledged that, even for Him, everything came from God (James 1:17): it was God the Father's provision.[69]

As a little boy, my parents taught me to always pray before I ate. The first time of eating without being in the presence of my parents, I had a choice to make. I sat down at one of the big tables in the cavernous lunch room of Haslett Public Schools, opened my brown paper bag, and spread out the lunch my mother sent. Then came the moment of truth: sitting there surrounded by a food fight and other various distractions, I folded my hands, bowed my head, and prayed.

---

69 There was also a feeding of 4,000 in Matthew 15:36, but with a whole different crowd. It was actually in the Gentile portion of the Decapolis area. However, the lesson was the same: always give thanks to God for His provisions!

It got quiet around me as everybody noticed, and a lot of kids made fun of me. However, a couple came up to me and asked, "Can we eat lunch with you tomorrow? We pray too—or we should." Before long, we filled a whole table in the cafeteria where we ate lunch and prayed together. That gradually evolved into my first Bible study in school. The point is this: we never know who's watching when we give thanks to God in public. In my own life, after praying before a meal, it's not uncommon to be approached by someone who wants to know if I am a Christian. Often, that has led into a fruitful ministry opportunity for the Lord. So never forget to thank God for His provisions—both publicly and privately!

Lesson 3—
Reorder to God's priorities as needed.

In Matthew 14:23 we see an example of Jesus arranging a time and a place to find solitude with His Father: ... *When He had sent the multitudes away, He went up on the mountain by Himself to pray. Now when evening came, He was alone there.* Do you remember what happened? After Jesus fed the 5,000, He knew the crowd would want to make Him their king. After all, it would be normal to think: "Wow! This Jesus is great! He can make food from nothing, heal sick and broken people, and put back limbs and eyes and everything else … He would make the best king … We would never die in battle, or have to carry around ammunition or food—He could take care of it all!" So what did Jesus do? He withdrew from the supposed popularity, because He recognized it was part of Satan's temptation. Jesus never sought fame. He was fully aware of how transient, fickle, and how quickly the winds of people's emotions change. He sent them away and reoriented Himself in prayer.

If you are in any kind of public ministry, be careful you don't let the praise of people go to your head. Always give God the credit He deserves. The way to stay humble is to reorient your thinking with prayer. Even Jesus, as a man, had to learn that. Hebrews 5:8 says *though He was a Son, yet He learned obedience* …. How God in human flesh had to learn obedience is certainly hard to understand, but we do know He perfectly modeled what Word filled living is about—proving love for God through obedience to His commands.

The lesson: keep reordering your life to stay in step with how God wants you to live.

Lesson 4—
Ask that God's will be done in all things.

Matthew 26:36-39 contains the most extensive lesson the disciples learned from Jesus. By the way, the lessons they were taught are in the Gospels. Jesus prayed a lot more than this, but the whole world couldn't contain all the books that could be written about His life. The lessons recorded in the Scriptures were inspired by the Holy Spirit who guided Jesus' students to remember and write down what He had taught in His School of Prayer, so we could learn as well.

Now look at Matthew 26:36-39: (Emphasis added.)

> *Then Jesus came with them to a place called Gethsemane, and said to the disciples, "Sit here while I go and pray over there." And He took with Him Peter and the two sons of Zebedee, and He began to be sorrowful and deeply distressed. Then He said to them, "My soul is exceedingly sorrowful, even to death. Stay here and watch with Me." He went a little farther and **fell on His face**, and prayed, saying, "O My Father, if it is possible, let this cup pass from Me; nevertheless, **not as I will, but as You will.**"*

The main lesson we see from Christ's life in these verses is *He fell on His face* and said, "Not My will, oh Father, but Yours be done!" What a great prayer! There is something profound that Jesus ... fell on His face. This is what a servant does before his master; what a conquered military person does before his conqueror. Such submission means: "You're in charge," and is what Jesus was saying to His Father.

Why would Jesus pray to His Father in this manner? Because God is a God of order. The Scriptures always reflect this order: Father, Son, and Holy Spirit. God is always referred to as the Father who is over all; Christ, the Son, who loves the Father and always fulfills the Father's bidding; and the Holy Spirit who is the One who points to Christ and to the Father.

And so we see because of order the Son prayed to the Father in the role of humbling Himself as being the Servant of the Father who was in charge; Jesus wanted to do His will. As God the Son, and as our 100 percent human representative, Jesus thus fell on His face and said, "I want Your will—not Mine!"

That is a wonderful prayer for us to regularly practice. We should "fall on our faces" and ask God to show us things like how He wants us to live our lives, who He wants us to marry, how to succeed in a career or in the home, how much He wants us to accumulate here on earth, and so forth. And we need to always pray with this spirit: "I don't want my own way; I want Your will to be done." A lesson those disciples never forgot!

Lesson 5—
Prayer is to be a discipline.

In Matthew, we've already seen the Garden of Gethsemane account where Jesus fell on His face and prayed, "Not My will, but Yours be done!" Now look at what was going on with His disciples: *Then He came and found them sleeping, and said to Peter, "Simon, are you sleeping? Could you not watch one hour? Watch and pray, lest you enter into temptation. The spirit indeed is willing, but the flesh is weak." Again He went away and prayed, and spoke the same words* (Mark 14:37-39).

Jesus' question to Simon—*"Could you not watch one hour?"*—is what inspired Dick Eastman to write his great little book called The Hour That Changes The World. Eastman's premise is most people don't know how to pray for even an hour. Because it is hard for us at times to keep focused on prayer, some people have trouble praying for even five minutes. So we can certainly relate to the disciples, and understand why Jesus said, "… *The spirit indeed is willing, but the flesh is weak*" (Mark 14:38). However, through the Holy Spirit's empowerment, we can learn to discipline ourselves to have more extended periods of prayer.

Let's look at Mark 14:39 again where Jesus … *spoke the same words*. Once again, He prayed the same prayer. Jesus never said repetition itself is wrong; He only said vain repetition is wrong (Matthew 6:7). Vain repetition means praying without any heart attachment simply because it's supposed to be done. An example would be reciting the

Lord's Prayer without thinking about the words. When you pray biblically, you *should* be praying a lot of the same things over and over again—especially when praying Scripture back to God.

What wonderful lessons were taught by Jesus in His School of Prayer! The last one we're going to cover is from the third chapter of the book of Luke. Did you know Luke was a great student of prayer? If God hadn't given us Luke, we would know very little about prayer. The Holy Spirit used Luke to record more about prayer than anyone else in the Bible, and he gave an account of nine different times Jesus prayed, including how He prayed at every great event in His life. Luke provided intimate details into prayer as no one else did, and then he wrote a sequel—The Acts of the Apostles. There's barely a chapter in the book of Acts without a recorded prayer, prayer meeting, or result of a prayer. Luke was definitely a man touched by prayer!

Lesson 6—
Acknowledge your neediness before God.

In verses 21-22 of chapter 3, Luke reported: *When all the people were baptized, it came to pass that Jesus also was baptized; and while He prayed, the heaven was opened. And the Holy Spirit descended in bodily form like a dove upon Him, and a voice came from heaven which said, "You are My beloved Son; in You I am well pleased."*

Although Jesus was baptized in the midst of the others being baptized, this is what Luke saw through the eye of his research and the inspiration of God's Spirit. What the disciples remembered about Jesus at His baptism is He prayed, and as He prayed, the heaven opened. And when God said: "I love this Man! He is my Son and I am going to be glorified through Him," Jesus was *praying*. You see, Luke began his look at the prayer life of Christ by saying Jesus humbled Himself before His Father by acknowledging His dependence, His need, and His utter longing to commune with God. And it was then God the Father launched Jesus' public ministry.

These are only six of many "How to Talk to Me" lessons Jesus taught His students in His School of Prayer. Jesus had thirty perfect years—He prayed all the time. Jesus had three wonderful fruitful years of ministry—He prayed all the time. Jesus had one incredible moment of death—He prayed to His last breath. And Jesus is still praying! Jesus emphasized prayer throughout His earthly ministry so we would well learn the "How to Talk to Me" lessons from His School of Prayer.

How to Pray Like Jesus Prayed

To exercise "the discipline of supplication" we should pray like Jesus taught through His life and words. The posture, place, time, or circumstance is not the issue of prayer. Prayer is a total way of life—an ongoing, open communication with God all the time. Since prayer is meant as a way of life, we need to understand how to pray, and what better example than the one Jesus set for us?

How did Jesus pray? He didn't teach us about the circumstances of prayer because any circumstance will do. Jesus Himself prayed:

- **While standing:** ... *He took the five loaves and the two fish, and looking up to heaven, He blessed and broke and gave the loaves to the disciples; and the disciples gave to the multitudes* (Matthew 14:19).

  ...*They took away the stone from the place where the dead man was lying. And Jesus lifted up His eyes and said, "Father, I thank You that You have heard Me"* (John 11:41).

- **On His face:** *He ... fell on His face, and prayed, saying, "O My Father, if it is possible, let this cup pass from Me; nevertheless, not as I will, but as You will"* (Matthew 26:39).

- **Kneeling:** ... *He was withdrawn from them about a stone's throw, and He knelt down and prayed ...* (Luke 22:41).

- **When sweating blood:** ... *Being in agony, He prayed more earnestly. Then His sweat became like great drops of blood falling down to the ground* (Luke 22:44).

- **Walking with uplifted eyes:** *Jesus spoke these words, lifted up His eyes to heaven, and said: "Father, the hour has come. Glorify Your Son, that Your Son also may glorify You ..."* (John 17:1).

- **With loud crying:** ... *In the days of His flesh, when He had offered up prayers and supplications, with vehement cries and tears to Him who was able to save Him from death, ... was heard because of His godly fear* ... (Hebrews 5:7).

- **Always from the Scriptures:** ... *" 'Behold, I have come—In the volume of the book it is written of Me—To do Your will, O God' "* (Hebrews 10:7).

Where did Jesus teach us to pray? He didn't teach us about the place of prayer—because we are to pray everywhere. In the Bible, people prayed in all different places.

- **In a private room:** *"... When you pray, go into your room, and when you have shut your door, pray to your Father who is in the secret place; and your Father who sees in secret will reward you openly"* (Matthew 6:6).

- **In a garden:** ... *Jesus came with them to a place called Gethsemane, and said to the disciples, "Sit here while I go and pray over there"* (Matthew 26:36).

- **On a mountain:** ... *He went out to the mountain to pray, and continued all night in prayer to God* (Luke 6:12).

- **In solitude:** ... *He went out and departed to a solitary place; and there He prayed* (Mark 1:35).

- **In the wilderness:** ... *He Himself often withdrew into the wilderness and prayed* (Luke 5:16).

- **On a cross:** ... *Jesus said, "Father, forgive them, for they do not know what they do." ... And when Jesus had cried out with* a loud voice, He said, "Father, 'into Your hands I commit My spirit.' " Having said this, He breathed His last (Luke 23:34, 46).

When did Jesus Pray? He didn't teach us about the times of prayer— because we are to pray unceasingly. In the Bible, people prayed at all different times:

- **Early morning:** ... *Having risen a long while before daylight, [Jesus] went out and departed to a solitary place; and there He prayed (Mark 1:35).*

- **Day and night:** ... *This woman was a widow of about eighty-four years, who did not depart from the temple, but served God with fastings and prayers night and day (Luke 2:37).*

  ... Shall God not avenge His own elect who cry out day and night to Him, though He bears long with them? (Luke 18:7).

- **Often:** ... *They said to Him, "Why do the disciples of John fast often and make prayers, and likewise those of the Pharisees, but Yours eat and drink?" (Luke 5:33).*

- **Before meals:** ... *He took the five loaves and the two fish, and looking up to heaven, He blessed and broke and gave the loaves to the disciples; and the disciples gave to the multitudes (Matthew 14:19).*

- **Always:** ... *He spoke a parable to them, that men always ought to pray and not lose heart ... (Luke 18:1).*

- **At death:** ... *When Jesus had cried out with a loud voice, He said, "Father, 'into Your hands I commit My spirit.'" Having said this, He breathed His last (Luke 23:46).*

What did Jesus ask for as He prayed? Luke records nine occasions when Jesus prayed:

1. At His baptism **He prayed for consecration for ministry:** *... Jesus also was baptized; and while He prayed, the heaven was opened* (Luke 3:21).

2. After a day of miracles **He prayed for daily strength:** *... Great multitudes came together to hear, and to be healed by Him of their infirmities. So He Himself often withdrew into the wilderness and prayed* (Luke 5:15-16).

3. Before choosing His disciples **He prayed for specific guidance:** *Now it came to pass in those days that He went out to the mountain to pray, and continued all night in prayer to God* (Luke 6:12). Jesus also prayerfully sought God's direction for facing stresses like the multitudes who wanted to hear Him or be healed of their infirmities (Luke 5:15-16); sick people who wanted healing of their diseases or freedom from demon possession (Mark 1:33-35); and ministry needs when crowds tried to keep Him from leaving them (Luke 4:42).

4. Before the first prediction of His death **He prayed for personal encouragement:** *... As He was alone praying, ... His disciples joined Him, and He asked them, saying, "Who do the crowds say that I am?"* (Luke 9:18).

- Discouragement over misguided followers was prevented by prayer: *... When Jesus perceived that they were about to come and take Him by force to make Him king, He departed again to the mountain by Himself alone* (John 6:15).

- His emotions were sheltered by resorting to prayer even in the presence of uncaring friends (Matthew 26:36-46).

- He was protected from the unbecoming attitudes and words of friends and the pain of His calling—the cross: *"Father, glorify Your name." Then a voice came from heaven, saying, "I have both glorified it and will glorify it again"* (John 12:28).

5. On the Mount of Transfiguration **He prayed for awesome worship:** *As He prayed, the appearance of His face was altered, and His robe became white and glistening (Luke 9:29).*

6. Before teaching the disciples to pray **He prayed for wisdom in ministry:** *… As He was praying in a certain place, when He ceased … one of His disciples said to Him, "Lord, teach us to pray, as John also taught his disciples" (Luke 11:1).*

7. When the seventy returned with their report **He prayed for insight for ministry:** *… Jesus rejoiced in the Spirit and said, "I thank You, Father, Lord of heaven and earth, that You have hidden these things from the wise and prudent and revealed them to babes. Even so, Father, for so it seemed good in Your sight" (Luke 10:21).*

8. In the Garden of Gethsemane **He prayed for personal victory:** *… He knelt down and prayed, saying, "Father, if it is Your will, take this cup away from Me; nevertheless not My will, but Yours, be done." Then an angel appeared to Him from heaven, strengthening Him. And being in agony, He prayed more earnestly. Then His sweat became like great drops of blood falling down to the ground. When He rose up from prayer, and had come to His disciples, He found them sleeping from sorrow. Then He said to them, "Why do you sleep? Rise and pray, lest you enter into temptation" (Luke 22:41-46).*

9. On the cross **He prayed for steadfast obedience:** *… Jesus said, "Father, forgive them, for they do not know what they do." And they divided His garments and cast lots. … And when Jesus had cried out with a loud voice, He said, "Father, 'into Your hands I commit My spirit.'" Having said this, He breathed His last (Luke 23:34, 46).*

Jesus prayerfully and consistently sought God's goals. His earthly prayer life can be seen as harmonious with God's plan because this was His passion (John 17:4). Thankfulness was a part of His entire life (Luke 10:21). God's glory, not His personal needs, was His top priority. Therefore, he always had confidence in God's hearing and answering Him: ... *I know that You always hear Me* ... (John 11:42). Every single area of His life demonstrated submission!

Have you learned that apart from Him you can do nothing (John 15:5)? Do you see why God's "How to Talk to Me" lessons are so important? If Jesus, who lived a perfect life in every way, saw the need continually pray, how much more should we who are sinners—whose spirit is willing but our flesh is weak? I urge you to continually ask the Holy Spirit to teach you how to glorify God through your prayer life!

My Prayer for You:
Father in Heaven, thank You for Your Word, for giving it to us, and letting us come by way of Your Word into the School of Prayer with Christ. I pray some part of what You did would affect us this week so we remember to pray before our meals—in public and in private. Help us to acknowledge how everything comes from You. Maybe we need to fall on our faces on a regular basis, laying prostrate before You saying, "I don't want to go my way, I want You to show me Your way in all I do." But Father You won't show anything to those who won't first show themselves as in need of Your salvation. If any readers are without Christ, I'm thankful Your invitation is open if they will call on Your name as the only hope of salvation, believing in Your sacrifice on the cross that they will be saved. For the rest of us, help us to linger long in Your presence through prayer. In Jesus' name I pray. Amen.

15

"If you ask anything in My name, I will do it."
—**John 14:14**

Supplication:
How to Unleash the Power of Prayer

PERHAPS THE MOST EXTRAORDINARY TESTIMONY to the power of prayer in modern times is seen in the life of a quiet man from Bristol, England.[70] Born in the early nineteenth century, George Mueller lived a Word filled life of powerful praying. For sixty years he served the Lord through prayer, and chronicled God's hand of provision as He intricately and miraculously worked in his life. Mueller's prayers touched 120,000 individual orphans and poor children, whom, solely by secret prayer, he fed, clothed, educated, and trained in God's Word in his five orphan homes and seventy-two day schools located in England and three other countries.

70 MP3 CD Audio DYG-12:030330AM, MP3 CD Audio DYG-13:030406AM, MP3 CD Audio DYG-14:030427AM

Mueller started his first orphan home in 1835 with a rented facility for thirty children. During the next ten years, he rented four more homes to accommodate 120. In 1849 he built a home for 300 orphans that included rooms for the staff plus classrooms where the children learned a trade. He added two more homes for 950 children in 1858, and in 1869-1870 built the fourth and fifth homes to house an additional 850. At that time, he had 2,100 orphans to care for by prayer.

Mueller's extensive diaries recorded his remarkable ninety-three years of life, piecing together a picture of powerful prayer. Amazingly, this man raised 7.2 million nineteenth-century dollars during his sixty years of ministry. In today's currency, that would be equal to $111.6 million![71] He had no mass mailings, TV ads, web blitzes, or huge financial machine behind him. All he did was pray!

He began his ministry by reading the Bible—and ended it the same way. The first 100 times, he read sitting down; the second 100 times, he read on his knees. As he read, he always *prayed*. Every time he came to a promise, he held a finger on it and earnestly asked God to show Himself powerful in that realm. Through simple faith, Mueller saw God open the windows of heaven and pour out boundless blessings!

His prayers touched countless individuals around the world who were led to freely give him staggering sums of money. He never asked for even one penny. Day after day, the exact amount of money flowed in to supply a home, food, clothing, and education for whatever number of orphans he was caring. All this was accomplished through reading God's Word and praying, telling only the Lord his requests—and the gifts kept coming in at an astounding rate. Were you to spread the amount received in today's currency over Mueller's entire ministry, this is how it would average out: annually, he would have received $1.86 million in gifts; monthly, he would have received $155,000; and weekly gifts would total $35,769.

When Mueller died, he had just enough money to pay for his burial and food for the orphans. He did not hold on to even a dime of the Lord's money. He never asked God for personal profit, but only what was for His kingdom and glory! This modern-day giant of the faith could therefore be considered a "valedictorian" of Jesus' School of Prayer! He truly believed Matthew 6:33 and acted upon it.

---

[71] http://www.cwc.lsu.edu/cwc/other/stats/warcost.htm has a war costs comparison that reveals that Civil War dollars would buy sixteen times the worth then.

Ask and You Shall Receive

God was always there for George Mueller, and He is always there for us because He wants to hear and answer when we pray His promises back to Him. Consider what a marvelous lesson Jesus taught in this verse:

> "**Ask, and it will be given to you; seek, and you will find; knock, and it will be opened to you.** For everyone who asks receives, and he who seeks finds, and to him who knocks it will be opened. Or what man is there among you who, if his son asks for bread, will give him a stone? Or if he asks for a fish, will he give him a serpent? If you then, being evil, know how to give good gifts to your children, how much more will your Father who is in heaven give good things to those who ask Him!" (Matthew 7:7-11, emphasis added).

Read these verses and ask yourself: What does this really mean? How does God want me to apply this to my life? Here are some more wonderful passages to meditate upon: (Emphasis added in the verses below.)

- "… *If two of you agree … concerning* **anything that they ask, it will be done for them** *by My Father in heaven*" (Matthew 18:19). Perhaps you are thinking: *Wait a minute. Isn't Matthew 18 talking about how to deal with order in the church, discipline, and sinning brethren?* Yes, but this is not the only time Jesus said the little phrase *"anything that they ask, it will be done for them."* I hope that unsettles you. Is anything you pray for answered? We should ask ourselves that question because of who is talking—Jesus.
- "… **Whatever things you ask in prayer, believing, you will receive**" (Matthew 21:22). Our Lord Jesus Christ was again the One who was speaking, and He was making a very powerful statement.
- "… **Ask, and it will be given to you;** *seek, and you will find; knock, and it will be opened to you*" (Luke 11:9). Jesus spoke more about prayer in Luke than in any other Gospel. Here, Jesus said the same thing: "Just ask!" This is an incredible promise!
- "… **Ask anything in My name, I will do it**" (John 14:14). This is a clear-cut expression of this concept of prayer—a very personal promise: "What you ask for, I will do!" That is simply amazing!

- *"You did not choose Me, but I chose and appointed you to go and bear fruit, so your fruit should remain, that **whatever you ask the Father in My name He may give you**"* (John 15:16). Though Jesus was talking to His disciples in this verse, by the time we get done you can see He was actually talking to us. Note Jesus had been making all these promises, and now He was bringing our Father in heaven into it so whatever we ask in *Jesus'* name, His Father will give us!
- *"**... Whatever you ask the Father in My name He will give you.** ... Ask, and you will receive, that your joy may be full"* (John 16:23-24). Jesus emphasized again, "Ask, and I will answer! I will respond, and give it to you."
- *... This is the confidence that we have in Him, that **if we ask anything according to His will, He hears us.** And if we know that He hears us, **whatever we ask, we know that we have the petitions that we have asked of Him*** (1 John 5:14-15).

The last passage was at the end of the New Testament canon. It was one of the last things the early church received. Since there weren't any apostles left, John was talking to the pure church—those alive at the end of the first century as well as future believers. He was saying, "You can have confidence in what I am about to say because the Lord Himself is speaking; the Spirit inspired me to write this." Do you have such a confident walk with the Lord that He will answer anything you ask in His name?

God's Qualifying Condition for Answered Prayers: When you think about George Mueller's incredible life testimony, does the level of prayer sound too good to be true in your own life—even on a smaller scale? Have you ever wondered if it is possible to have all of your prayers answered? It certainly seems so for many believers. Some who have been through decades in the faith know numerous verses about prayer, but when they don't understand them, they simply don't do what Jesus says to do. Why? I believe they overlook this one qualifying condition for answered prayers: *obedience*. That really gets to the heart of the problem, doesn't it? *Obedience is necessary to unleash the great power of prayer.*

Understanding just one little phrase in John 15:7 can launch some of your life's greatest prayers. I am listing that verse in a variety of popular Bible translations so you can get the full impact of what Jesus said about prayer in this verse. (Emphasis added in the verses below.)

- *"If you abide in Me, and **My words abide in you,** you will ask what you desire, and it shall be done for you" (NKJV).*
- *"If ye abide in me, and **my words abide in you,** ye shall ask what ye will, and it shall be done unto you" (KJV).*
- *"If you abide in Me, and **My words abide in you,** ask whatever you wish, and it will be done for you" (NASB).*
- *"If you remain in me and **my words remain in you,** ask whatever you wish, and it will be given you" (NIV).*
- *"But if you remain in me, and **my words remain in you,** you may ask for anything you want, and it will be granted!" (NLT).*
- *"But if you make yourselves at home with me and **my words are at home in you,** you can be sure that whatever you ask will be listened to and acted upon. This is how my Father shows who he is—when you produce grapes, when you mature as my disciples" (vv. 7-8 The Message).*

Note all say the same thing: "My words." Because Peter was inspired by the Holy Spirit to proclaim that every prophet in the Old Testament who wrote any portion of the Bible was inspired, we know all sixty-six books were inspired by the Spirit of Christ (2 Peter 1:19-21). So, every word in the Bible is the word of Jesus—literally, truly, and biblically.

The more you abide in the written Word of God, the more the precious living Word will abide in you! When you delight in the Lord … He shall give you the desires of your heart (Psalm 37:4), because delighting in Christ and His Word produces a heart in line with God's. Anytime a need arises, the Holy Spirit will bring to mind an appropriate Scripture to pray back to God—who in turn will respond in faithfulness to His Word! That type of ongoing communication is how to unleash the power of prayer that produces the joy of living a Word filled life!

The Biblical Motivation for Prayer

The more you love Jesus and understand what He taught about prayer, the more you should want to pray like He prayed. To encourage you, here are more reasons to pray.

You should pray out of obedience. You can only avoid sin by prayer. Without beginning a day by praying, how will you ever know if you are fulfilling what God wants? Look at these verses:

- "... *Pray the Lord of the harvest to send out laborers into His harvest*" (Matthew 9:38). Pray for villages and cities around the world that have no witness for Christ. Pray for people you see. Usually, if you pray for something, your heart is open to being a part of it. If you are praying to the Lord of the harvest, you should be willing to be one of those laborers.

- "... *Far be it from me that I should sin against the LORD in ceasing to pray for you ...*" (1 Samuel 12:23). You should faithfully pray for those whom God lays on your heart because it would be a sin to not do so.

- "*If My people who are called by My name will humble themselves, and pray and seek My face, and turn from their wicked ways, then I will hear from heaven, and will forgive their sin and heal their land*" (2 Chronicles 7:14). How many Christians believe in prayer enough to regularly pray like this for our country? How many are serious enough to humble themselves, and get right with God so He can heal our land of its wickedness? Are you one of them? I hope so!

- "*Watch and pray, lest you enter into temptation. The spirit indeed is willing, but the flesh is weak*" (Matthew 26:41). Be vigilant! Be alert to anything that would hinder you from serious prayer times. For ... *the devil walks about like a roaring lion, seeking whom he may devour* (1 Peter 5:8). When Peter denied Christ three times, he learned his lesson the hard way—*prayerlessness leads to disobedience.*

- *You ought to be praying always with all prayer and supplication in the Spirit, being watchful to this end with all perseverance and supplication for all the saints* — (Ephesians 6:18).

You should pray so you become strong. If you don't keep your cell phone battery charged, it will wear down. My family has an upward plug-in to remind me that we have to be plugged into God. Jesus was strengthened as He prayed. Most of us get worn down and think prayer is such a hard thing. We don't realize just coming into the presence of God strengthens our lives. You can only experience the power God has for you as you wait upon Him, seek the fullness of His Spirit, and yield to His work through you moment by moment.

- [Jesus] said to them, *"This kind can come out by nothing but prayer and fasting"* (Mark 9:29). Supplication is an intense, self-denying, discipline of seeking God.

- *My soul melts from heaviness; strengthen me according to Your word* (Psalm 119:28). Ezra felt the oppressiveness of the world just as you and I. There is so much pressure, so many options, and so many voices a heart can melt from heaviness in the soul. But the Lord says if you communicate with Him you will be strengthened: ... *He [will] grant you, according to the riches of His glory, to be strengthened with might through His Spirit in the inner man* ... (Ephesians 3:16). If you want to make it through life, PRAY. If you want to be strong, PRAY.

You should pray so you can understand God's Word. You can only understand and comprehend the Lord's ways in His Word through prayer for illumination, guidance, and obedience. I meet people all the time who claim they can't get anything out of the Bible. So I ask, "Did you pray for illumination and guidance? Did you talk to the Author?" You have the wonderful privilege of having the greatest Teacher of all times with you—the Holy Spirit of God who will open your heart to the Scriptures every time you ask Him and seek His illumination!

- *... He opened their understanding, that they might comprehend the Scriptures* (Luke 24:45). Don't ask for this and you will become blind to God's Word.

- *Open my eyes, that I may see wondrous things from Your law* (Psalm 119:18). Ezra understood to comprehend the Scriptures, he needed God's insight. This is a precious prayer to pray, and you should do so regularly.

You should pray so you become wise. God wants you to come to Him for wisdom regarding marriage, parenting, relationships, work, ministry, and so forth.

- *If any of you lacks wisdom, let him ask of God, who gives to all liberally and without reproach, and it will be given to him* (James 1:5). God loves to give His wisdom, but you must first remember to ask for it.

- *... The men of Israel took some of their provisions; but they did not ask counsel of the Lord* (Joshua 9:14). Joshua and the Gibeonites learned a tough prayer lesson. God had instructed the mighty army of Israel to utterly destroy everyone in Canaan due to their wickedness. However, a delegation came from a far country and deceived Joshua and the elders of Israel, because these leaders of God's people failed to consult Him first about the matter. Similarly, if you fail to ask God's counsel on how to raise your children, they could be a lifelong grief to you. If you don't ask God's counsel on whom you should marry, you could suffer great heartache for many years. If you don't ask for wisdom regularly, you will often act foolishly. In other words, choose to go your own way instead of God's, and reap what you have sown (Galatians 6:7).

You should pray so you become spiritually rich. If you fail to pray, God says ... *you [will] not have because you [will] not ask* (James 4:2). Think about this:

- We can only lay up treasures in heaven by a prayerful life on earth.
- We can only fill our bowls of worship around God's throne by prayerful living.
- We can only stay in touch with God by prayer.
- We can only stay in love with Jesus by prayer.
- We can only stay in step with the Spirit by prayer.

When I was a poor graduate student in Greenville, South Carolina, I met my Bonnie when she was a first grade teacher. On our first date, I told her she was the one I'd asked God for my whole life (What a line *that* was—but it was *true*). From the moment I laid eyes on her, I knew Bonnie was "the one" for me. But I barely got to see her in those early days because her schedule was different than mine. So I did all I could to catch even a glimpse of her. When I found out there was one window in her first grade classroom close to the street, I drove slowly by hoping to spot her. In fact, I made so many laps around the school a policeman started to keep an eye on me. But when he wasn't looking, I would park and watch Bonnie. I even put notes in her box in the school office. Why? If you deeply love someone, you can't stand not getting to communicate with that person. God wants you to feel this way about communing with Him. He wants you to love Him so much you can't stand not being in touch with Him!

Be constantly vigilant so you don't lose or diminish the rich communication treasure of prayer! Never forget we have an adversary who wants believers to think prayer really doesn't matter. That sly old serpent, *"the father of lies"* (John 8:44), loves to whisper lies to us like: *Why pray? After all, you haven't had any prayers answered lately… Maybe He's not even listening to you … And, because He is GOD, He'll just do whatever He pleases anyhow … so why even bother?* If Satan can convince you prayer doesn't work, you'll be cut off from the power needed to live a Word filled life, and he wins a huge victory! There's a lot at stake. Prayerlessness leads to poverty in all truly important matters. Until you ask, you will have no idea how much God wants to do through you!

Gaining a better understanding of what Jesus taught in His School of Prayer, and applying it to your life, will lead to the most fruitful, joyful, and powerful spiritual life there can be this side of heaven.

How to Have a Powerful Prayer Life

This is where Jesus' "How to Talk to Me" lessons become even more practical. You might say this is a recap. So if you are among those who have not formed a faithful prayer habit, here are basic suggestions to have a powerful prayer life.

Make the time to pray. Take time—it is not possible to "find time." If you prioritize the time God gives you, you will be more effective for eternally important things. Remember to follow "the discipline of simplicity" (Matthew 6:33). When you find yourself falling short of His expectations, reorder your priorities back to God's!

Choose a place to pray. Establish a specific place to pray, just as Jesus had ... a solitary place, where he prayed (Mark 1:35 NIV). In Matthew 6:6 He even spoke of entering an inner room or closet to have a quiet time of prayer.

Pray as often as possible. Pray many times day and night. May this be your spirit: Evening and morning and at noon I will pray, and cry aloud, and He shall hear my voice (Psalm 55:17). Ask the Holy Spirit to make you so God-conscious your prayers continually fly heavenward as you talk with Him about everything going on in your day.

I once read a wonderful article in a missions newsletter called "Non-Stop Prayer."[72] The article challenged me to start cultivating some fresh habits of prayer. In 1 Thessalonians 5:17, we are told to pray without ceasing. We have the ability to do so, and simple methods make unceasing prayer less difficult:

- **Reading Prayer:** Don't simply read through letters, but read and pray. After each paragraph quickly pray about what you just read. Missionary prayer letters, ministry updates, and letters from Christian organizations are all good resources to prompt intercessory prayer.

---

[72] These ideas were in an article by George Verwer, "Non-Stop Prayer," Interest Magazine, March, 1991, p. 13.

- **Watching Prayer:** When you watch something take place live, or on TV, immediately pray about what you are seeing. Especially do so after news programs, but if what you are watching deadens your heart to God stop watching. Countless times I've prayed Christians would share with people in tragedies. As the World Trade Center came down on September 11, 2001, I prayed believers would share the gospel with those around them.

- **Talking Prayer**: When you talk on the telephone, pray for the person with whom you are talking. If it is a believer, you can pray together on the phone, and it will likely lead you to a double ministry of prayer and encouragement. Discipline yourself to see persons as prayer signals (Nehemiah 1:11; 2:4; etc.; Luke 22:31-32).

- **Listening Prayer:** As you hear things in a meeting, on the radio, or almost anywhere, quickly lift needs to God in prayer.

- **Writing Prayer:** As you send e-mails, do so with a touch of God through prayer for the people receiving the communications. When writing a letter or card, pray about what you are writing and, of course, for the person receiving it. These are simple things you can include into the fabric of life while asking for God's wisdom and blessing on the people with whom you communicate.

- **Witnessing Prayer:** One of my prayer habits is to pray all the time when I travel. Part of my morning routine is to put a tract in my pocket when getting dressed. I then pray over it, asking God to give me a supernatural divine appointment to share His Word that day, and to help me be ready (1 Peter 3:15).

Once while in California, I was driving around looking for the first Starbucks Coffee™ shop to open. When it did, I walked in and the attendant looked like he had just gotten out of bed. I greeted him by looking into his droopy eyes and saying, "I FEEL WONDERFUL!" He looked astonished and told me he'd never heard anybody say that. Right then, I had a divine appointment and an opportunity to share

Christ. So I asked him, "Do you know why I feel wonderful? Because I have a new heart! And I have something I would like you to read. If you're willing, I'll give it to you." This method works. Most people don't share the gospel because they never ask God for an opportunity. If you ask, seek, and knock—God will respond.

On another occasion, before returning my rental car, I pulled into a gas station to fill up. I soon spotted an old homeless man pushing his shopping cart. I had prayed over my tract that morning, and this was my opportunity. The homeless man came to ask for money and I said, "I'll be glad to give you some money if you will listen to me." So he stood there to listen. I started off by asking him, "Are you going to heaven?" He looked around as if I was going to send him there right then! I explained, "God allows sinners like me into heaven, but have you ever sinned?" He said he had not sinned for three months—the last time he was drunk. I pulled out the tract and shared the good news Someone died for sinners if he would confess he was totally unfit and unable to get to heaven on his own. I asked him next, "Do you know who Jesus is?" He replied, "Jesus is the Way and the Truth." That was the only thing he had ever heard about Him. I then asked, "What is your name?" "Robert." I said, "Robert, if you will repent of your sins, Jesus Christ will offer you a free gift, just like I'm offering you today." As this person looked at me, a man with everything he owned in a shopping cart, I will never forget what I saw in his eyes when he responded, "I never heard that before …" Robert promised to read the tract; I gave him the change in my pocket, and off he went. I won't be surprised if we may meet Robert some day in heaven—that is how gracious God is.

Pray systematically. Paul called it the … deep concern for all the churches (2 Corinthians 11:28). Be organized; use whatever means will help you feel more organized, such as a prayer list or prayer book. But depend on the Lord, not on the means. Take advantage of time to pray during showers, shaving or putting on cosmetics, mowing the lawn, driving, waiting in a doctor's office, exercising, and during other situations which allow the mind freedom to do this.

Pray with people throughout the day. Seek some meaningful opportunity to pray with others (Matthew 18:19). Note most of the passages on prayer in Acts are group prayer situations, as Acts 13:1-3.

- Pray with your marriage partner to start the day.
- Pray with your children to start their day.
- Pray at meals to show thanksgiving.
- Pray in the car before you drive away.
- Pray at the airport when departing, and at arrival.
- Pray with *thanksgiving* when you hear good news, and with *intercession* when you hear bad news.

You can further exercise "the discipline of supplication" by starting a daily family system, emphasizing a different element of prayer each day of the week. It is good to introduce a note of variety into family prayer.[73] For instance, each day of the week you can concentrate on a different prayer project, like this:

- **Monday—The Prayer of Faith.** Each member of the family picks out a prayer project with the objective of obtaining an answer before the week is out. It is important to distinguish between the different kinds of prayer, because each has a different objective and approach. If we come to pray in a vague way, it may be well enough, but we may pray the wrong kind of prayer for the particular situation. The object of faith prayer is to get a job done. Pray that a child afraid of the nursery will be comforted this Sunday, or a newcomer to Sunday school will feel welcome, or a witnessing opportunity will open and courage to speak will come—all of these are prayers of "faith."

- **Tuesday—Prayer for Family** (Far or Near). Each one picks a relative or immediate family member and prays for some specific need the person has.

- **Wednesday—The Lord's Prayer.** To provide variety, one method I use is to pray the Lord's Prayer (Matthew 6:9-13) a sentence at a time. After each sentence prayer, family members offer specific petitions related to that prayer. For example, under *"Your kingdom come"* may bring prayer for the peace of His kingdom to come in our own home or nation. The prayer sentence

[73] For a powerful presentation of family prayers see Larry Christenson's The Christian Family (Minneapolis: Bethany Fellowship, Inc., 1974), pp. 174-176. This prayer week is adapted from his book.

"Forgive us our debts, as we forgive our debtors" may prompt confession of a resentful and unforgiving attitude toward a playmate.

- **Thursday—Prayer for Missionaries.** Each person picks a missionary to pray for. This helps project the family's concern for Christ's Kingdom *"to the ends of the earth."* Sometimes it is fun to vary this by first praying silently for one's particular prayer project. Afterward, each has an opportunity to act out his or her missionary as a charade while the others try to guess for whom or what the prayer directed.

- **Friday—Prayers of Confession.** Each family member openly confesses one sin that disturbed peace and harmony within our home. This may, at first, be more difficult for parents than children. Children are used to being corrected and chastened within the family, but not parents. Yet parents, too, stand in need of forgiveness. In this setting, irritations and resentments can be dealt with—not in the context of anger and recrimination, but in the healing light of forgiveness. If on Friday one of the children seems at a loss to recall anything to confess, brothers and sisters make fine auxiliary consciences! Parents can both give and receive suggestions in order that genuine sins and hurts receive light, and then closely watch so no spirit of impudence or bitter accusation develops. When done in love, genuine and even deep repentance is produced.

- **Saturday—Prayers for Our Church.** Each can pick out some aspect of the Sunday services to pray about: choir, Sunday school, sermon, Communion, particular individuals in the congregation, or any other worship needs.

- **Sunday—Prayers for Our Worship.** On the way to church ask for God's blessing and power to flow in and through as all gather with our brothers and sisters to worship. At the lunch, we try to capture some of what we just experienced, and we ask for the worship we have enjoyed to flow through the week ahead.[74]

The key to unleashing prayers God always answers is to have them

---

[74] Dr. John S. Barnett, The Joy of a Word Filled Family (Tulsa: Mullerhaus Publishing, 2004), pp. 303-305.

flow from a Word filled life of obedience. Jesus wants His Word to stay with us, live with us in all phases of our lives. He wants His Word to fill our hearts, fill our minds, fill our days, and fill our ways.

What If Your Prayers Are Not Getting Through to God?

One more important area to cover on "the discipline of supplication," is how the great Old Testament saints could maintain a lifelong habit of powerful praying? They had two special traits in common: (1) they judged themselves, and (2) they prayed habitually. Because their lives were open before Him, God could cleanse and commune with them at all times. This is vital for staying in touch with God in a powerful way.

Failure to maintain constant vigilance in exercising "the disciplines of a godly life" hinders your prayers, making you slip in your walk with the Lord. As soon as you sense that happening, refresh your mind with God's *"How to Talk to Me"* lessons. Start by praying: *Search me, O God, and know my heart; try me, … and see if there is any wicked way in me …* (Psalm 139:23-24).

While you wait upon God to answer prayer, examine your life to see if you've slipped in any of the areas like the following, and thus need to reorder your priorities back to God's:

ROADBLOCK 1 —*Prayers Loosely Connected to Scripture:*
"If you abide in Me, and My words abide in you, you will ask what you desire, and it shall be done for you" (John 15:7).

Loose prayers—praying apart from a connection to God's Word and a living, vital relationship with God Himself through His Son—are sent to the "Dead Prayer Office." Loosely praying is being unaware of what God has already said about something. Because 99 percent of the revealed will of God is in His Word, exercising "the discipline of the Scriptures" is essential. The connectors are what you wait on Him for, asking Him to make your path straight and clear (Psalm 16:11). When you pray according to the will of God, as revealed through His Word, and to you personally, those prayers will be heard (1 John 5:14-15).

ROADBLOCK 2 —*Prayers That Are Hypocritical:*
"... When you pray, you shall not be like the hypocrites. For they love to pray ... that they may be seen by men ..." (Matthew 6:5).

This does not mean public praying is wrong, but proud public praying is wrong. Always come before God's throne in humility. Prayers voiced so others will admire your eloquence or spirituality will never be heard.

ROADBLOCK 3 —*Prayers That Are Mechanical:*
... When you pray, do not use vain repetitions as the heathen do. For they think that they will be heard for their many words (Matthew 6:7).

Just as hypocritical prayers never have God's ear, so it is with mechanical praying. I have heard some people pray for years and it is always the same prayer every time. There is nothing wrong with repetition in humble, sincere prayer; mechanical, mindless repetition is wrong. Your prayers must have freshness and intimacy.

ROADBLOCK 4 —*Prayers From a Heart Lacking Forgiveness:*
"... Whenever you stand praying, if you have anything against anyone, forgive him, that your Father in heaven may also forgive you your trespasses" (Mark 11:25).

If you are angry, troubled, or holding to a grudge, it ruins your connection with God. A psalmist said if God should mark iniquity, none of us would stand. We are all sinners by nature, by choice, by habit: we default to self and not to God. We should never allow bitterness to cut our connection with the Lord. If we forgive those who have hurt us, He will give them what they deserve. If you struggle in this area, and don't let go of bitterness, it will prevent your prayers from going through to God.

ROADBLOCK 5 —*Prayers That Are Self-Seeking:*
"I delight to do Your will, O my God, and Your law is within my heart" (Psalm 40:8).

Psalm 40:8 verse represents the spirit with which we are to pray. Self-prompted and self-empowered prayers—where you try to seek your own will instead of God's—cannot get through. Jesus in His humility chose to never operate on earth other than through the will of His Father in heaven.

ROADBLOCK 6 —*Prayers That Lack Self-Denial:*
Jesus said, … "This kind can come out by
nothing but prayer and fasting" (Mark 9:29).

Although this verse refers to a demonized boy, there is a spiritual principle here: prayer is seeking God, and fasting is denying self and the flesh. In the first-century church, when they conquered the whole world for Jesus Christ, fasting and prayer went hand in hand. In contrast, our twenty-first century is a very consumptive society, one in which everybody is preoccupied with self-need and self-fulfillment. The Lord says if you get tainted by that selfishness, He can't hear because you are so "full of yourself." To get your prayers through, you must fast by denying yourself and … *"seek first the kingdom of God and His righteousness, and [THEN] all these things shall be added to you."*

ROADBLOCK 7 — *Prayers That Are Out of God's Will*
"… Whatever you ask in My name, that I will do, that the Father
may be glorified in the Son. If you ask anything
in My name, I will do it" (John 14:13-14).

To pray and never once say the name of Jesus is "nameless praying." Jesus said we are to ask in His name. There is nothing magical or mystical about the name of Jesus, but there IS something powerful. When we pray in His name, we are saying to God, "I am coming to You in the Person and the Character of Jesus, God the Son." Don't get so concise you neglect the important part of prayer and cut off your connection to heaven.

ROADBLOCK 8 —*Prayers From a Heart of Untoppled Idols:*
"… These men have set up their idols in their hearts, and
put before them that which causes them to stumble into iniquity.

Should I let Myself be inquired of at all by them?" (Ezekiel 14:3).

Perhaps you heaved a sigh of relief when you read that because you don't worship Baal or Buddha. But do you recall the New Testament says idolatry is covetousness—wanting something so badly you won't let go of it? There are people who want security, money, power, pleasure, entertainment, or recognition so much it is all they think about. An idol is whatever captivates you. If you let anyone or anything capture your attention more than God, this will prevent your prayers from getting through.

ROADBLOCK 9 —*Prayers From an Unharmonious Marriage:*
> *... Husbands, dwell with them according to knowledge, giving honour unto the wife, as unto the weaker vessel, and as being heirs together of the grace of life; that your prayers be not hindered. Finally, be ye all of one mind, having compassion one of another, love as brethren, be pitiful, be courteous: not rendering evil for evil, or railing for railing: but contrariwise blessing; knowing that ye are thereunto called, that ye should inherit a blessing (1 Peter 3:7-9 KJV).*

In today's society, so many marriages are in trouble, and the Apostle Peter had a lot to say about how this affects a couple's prayer life. As he wrote to Christian husbands, he reminded of specific areas of responsibility in their relationship with their mates. The gifted author and pastor Warren Wiersbe has some very helpful words to encourage us in this area. Look at what he has to say about this vital topic:

> • **Physical—"dwell with them."** This implies much more than sharing the same address. Marriage is fundamentally a physical relationship: "The two shall be one flesh" (Eph. 5:31). A truly spiritual husband will fulfill his marital duties and love his wife. The husband must make time to be home with his wife. ... "Dwell with them" also suggests the husband provide for the physical and material needs of the home. While it is not wrong for a wife to have a job or career, her first responsibility is to care for the home (Titus 2:4–5). It is the husband who should provide (1 Tim. 5:8).

- **Intellectual—"according to knowledge."** … In my premarital counseling as a pastor, I often gave the couple pads of paper and asked them to write down the three things each one thinks the other most enjoys doing. How can a husband show consideration for his wife if he does not understand her needs or problems? To say, "I never knew you felt that way!" is to confess, at some point, one mate excommunicated the other. When either mate is afraid to be open and honest about a matter, then he or she is building walls and not bridges.

- **Emotional—"giving honor unto the wife."** … The husband should treat his wife like … a precious treasure. … [M]any a husband forgets to be kind and gentlemanly and starts taking his wife for granted. He forgets that happiness in a home is made up of many *little* things, including the small courtesies of life. … "Giving honor" means the husband respects his wife's feelings, thinking, and desires. He may not agree with her ideas, but he respects them. The husband must be the "thermostat" in the home, setting the emotional and spiritual temperature. The wife often is the "thermometer," letting him know what the temperature is! … The husband who is sensitive to his wife's feelings not only makes her happy, but also grows himself and helps his children live in a home that honors God.

- **Spiritual—"that your prayers be not hindered."** Peter assumed husbands and wives would pray together. Often, they do not; and this is the reason for much failure and unhappiness. … In fact, the prayer life of a couple indicates how things are going in the home. If something is wrong, their prayers become hindered. A husband and wife need to have their own daily, private, individual prayer time. They also need to pray together and to have a time of "family devotion." …The Word of God and prayer are basic to a happy, holy home. A husband and wife are "heirs together." If the wife shows submission and the husband consideration, and if both submit to Christ and follow His example, their marriage will have an enriching experience. If not, they miss God's best and rob each other of blessing and growth.[75]

[75] Warren W. Wiersbe, The Bible Exposition Commentary (Wheaton: Victor Books, 1997), p. # needed.

ROADBLOCK 10—Prayers From a Heart of Unconfessed Sin:
If I regard iniquity in my heart, the Lord will not hear.
... Behold, the LORD's hand is not shortened, that it cannot save; nor His ear heavy, that it cannot hear. But your iniquities have separated you from your God; and your sins have hidden His face from you, so that He will not hear (Psalm 66:18; Isaiah 59:1-2).

These are very sobering verses. Without regularly confessing your sins, allowing God through the conviction of His Word and the work of His Spirit to make you agree with Him about your sins (1 John 1:9), He will not hear your prayers. You need to constantly confess and agree with God about your fleshliness, and be painfully aware of your sins. Remember: obedience is the one qualifying condition for answered prayers, and unrepentant sin disconnects those prayers.

The Heart God Desires in Prayer

After reading about the various ways your prayers can be hindered, perhaps you're feeling a little discouraged and are even thinking: *Oh, why bother ... I shouldn't even try to pray ... I can never measure up to God's expectations.* Beloved of God, be encouraged! He isn't expecting perfection, because that will never occur this side of heaven. Our weaknesses are the very reason God gave us Romans 8:26-27:

> *... The Spirit also helps in our weaknesses. For we do not know what we should pray for as we ought, but the Spirit Himself makes intercession for us with groanings which cannot be uttered. Now He who searches the hearts knows what the mind of the Spirit is, because He makes intercession for the saints according to the will of God.*

Based upon God's very own Word, you can have confidence the Holy Spirit's intercessory prayers on your behalf WILL be heard. So when you get off-track, simply reorder your priorities back to God's and keep on praying. The Holy Spirit will sort out your prayers according to God's perfect will, and in the process teach you more of

His valuable "How to Talk to Me" lessons. That is why the Lord said the Christian life is but a series of new beginnings!

God will help you be compassionate, humble, self-denying, forgiving, and selfless. The heart of "the discipline of supplication" is this: when Christ's Words abide in you, and you abide in His Word, simple, direct, and biblical prayers will flow from your life. If you seek to pray simply, directly, and biblically, it will harmonize your prayers to the Lord, His will, His Spirit—and you will experience the power and joy of a Word filled life!

My Prayer for You:
Father in Heaven, may we never forget to unleash the power of prayer. We should, like Jesus, be giving ourselves continually to prayer, seeking Your intervention in the events and people of our lives and the ministry of Your Word. We want to do Your will as we walk through life; we want to minister Your truth and live it because so many things in life cannot come except by prayer. We will miss the greatest blessings in life if we live in our own strength. May Your Holy Spirit teach us to make the time and place to pray specifically for and with individuals—to pray continuously throughout the day as well as systematically in private. Lord, how we look forward to the day around Your throne when we rise and bow in worship of You—when our eyes catch the answers to our prayers one after another. Help us to discipline ourselves to pray like Jesus prayed, to do as Jesus did, that in all things we might be pleasing to You, oh Father. In the name of Jesus I pray. Amen.

16

This is my comfort in my affliction, for Your word has given me life. ...It is good for me that I have been afflicted, that I may learn Your statutes.

—**Psalm 119:50, 71**

Discipline Seven—Suffering Affliction:
Building the Best Life Possible

ONE OF THE GREATEST BLESSINGS of life is to know God! Knowing God means He also knows us. God knowing us means He knows life hurts at times. So whenever I go through hard times, sad times, dark times, discouraging times—I can testify with many of you that the greatest cure comes from looking at Jesus!

I love how Isaiah 53:3 describes Jesus: ... *a Man of sorrows and acquainted with grief* .... To me, this description sounds like the Person to know when troubles, pains, and afflictions come! Where do I personally look for comfort in the Scriptures when life hurts? I start with Hebrews 4:15-16 (emphasis added):

> ... *We do not have a High Priest* **who cannot sympathize with our weaknesses,** *but was in all points tempted as we are, yet without sin. Let us therefore come boldly to the throne of grace, that we may obtain mercy and find grace to help in time of need.*

Did you grasp the impact of what God just said? Jesus can "feel the pain with us of our weaknesses." What would you call depression, discouragement, sadness? Weaknesses. And what does Jesus do? He feels the pain with us. The word is *sum-pascho*, which *means* "with pain." In fact, the pain of the cross is called "the paschal time" or "pain time," and is what Jesus feels for us when we suffer.

How does knowing this truth help us? Well, to bridge the chasm between the High and Mighty, Sinless Jesus Christ, the Lord of Glory, and you and me, God gave us the promises of His Word, lived out in the shadow of Christ's cross, through the power of His Spirit!

Affliction Is God's Tool

As you've read in the first pages of this book, no matter who you are, how old you are, where you are in life, or what your past might be, God's perfect plan for you is described in the Scriptures.[76] He wants to write Himself across all the pages of your life by letting you have a complete takeover of your heart, soul, and mind through His Word—as Ezra experienced in his Psalm 119 testimony.

Ezra lived a Word filled life of holy habits cultivated out of a deep love for God. He thought about biblical principles so extensively they became ingrained in his mind, and invoked an automatic scriptural response and resolve in him. Without even thinking, holy habits just flowed from godly choices he routinely made. Long before 1 Timothy 4:7 was written, Ezra lived according to … *exercise yourself toward godliness*. In every circumstance, he sought to practice "the disciplines of a godly life"—what the Lord wants for your life as He unfolds His perfect plan.

The best life possible is to fulfill whatever God plans for only you and He together to accomplish. The most effective way to do this is for Him to provide opportunities to *apply* what He's been teaching about how to live a Word filled life. The seventh godly discipline— "the discipline of suffering affliction"—comes in here. As regular exercise builds strong muscles and keeps you physically healthy, so regular exercise of "the disciplines of a godly life" builds strong

---

[76] MP3 CD Audio DYG-27:030831AM, MP3 CD Audio DYG-28:030907AM

muscles of faith and keeps you spiritually healthy. What better way to get such exercise than through "Tribulation 101" lessons in God's School of Affliction?

"... In the world you will have tribulation ..." Jesus said, *"but be of good cheer, I have overcome the world"* (John 16:33). What a comfort! The word "tribulation," or thlipsis in the Greek, primarily means "a pressing pressure," anything which burdens the spirit.[77] It comes from the root word *thlibo*, which means "to suffer affliction, to be troubled," [and] has reference to sufferings due to the pressure of circumstances, or the antagonism of persons.[78] We can all identify with the pain of pressing pressures, burdens of the spirit, afflictions, trying circumstances, and people who are antagonistic toward us.

[77] Strong's #2347.

[78] Strong's #2346.

What is God's ultimate purpose for enrolling believers in His "Tribulation 101" class? He wants each of His children to excel in learning to ... *glory in **tribulations**, knowing that tribulation produces **perseverance**, and perseverance, **character**; and character, **hope*** (Romans 5:3-4, emphasis added).

A master teacher follows a scope and sequence with lesson plans and objectives to teach students what they need to know, and at a pace they can handle. So it is with our Master Teacher in the School of Affliction. God tailors "homework assignments" according to a pace He knows you and I can bear in His strength (1 Corinthians 10:13; Philippians 4:13). If we respond in faith to those assignments, viewing them as blessings rather than curses, we will one day receive an "A+" by hearing Jesus say, "Well done!"

Teaching His children how to exercise "the discipline of suffering affliction" with a godly spirit is therefore a main objective of God's Master Lesson Plan. For He knows this a major key to living the best life possible—a Word filled life that leads to pleasures forevermore at His right hand (Psalm 16:11). *Thus, Ezra could confidently say: This is my comfort in my affliction, for Your word has given me life. ... It is good for me that I have been afflicted, that I may learn Your statutes (Psalm 119:50, 71).*

Lessons in the School of Affliction

To get started in our lessons on affliction, we will first trace the word *"affliction"* through the 119th Psalm. The English word *"affliction"* is translated from two different Hebrew words: the first, *onee* (Strong's #6040), portrays an **emotional affliction** of being in a state of misery; the second word, *anah* (Strong's #6031), portrays a **physical affliction** of being bowed down or squashed beneath a physical load. Distinguishing those differences makes the following seven verses sound more powerful: (Emphasis added in the verses below.)

1. **Psalm 119:50:** *This is my comfort in my **affliction** [#6040—emotional], for **Your word** [#565—reading the divine Word to obtain the will of God]*[79] *has given me life.*

Only God's Word can really help us in afflictions. Cards, visits, gifts, and activities only offer temporary relief through distractions or amusement. Suffering through emotional affliction ought to drive us to read the Word of God to find comfort. Affliction can deaden us, but the Word gives us life.

The Blessing: Affliction causes us to see God's perfect Word more clearly.

2. **Psalm 119:67:** *Before I was **afflicted** [#6031—physical] I went astray, but now I keep **Your word** [#565—reading the divine Word to obtain the will of God].*

A consistent life is built by afflictions. God uses physical afflictions to pull us back and keep our lives on His path. It's common to hear someone who has gone through physical affliction say, "I was going my own way before I had this problem (car accident, illness, disability), but I am once more following God's path!"

The Blessing: Affliction causes us to see God's path of holiness more clearly.

---

[79] As discussed in chapter 2, there are ten synonyms for the Bible in Psalm 119; verses 50, 67, 71, 75, 92, 107, and 153 contain four of these synonyms. Their number designations are from Strong's Exhaustive Concordance of the Bible; their descriptions are from the "Psalm 119's Ten Synonyms for the Bible" list at Appendix A.

3. **Psalm 119:71:** *It is good for me that I have been* ***afflicted*** *[#6031—physical], that I may learn Your statutes [#2706—using the divine plans, or specifications, to build the ultimate life].*

The Hebrew word behind the English word "statutes" means "God's divine plans." God has plans, similar to a schematic or blueprint. They are like engineering drawings for how He designed life to be lived. Verse 71 says to understand or learn those plans, it's good that we be afflicted, because there are truths and lessons we can only learn in God's School of Affliction. Affliction scrapes away what is not part of His plan for our lives—people, possessions, positions, and so forth. Physical problems teach us to follow the Lord's plan.

The Blessing: Affliction causes us to see God's plan for our lives more clearly.

4. **Psalm 119:75:** *I know, O LORD, that Your judgments [#4941—building life upon the divine decisions—judgments that are always true and vindicate] are right, and that in faithfulness You have* ***afflicted*** *[#6031—physical] me.*

God's unchanging faithfulness is learned best in affliction; everything He does is good, right, and the most loving choice possible for His children. Isn't it a great blessing to realize He knows us, and is monitoring our entire lives.

The Blessing: Affliction causes us to see God's pruning of our lives more clearly.

5. **Psalm 119:92:** *Unless Your law [#8451—receiving the divine instructions from the Ultimate Teacher who gives perfect instructions that restore and transform] had been my delight, I would then have perished in my* ***affliction*** *[#6040—emotional].*

The onset of troubles marks the beginning of our Divine Teacher's personal tutorial. Afflictions are opportunities to either delight in Him or perish in our troubles. Many people go through life without knowing the reviving power of God's Word. As a result, they become buried in an emotional avalanche when tribulation comes—and some even give up. So Ezra was saying in verse 92: "Unless You instruct me as my Divine Teacher, I will perish by becoming smothered or buried in my emotional affliction!"

When Americans have emotional afflictions, many seek escape through medication, alcohol, or a variety of amusements. Do you know the meaning of "amusement"? The alpha primitive "a" means "not"; "muse" means "to think." In other words, they look for distractions to divert thinking so their minds can go into neutral. But God says, "What you need is My Law; you need to get My Divine Instructions in you to restore and transform you so you don't perish when you feel buried emotionally." The Lord will bring us back with His Word (Psalm 119:25-32), restore our soul (Psalm 23:3), and make us whole again (Psalm 19:7-14).

The Blessing: Affliction causes us to see God's source of hope more clearly.

6. **Psalm 119:107:** *I am **afflicted** [#6031—physical] very much [all kinds of physical afflictions]; revive me, O LORD, according to **Your word** [#1697—hearing the Divine Voice walking us all the way through life].*

As we age, it's common to think life will get easier because we won't have to face as many struggles just to survive. But that's not really true. Going through afflictions is a lifelong process. As we get older, the nature of the afflictions simply changes. But one thing will never change: God's Word will always renew, refresh, and revive. Having witnessed many of God's children at the final stages of their life, I've found what has comforted them most is the reading of God's Word because they hear the Divine Voice walking with them in their afflictions.

The Blessing: Affliction causes us to see God's offer of personal revival more clearly.

7. **Psalm 119:153:** *Consider my **affliction** [#6040—emotional] and deliver me, for I do not forget **Your law** [#8451—receiving the*

divine instructions from the Ultimate Teacher who gives perfect instructions that restore and transform].

Affliction comes with a promise from God for a special deliverance once we've learned the lessons He's designed for us. In the meantime, through His Word He draws near to us and provides everything we need to bear up under the trials.

The Blessing: Affliction causes us to see God's ability to rescue us more clearly.

Because seven is the number of divine completion, it seems God has engineered a complete set of messages on affliction in these seven verses in Psalm 119. The primary lesson is affliction is purposed to drive us to God and His Word: to find comfort (v. 50); to obtain the will of God (v. 67); to follow His divine plan (v. 71); to learn of God's faithfulness (v. 75); to find restoration and transformation (v. 92); to hear His voice walking with us in our affliction (v. 107); and to get special deliverance (v. 153). With these verses the Lord as our Ultimate Teacher has traced how He uses afflictions as a part of His divine plan to build our lives into a masterpiece for His glory!

What Qualifies as an Affliction?

Have you ever asked yourself: *What qualifies in God's eyes as an affliction?* Do you know how to find an answer to such questions? Simply trace a topic as it unfolds in the Scriptures from its first occurrence onward. For example, to find where "affliction" occurs in the Scriptures, you can look the word up in a Bible study tool such as *Strong's Exhaustive Concordance of the Bible* and then read each reference in your Bible, along with any surrounding verses that affect its context. When I did this with the word "affliction," I found thirty-seven occurrences in the Old Testament and takes at least seven forms, as follows: (Emphasis added to the verses below.)

1. Ill treatment by others qualifies as an affliction: ... *The Angel of the LORD said to [Hagar]: "Behold, you are with child, and you shall bear a son. You shall call his name Ishmael, because the LORD has heard your **affliction**" (Genesis 16:11).*

In God's sight, being ill treated by jealous and vengeful bosses is an affliction. Hagar's boss—her mistress, Abram's wife Sarai—was jealous when Hagar became with child by Abram, and Sarai held Hagar in contempt. But God said, "I am the God who sees your affliction, Hagar, and it is not right for Sarai to mistreat you this way, so I will bless you." If you are mistreated by someone who has authority over you and it is making life hard at home, at work, or at school, God says, "I want you to learn from Me in that situation; I know about it and will work good for you through it." (See Romans 8:28.)

2. Lack of love qualifies as an affliction: ... *Leah conceived and bore a son, and she called his name Reuben; for she said, "The LORD has surely looked on my **affliction**. Now therefore, my husband will love me" (Genesis 29:32).*

God considered Jacob's lack of love for Leah to be her affliction. After Jacob labored for seven years to earn Laban's permission to marry Rachel, the pretty and well-favored daughter, he was tricked by Laban who gave him Leah instead—the older and less-favored daughter. Jacob never wanted Leah as his wife, so when he had to work another seven years to marry the one whom he really loved, that carried over into the marriage. Just as it wasn't right for Hagar to be mistreated by her mistress, it wasn't right for Leah to be unloved by her husband. God said, "I see your affliction, Leah. Your husband should love and cleave to you, and I want you to know I care about your suffering." Can you relate to that? Do you have a lack of love in some relationship? Are you experiencing an undeserved lack of love simply because of not being liked? That's an affliction, and God wants to teach you some great things through suffering.

3. Lost wages and broken promises qualify as an affliction: ... *Jacob was angry and rebuked Laban, and Jacob answered and said to Laban: "What is my trespass? What is my sin, that you have so* *hotly pursued me? ... Thus I have been in your house twenty years; I served you fourteen years for your two daughters, and six years for your flock, and you have changed my wages ten times. Unless the God of my father, the God of Abraham and the Fear of Isaac, had been with me, surely now you would have sent me away empty-handed. God has seen my **affliction** and the labor of my hands, and rebuked you last night" (Genesis 31:36, 41-42).*

God viewed Jacob's lost wages and Laban's broken promises to him as an affliction. A modern-day example of such a trial is the plight of many American workers who suffer because of the downsizing of the large companies to which they'd given the best years of their lives. In an effort to save money, the oldest employees are let go first so the companies don't have to pay retirement benefits. God says to those enduring such a hardship, "I know about your lost wages and the company's broken promises, and I intend to work out My perfect plan for your life through that affliction." Your job situation is part of the afflictions God promises to use for your good—no matter how it may look at the time.

4. **Hatred, jealousy, and betrayal qualify as an affliction:** *... The name of the second he called Ephraim: "For God has caused me to be fruitful in the land of my **affliction**" (Genesis 41:52).*

The hatred, jealousy, and betrayal Joseph suffered at the hands of his family and employers, plus the neglect and broken promises of his friends, was seen by God as "affliction" (Psalm 105:17-19). Yet, his trials were not removed for a long time; instead, the Lord worked behind the scenes to make Joseph fruitful in the midst of it all. After Joseph's character had been thoroughly proven, so he had unshakable confidence in the Lord, He took him from rags to riches by making him second in command in all of Egypt. Then God used him to save His people, Israel!

What is the lesson from Joseph's life? If you are experiencing any suffering, God says to you, "I am aware of every situation, but you need to go through the furnace of affliction to become more fruitful for Me. Do you remember when Shadrach, Meshach, and Abed-Nego were thrown into the fiery furnace because they refused to worship King Nebuchadnezzar's golden image? (See Daniel 3) The fire was so strong it burned up the soldiers who threw them in! But the only thing God allowed to burn on the three Hebrews was the ropes binding their hands and feet. Then they were set free to walk with God in that fiery furnace! And He will walk with you through your own afflictions.

5. **Underpayment and overwork qualifies as an affliction:** ... *The LORD said: "I have surely seen the **oppression** [affliction] of My people who are in Egypt, and have heard their cry because of their taskmasters, for I know their sorrows" (Exodus 3:7).*

The word "oppression" means "affliction." The underpayment and overwork of the Hebrews by unkind and evil masters was an affliction, and happens all the time to American workers. Many are underpaid and practically kill themselves overworking just to make ends meet. But God says, "I see that affliction of yours, but instead of fighting, I want to strengthen and teach you some valuable lessons as you go through it."

6. **The inability to have children qualifies as an affliction:** ... *[Hannah] was in bitterness of soul, and prayed to the LORD and wept in **anguish** [affliction] (1 Samuel 1:10).*

Anguish is "affliction"—a squashing—which is the depth of emotion Hannah displayed as she wept. Her inability to have children caused her great suffering, but the cruelty of her "fellow wife" and the insensitivity to Hannah's pain compounded the problem.

Are there things you are unable to do and have no control over it? Perhaps you have limitations or inabilities for which people afflict you and give you pain. God says to you, "I know all about your struggles; I am not blind to them, and through your furnace of affliction I am going to teach you something valuable you can never learn any other way." That is always the lesson of affliction.

7. **Unkind words, slander, accusations, and insults qualify as an affliction:** *"It may be that the LORD will look on my **affliction**, and that the LORD will repay me with good for his cursing this day" (2 Samuel 16:12).*

This was a real low point in David's life. His adversary, Shimei, hurled unkind words, slander, accusations, and insults at him when David's son, Absalom, won the heart of the people and ran his father out of town. On top of that, Shimei, a descendant of King Saul, screamed venomous words and cursed David, and threw dirt and kicked rocks at him? But David responded well in spite of his heartache, "Maybe You, oh Lord, will repay me with good for the cursings I've endured today. I want to walk with You through this fiery furnace of affliction so You can burn away anything from my life keeping me from serving You more fully." This is the attitude God wants to see in us as well.

What do you sense is the most important lesson the Ultimate Teacher wants you to personally learn from these seven beautiful portraits of affliction? If you are struggling emotionally or physically right now, stop and reflect upon the lives of these Old Testament saints and what they faced: hatred, jealousy, and betrayal; a bad job situation; family disharmony; infertility; and verbal insults, accusations, and unkind words. How did they survive such afflictions? They turned to God and His Word and found comfort, strength, and deliverance in His perfect timing. So instead of opting to escape afflictions through distractions, or getting even with those who are mistreating you, pray: "Oh Lord, my Divine Teacher, what do You want me to learn in this situation? Is there anything keeping me from walking more closely with You? If so, reveal what it is and then remove it. As I go through this furnace of affliction, teach me to find comfort through Your Word and to follow Your will for my life."

Great Is God's Faithfulness!

If anybody ever had the right to say "I quit, God! I can't take any more of these afflictions!"—it would have been Jeremiah. Known to us as the weeping prophet, he had an extremely hard life: no family, no friends, no ministry—he was a complete failure from an earthly perspective. Yet, what rose from his life was the greatest testimony possible:

*This I recall to my mind, therefore I have hope. Through the
LORD's mercies we are not consumed, because His compassions
fail not. They are new every morning; great is Your faithfulness
(Lamentations 3:21-23).*

It's one thing to sing "Great Is Thy Faithfulness" in a comfortable church while dressed in finery and enjoying the fellowship of the saints. However, it is quite another thing to sing "Great Is Thy Faithfulness" when you have no family, no friends, no success, and suffer both physical and emotional pain—feeling trapped, hopeless, and having no future. That was a daily reality for Jeremiah. If we had to endure even a small part of what he went through, I wonder whether we could sing or say what he did in verse 23? God's grace is certainly sufficient to make that happen, but we're not always good receptors of His grace, are we?

What possible blessing could ever come from Jeremiah's desperate condition of affliction and pain? Let's look at what he had to say, beginning in Lamentations 3:22-23 because those verses contain the greatest message of hope in all of God's Word—and our faithful God still offers the same hope to His children today.

In our failures God always offers His unfailing love:
*Through the LORD's mercies we are not consumed,
  because His compassions fail not (Lamentations 3:22).*

Jeremiah never claimed to be perfect, but often confessed he was weak, so the Lord revealed to him that even when His children fail, His love never fails. God's mercies, compassions, and love are endless and unconditional.

Into our monotonous lives God gives His daily freshness:
*[Your mercies] are new every morning;
  great is Your faithfulness (Lamentations 3:23).*

Have you ever thought about how monotonous life could be without God's faithfulness, His newness, and His freshness? Basically, I have done the same thing in my life every day for twenty-five years. I spend a portion of my day wrestling with God's Word

(I have been reading the Bible a lot longer, but it's been part of my full-time vocation for twenty-five). Many believers get bored with the same routine and constantly search for something different. But if we will allow God, He promises to insert freshness into our monotonous lives. Because He is so faithful, we can find newness in our daily walk with Christ. And when we go through affliction, His faithfulness will be even more evident as He draws near to comfort us during those trying times.

In our weaknesses God gives us a personal dose of strength:
"The LORD is my portion," says my soul,
  "therefore I hope in Him!" (Lamentations 3:24).

When our eight children were little, like all parents, Bonnie and I fed them in the usual growth sequence: milk, chopped up or mashed food, small finger foods, and then whole meals. When they were able to eat only a small portion at a time, we used a tiny spoon so they wouldn't choke. Similarly, our heavenly Father knows His children's weaknesses and just what size "portion" is right for each of us so we won't choke on the affliction, but find hope in Him.

In our frantic lifestyles God gives His promise of blessings:
The LORD is good to those who wait for Him,
  to the soul who seeks Him (Lamentations 3:25).

Would you like to do a great study? The word "wait" is one you will find all the way through the Old Testament. Eight different Hebrew words are translated into the English word "wait." Waiting is really important to God, but foreign to most people, so God reminds us He's ... *good to those who wait for Him.* Although our lives may often be frantic, the Lord promises blessings to those who don't try to run away from or escape the common tribulations of life. Instead, He wants us to pray, "Lord, because You don't change, and Your judgments are right, I realize in faithfulness You are allowing this in my life. So please speak to me; teach me to be patient in this tribulation and learn whatever is needed so I have unshakable confidence in You, and thus serve You more fully."

Into our anxious lives God's salvation gives quiet hope:
It is good that one should hope and wait quietly
for the salvation of the Lord (Lamentations 3:26).

In Lamentations 3, Jeremiah reported his many afflictions: broken physical health and deep emotional strain (v. 5); dark depression (v. 6); desperation and feeling trapped (v. 7); being out of touch and distant from God (v. 8); feeling frustration and confusion (v. 9); struggling with anxiety and sadness (v. 17); experiencing physical weakness and hopelessness (v. 18); and suffering bitter affliction (v. 19).

What did he learn during such afflictions? Jeremiah concluded: "Though I fail, God's love never fails. When my life is monotonous and terrible, His freshness pervades my life. Every single time I open the Scriptures, they are like a breath of fresh air to me." Whenever we open God's Word in the hot, triple-digit temperatures of life's tribulations, a breath of freshness will come as we wait on the Lord. For great is the Lord's faithfulness!

Into our confusing lives God writes His perfect plan:
... He does not afflict willingly,
nor grieve the children of men (Lamentations 3:33).

Jeremiah was saying, "God is not just capricious in what He does, as in roulette living or simple happenstance; He has a perfect plan." When affliction comes, as this verse says, it's not an affliction to just "rattle your cage" and cause you some problems. No, God has a specific objective in mind.

What is that plan? Look at Psalm 119:75 again: *I know, O LORD, that Your judgments are right* [You don't ever change], *and that in faithfulness You have afflicted me. You know what?* God wants to teach us that He is faithful! The way He does so is to bring affliction into our lives. If you will wait quietly before Him, and say, "Lord, I want what You are teaching me," He will bring into your life everything I just shared with you from Lamentations 3:22-33. Isn't that worth whatever price you might have to pay?

Find Hope in the Lord!

When you're in the furnace of affliction, you will be blessed if you do a word study in Scriptures that offer HOPE. The Bible is full of them! To get you started, listed below are some verses from the Psalms I urge you to memorize and meditate upon, then pray back to the Lord.

- **Hope unlocks divine strength:** *Be of good courage, and He shall strengthen your heart, all you who hope in the LORD (Psalm 31:24).*
- **Hope attracts God's attention:** ... *The eye of the LORD is on those who fear Him, on those who hope in His mercy ... (Psalm 33:18).*
- **Hope opens God's ears:** *For in You, O LORD, I hope: You will hear, O LORD my God (Psalm 38:15).*
- **Hope is God's desire for us**: *"And now, Lord, what do I wait for? My hope is in You" (Psalm 39:7).*
- **Hope dispels gloom:** *Why are you cast down, O my soul? And why are you disquieted within me? Hope in God, for I shall yet praise Him for the help of His countenance (Psalm 42:5).*
- **Hope in God is to be lifelong:** ... *You are my hope, O LORD GOD; You are my trust from my youth. ... But I will hope continually, and will praise You yet more and more (Psalm 71:5, 14).*
- **Hope is a choice:** *That they may set their hope in God, and not forget the works of God, but keep His commandments ... (Psalm 78:7).*
- **Hope in His Word:** *Remember the word to Your servant, upon which You have caused me to hope (Psalm 119:49). (See also vv. 81, 114, and 116.)*
- **Hope in your Creator:** *Happy is he who has the God of Jacob for his help, whose hope is in the LORD his God, who made heaven and earth, the sea, and all that is in them; who keeps truth forever ... (Psalm 146:5-6).*

Rest in His Great Faithfulness

What a great God! Doesn't the very thought of His awesomeness make you want to burst forth into singing "Great Is Thy Faithfulness"?

I encourage you to rejoice in the Lord as you worshipfully sing these verses to Him!

Great is Thy Faithfulness, O God my Father!
There is no shadow of turning with Thee;
Thou changest not, Thy compassions, they fail not:
As Thou hast been Thou forever wilt be.

Pardon for sin and a peace that endureth,
Thine own dear presence to cheer and to guide,
Strength for today and bright hope for tomorrow—
Blessings all mine, with ten thousand beside.

Refrain:
Great is Thy faithfulness, Great is Thy faithfulness,
Morning by morning new mercies I see;
All I have needed Thy hand hath provided—
Great is Thy faithfulness, Lord, unto me! Amen.[80]

—**Thomas O. Chisholm**

[80] Thomas O. Chisholm (1866-1960). © Copyright 1923. Renewal 1951. Hope Publishing Company.

My Prayer for You:

Father in Heaven, we bow reverently before You as we ask for help to understand there are blessings in affliction we will miss if we run away, if we don't accept the fact You are faithful and will only afflict us in love because You want to build the best life possible for us—a Word filled life. Sometimes the most effective way You can do that is to simply stop us in our tracks to get our complete and undivided attention. Therefore, whatever You bring into our lives, we know it's good for us. We want to hope in You, and commit the keeping of our souls to You—the One who does all things well. As we trust in Your faithfulness, may You make the dark times, the sad times, the discouraging times, and the inexplicable times a blessing not only in our own lives but also in the lives of those observing our struggles. Thank you for Your greatest display of faithfulness in giving Your Son to be the sacrifice for our sins. Thank You that in His body He bore our sins on the cross as He gave Himself for us! In Jesus' name I pray. Amen.

17

... [If] you will seek the LORD your God, ... you will find Him if you seek Him with all your heart and with all your soul.

—**Deuteronomy 4:29**

Suffering Affliction:
Testing God's Promises

R EMEMBER: A GREAT BLESSING OF exercising "the discipline of suffering affliction" is through it we get to test the promises of God, which is one of the ways we are assured of our salvation.[81] Through affliction we get to see God fulfill what He has promised to do—the greater the trial, the greater the potential for blessing!

How can this be? In his *Confessions*, St. Augustine explains this seeming contradiction:

> What is it ... that goes on within the soul, since it takes greater delight if things that it loves are found or restored to it than if it had always possessed them? Other things bear witness to this, and all are filled with proofs that cry aloud, "Thus it is!" The victorious general holds his triumph: yet unless he had fought, he would never have won the victory, and the greater was the danger in battle, the greater is the joy in the triumph. The storm tosses seafarers about, and threatens them with shipwreck: they

[81] MP3 CD Audio DYG-30:030928AM, MP3 CD Audio DYG-32:031019AM

all grow pale at their coming death. Then the sky and the sea become calm and they exult exceedingly, just as they had feared exceedingly. A dear friend is ill, and his pulse tells us of his bad case. All those who long to see him in good health are in mind sick along with him. He gets well again, and although he does not yet walk with his former vigor, there is joy such as did not obtain before when he walked well and strong. Everywhere a greater joy is preceded by a greater suffering .... [82]

Our suffering can produce great blessings if it causes us to test God's promises and thus see more clearly: His Word (Psalm 119:50); His path (Psalm 119:67); His plan for our lives (Psalm 119:71); His pruning of our lives (Psalm 119:75); His source of hope (Psalm 119:92); His offer of personal revival (Psalm 119:107); and His ability to rescue us (Psalm 119:153).

God Can Use the Big Afflictions of Our Lives

One of those seven verses uniquely stands out: *I am afflicted very much; revive me, O LORD, according to Your word (v. 107).* Due to the immensity of its meaning, studying each phrase of that verse is fascinating.

I am afflicted very much ...: "Afflicted," (Strong's #6031) as in physical affliction, means "to bow you down," and speaks of pushing you down physically. Where it really gets interesting is the adverb "very much," which is the same Hebrew word used for the way the Flood waters covered earth (Genesis 7:18-19); the way the plagues covered Egypt (Exodus 9:3—pestilence; Exodus 9:18—hail; Exodus 10:14—locusts). Let's look at each example to grasp the full impact of what Ezra was saying. (Emphasis added to the verses below.)

> • **Genesis 7:18-19:** *The waters prevailed and **greatly increased** on the earth, and the ark moved about on the surface of the waters. And the waters prevailed **exceedingly** on the earth, and all the high hills under the whole heaven were covered.* ("Greatly increased" and "exceedingly" are the same Hebrew word.)

[82] As cited in Dr. Paul Brand and Philip Yancey's Pain—The Gift Nobody Wants (New York: Harper Collins, 1993), p. 300.

Have you ever considered what it was like for earth to suddenly have an overwhelming flood of water come upon it? That is the picture our Divine Engineer, the Holy Spirit of God, wanted to capture by the word He inspired His servant Ezra to record in verse 107.

Can you identify with how Ezra must have felt when troubles rained down on him like the waters that burst forth upon Noah during the Flood? Are troubles coming down on you, piling up until you feel like you're drowning? God wants you to test His promises so He can revive you as you learn to listen to His voice in His Word—guiding, rescuing, and comforting.

Perhaps your afflictions appear to be so complex you feel they're beyond remedy. As a result, you've let those struggles dominate your time and have been neglecting the Word. Do you realize what a treasure it is to have the Bible so readily available in the twenty-first century? Most people have several versions in their home. Ezra, however, had a far different situation. Unroll a large roll of paper towels for fifty-five feet, and that gives you a picture of how long the Bible was for him, and how hard it was to get into the Scriptures. Think about it: how would you like to have to roll out a fifty-five foot long scroll before you could even try to do a little Bible study? And, what if there was only one scroll for your entire community? Can you imagine how challenging that was for Ezra? To manage, Old Testament saints would sit, memorize, and inculcate the Word of God into their hearts to readily meditate on it day and night. The primary reason someone doesn't get into the Word isn't really a lack of time, but lack of desire. If your desire for the Word wanes, it is a wakeup call for asking the Holy Spirit to restore and transform you.

- **Exodus 9:3:** *"... Behold, the hand of the LORD will be on your cattle in the field, on the horses, on the donkeys, on the camels, on the oxen, and on the sheep—**a very severe** pestilence."*

In this verse, the Lord spoke about what He was going to do to Egypt through Moses. This is the same idea where Ezra said, "I am afflicted very much." It's the identical word, and describes the horrible plague that came down upon him.

• **Exodus 9:18:** " ' *"Behold, tomorrow about this time I will cause* **very** *heavy hail to rain down such as has not been in Egypt since its founding until now."* ' "

Do you see the intensity? God was not talking about having a little fogginess in the morning before having a cup of coffee—major events were involved here.

• **Exodus 10:14:** *And the locusts went up over all the land of Egypt and rested on all the territory of Egypt. They were* **very** *severe; previously there had been no such locusts as they, nor shall there be such after them.*

There are many ways the Lord could have said through Ezra in Psalm 119, "I am having trouble!" But He chose to use a word indicating the highest level possible for problems.

Are your life's pains sometimes like the plagues of Egypt, hardships that keep coming before you've recovered from the last? As you listen to God's voice in the Word, He wants to revive you by leading, rescuing, and comforting you; He wants to guide you into the place He wants you to be. That is His whole purpose in allowing afflictions. As they are raining down like the Flood, and coming in wave after wave like the plagues of Egypt, God wants you to look up and pray, "Lord, You promised that You would revive me in the midst of my affliction, and I am counting on that now!" As you test His many scriptural promises through "the discipline of supplication," He will faithfully fulfill them.

God Always Meets Us in the Furnace of Affliction

... *revive me, O LORD* ...: "Revive" is actually "save my life" and is the same word God used to describe His rescue of Rahab from Jericho. As the walls crumbled around her and everyone was destroyed, she and her family, alone, were rescued (Joshua 2:13; 6:17, 25). When I think of her rescue, it reminds me of an old cat and mouse cartoon I watched as a child. The cat chased the mouse all around the house, and then did something to cause the whole house to collapse—leaving the mouse standing all alone. That is what I see in my mind when I think of Rahab; I picture her in her little wall house and then the whole city crashing down—leaving Rahab standing there amazed, thinking: *How on earth did we ever manage to survive all this?* Then she praised the true and living God for delivering her safely through the trial! That is what Ezra was saying in this verse, "I am saved through my great flood and plagues of afflictions by the Lord! He is reviving me; He has saved me, and kept me alive!"

> • **Joshua 2:13:** *"… **spare the lives** of my father and mother, my brothers and sisters, and all who belong to them, and that you will save us from death" (NIV).*

This Hebrew word for "revive" is exactly the same in Psalm 119:107, but look how Joshua 2 translates it: "spare the lives," and that is what the word means. (The word for "save us from death" is a different word than "spare the lives.")

> • **Joshua 6:17:** *"Now the city shall be doomed by the Lord to destruction, it and all who are in it. Only Rahab the harlot **shall live**, she and all who are with her in the house, because she hid the messengers that we sent."*

"Shall live" is the same word as "*revive*" in Psalm 119:107.

> • **Joshua 6:25:** *And Joshua **spared** [revived] Rahab the harlot, her father's household, and all that she had. So she dwells in Israel to this day, because she hid the messengers whom Joshua sent to spy out Jericho.*

Isn't this fascinating? Joshua 2:13 says *"spare the lives"*; Joshua 6:17 says *"shall live"*; and now Joshua 6:25 says *"spared."* The context is this was the great city of Canaan, the gateway city. After crossing the Jordan River, you came to a gigantic fortress with impenetrable walls. Jericho, one of the oldest continuously inhabited cities in the world, was perfectly defensible. Yet, in this monstrous city sat one unrighteous woman who came to faith in the true and living God by believing what He said. So she got a scarlet cord—the scarlet cord of redemption—and stuck it out her window. Meanwhile, she was perched in one of the most dangerous places in the city: on the wall. As Rahab stood watching, the people of Israel marched silently around Jericho every day for six days. On the seventh time around the city, on the seventh day, the priests blew their trumpets and the people loudly shouted in expectation of God fulfilling His promise. Then kaboom! The walls came tumbling down—falling outward! But there was one tiny section where Rahab and her family were still standing; they had been spared.

Do you ever feel unable to survive what you are going through right now—the pain, the hurt, the crumbling of everything you have held onto? If that's how you feel, then you know what Rahab must have gone through as the city of Jericho was destroyed. Part of God's plan is for afflictions to tear things down, and cause us to test scriptural promises through which the Lord then revives, rescues, and spares us!

Do you realize the destruction of Jericho was an affliction Rahab had to go through—or she would not have been in the lineage of Jesus Christ? Nor would she be one whom the Bible records was still living in Israel, having been accepted into the community. Rahab was blessed because she followed God's lead when He said, "I want you to stay put. I am going to revive you when your whole world crumbles and falls apart, and everything around you is destroyed; I am going to spare you." Through faith, Rahab tested the promises of God and found Him to be faithful.

God Always Uses His Word During Affliction

- *... according to Your word:* Recall in chapter 2 how we looked at all ten synonyms for the Word of God in Psalm 119. "Word" in Psalm 119:107 means "His voice." Ezra was saying: "God, You have talked me through the complete flood of problems—the complete disaster that has totally made my whole world crumble around me. But I am still standing here because I hear Your voice through Your Word, and so I am surviving!"

One might think of the 119th Psalm as sort of a long summary of Ezra's life, as if he was saying, "I was afflicted, and I was afflicted, and I was afflicted, and now I'm still being afflicted. It's not over." The truth is, this life is typical as a whole. In fact, some of the hardest days in life are the latter years. When you're young, there's always something to look forward to, but when you get older, everything is running out: time, strength, energy, and hope (at least on a horizontal plain). That is what Ezra was going through when he said, "I am afflicted very much, but I know You are going to spare me because I am listening to Your voice and Your Word." Now here's the good news: although affliction usually increases as we get older, God's Word will always renew, refresh, and revive. Therefore, the Apostle Paul could say:

> … We do not lose heart. Even though our outward man is perishing, yet the inward man is being renewed day by day. For our light affliction, which is but for a moment, is working for us a far more exceeding and eternal weight of glory, while we do not look at the things which are seen, but at the things which are not seen. For the things which are seen are temporary, but the things which are not seen are eternal (2 Corinthians 4:16-18).

Lessons From Abraham in the School of Affliction

What if God asked you to leave all you'd grown up with to travel 1,500 miles with a huge family—but would not even tell you where you were going? How would you know when you got there? How would you know when to stop? Just think about the immense implications of such a dilemma and what faith it required! Abraham knew, because God chose him for just such a trial. In fact, the Lord summarized his entire journey through life as being one of faith (Hebrews 11:8-19).

What was it about Abraham to cause God to call him "the father of the faithful"? Simply this: Abraham did what the Lord asked him to do—he went on a journey even though he didn't know where, didn't know how, didn't know when, and didn't know why. Abraham was, therefore, one of the greatest men of human history. He is the second man after Adam to whom God had chosen to appear. God walked with Enoch, talked with Noah, but appeared to Abraham, making him very special. But with every blessing comes responsibility, so with the appearance of God to Abraham at age seventy-five came one hundred years of lessons in the promises of God—most of which we would call "afflictions."

What are these promises afflictions forced Abraham to test? Hebrews 11 can help us to consider some questions Abraham may have thought, or at least felt. (Emphasis added in the verses below.)

Where is this promised place we're going?

Abraham probably had thoughts such as: "If I am going to leave with my wife, my many servants, and all these animals, where exactly are we going?" But look what God says in verses 8-10:

> *By faith Abraham obeyed when he was called to go out to the place which he would receive as an inheritance. And he went out,* ***not knowing where he was going.*** *By faith he dwelt in the land of promise as in a foreign country, dwelling in tents with Isaac and Jacob, the heirs with him of the same promise; for he waited for the city which has foundations, whose builder and maker is God.*

Not only did Abraham not know where he was going, but he left the most civilized city in the ancient world to dwell in a tent for the rest of his life. Ur, that wealthy and highly populated city of the Chaldeans in Mesopotamia, even had multistory buildings with plastered walls and indoor plumbing. Its citizens were highly educated and many were skilled craftsmen. So Abraham was in the ultimate place to live, and yet he willingly moved into a tent because he wanted to confess by his lifestyle he was a stranger and pilgrim on earth.

Sometimes thoughts about leaving behind our highly developed civilization for heaven may occasionally prompt questions like: *Where is it I'm really going? Is it worth so much to sacrifice here and now? Do I really need my lifestyle to reflect where I am going? Do I really need my lifestyle to reflect whom I worship and believe? Where exactly is my REAL home?* When you face your own "Where" questions, it is time to test the promises of God—and find He is more than enough for whatever you need!

How is this promised son possible?

When God told Abraham a son would be born to Sarah, he ... laughed, and said in his heart, *"Shall a child be born to a man who is one hundred years old? And shall Sarah, who is ninety years old, bear a child?"* (Genesis 17:17). I love how the Lord responded in Genesis 18:14: *"Is anything too hard for the LORD? ..."* And God was faithful to keep His promise, as we see in Hebrews 11:11-12:

> *By faith Sarah herself also received strength to conceive seed, and she bore a child when she was past the age, because she judged Him faithful who had promised. Therefore from one man,* **and him as good as dead,** *were born as many as the stars of the sky in multitude—innumerable as the sand which is by the seashore.*

Sometimes we face seemingly impossible obstacles. Has God also called you to do what looks impossible to accomplish? Great! Just do what Abraham did: test the promises of God. When he concluded "This is humanly impossible," God replied, "I want to do something you can't figure, plan, orchestrate, or work out so when I do it, I'll get all the credit!" You see the idea: that is what these impossible situations are about, and the Lord loves to work mightily through them.

In America, we won't enter a war until we have counted the cost and are able to believe we can win. We have to have overwhelming firepower and superior troops and equipment. But God said to Abraham, "You will enter this situation in life not knowing what the outcome will be. Trust the outcome to Me, because that is what the life of faith is about." So when you face your own "How" questions, it is time to test God's promises—and find He is more than enough for whatever you need!

**When is this
promised inheritance going to happen?**

If you think about it, almost every possible question was being asked, but rather than answer each question, the Lord led Abraham to walk in faith, not by sight.

> *These all died in faith, not having received the promises,* **but having seen them afar off** *were assured of them, embraced them and confessed that they were strangers and pilgrims on the earth. For those who say such things declare plainly that they seek a homeland. And truly if they had called to mind that country from which they had come out, they would have had opportunity to return. But now they desire a better, that is, a heavenly country. Therefore God is not ashamed to be called their God, for He has prepared a city for them (vv. 13-16).*

Waiting is probably the hardest thing for us. Imagine how difficult it was for Abraham to wait 10-15 years between the promise and answer. If you wait at a stop light a moment too long, you're likely to hear honking coming from the car behind you. The driver might even get out, kick your car, and yell at you. Because it is so difficult to wait, Abraham probably asked God on many occasions: "When is this going to happen?" From God's Word, we know Abraham was expected to trust God to keep His promise in His own perfect timing. So when you have your own "When" questions, it is time to test the promises of God—and find He is more than enough for whatever you need!

**Why do You want
this great of a sacrifice?**

Now look at verse 17 for his greatest lesson in faith yet: *By faith Abraham, when he was tested,* **offered up Isaac,** *and he who had received the promises offered up his only begotten son ....*

Talk about the ultimate test of a lifetime! After all the years of waiting for Isaac, his promised son, it would be no surprise if Abraham cried out from the depths of his heart: "Why are you doing this, God?

Why would You want me to KILL Isaac? I simply don't understand what's going on …" Humanly speaking, "Why" questions commonly pour out of grieving and sorrowful hearts. In fact, when Jesus was dying on the cross, He Himself cried out in anguish: … *"My God, My God, why have You forsaken Me?"* (Matthew 27:46).

Abraham's supreme test of faith reminds me of one of our dear saints at Tulsa Bible Church who, for his whole Christian adult life, wanted to go to Bible school to become a missionary. But just before he was supposed to retire, and everything looked great for going to the mission field, he suddenly faced a life-threatening illness so severe he was expected to die at any moment. Instantly, many of his friends and family wondered: *Why would God allow this? If anybody should be able to make it to the mission field, it would have been Prince Platner! And now there he is in a hospital bed—about as close to dead as anyone could be and still come back. Why? I just don't understand* … Do you know what was happening? God wanted to put Prince, his wife, and all of his friends through that agonizing affliction so everyone would say what Abraham said, "Why are you allowing this? Why?" And after a season of intense suffering, the Lord miraculously restored Prince to his family and ministry, which testifies to the truth "greater joy is preceded by greater suffering."

"Greater joy is preceded by greater suffering" was also true in Abraham's life. He tested God's promise … *"In Isaac your seed shall be called" by concluding … that God was able to raise him up, even from the dead* … (vv. 18-19). And, having passed the supreme test of faith, God met Abraham's need and wonderfully spared Isaac! So when you face your own "Why" questions, it is time to test the promises of God—and find He is more than enough for whatever you need!

Trust in God With All Your Heart

Now reflect on Psalm 119:107 again: *I am afflicted very much; revive me, O LORD, according to Your word.* Like Ezra, wouldn't you like to test the promises of God and know He really is out there? The lessons the Lord has for us in His School of Affliction are absolutely amazing. They are so hard to come upon and go through—but oh, how wonderful they are afterward! So when God floods you, and storms you, and you experience what seems like the plagues of Egypt, don't lose heart! Remember ... *weeping may endure for a night, but joy comes in the morning* (Psalm 30:5).

Always test His promises in faith: listen for His voice in His Word guiding you to the place where He wants you to be. And for those times when you feel you're drowning in your afflictions, earnestly cry out to Him: "I don't think I'm going to survive this, Lord! If you don't reach down and rescue me, and keep me alive like Rahab and her family at Jericho, I'm going to perish! Revive me! Spare me! I need to hear Your voice in Your Word. I need to sense Your presence, and walk with You. I need You to bring Your promises to bear in my life so I can better believe You, God. Therefore, I'm choosing to trust that no good thing will You withhold from me!" He wants a response of absolute trust—no matter how things might look at the time—when you are ... *afflicted very much.*

This is the message of this poem which hung on the wall of Richard W. DeHann's office during his long Radio Bible Class ministry:

TRUST IN GOD
Courage, Brother, do not stumble,
Though your path be dark as night;
There's a star to guide the humble,
Trust in God and do the right.

Let the road be rough and dreary,
And its end far out of sight,
Foot it bravely, strong or weary;
Trust in God and do the right.

Perish policy and cunning,
Perish all that fears the light;
Whether losing, whether winning
Trust in God and do the right.

Trust no party, sect or faction,
Trust no leaders in the fight;

But in every word and action
Trust in God and do the right.

Simple rule and safest guiding,
Inward peace and inward might,
Star upon our path abiding;
Trust in God and do the right.

Some will hate you, some will love you,
Some will flatter, some will slight;
Cease from man, and look above you,
Trust in God and do the right.
—**By Norman Macleod**

So, when afflictions try your faith, make those times count for eternity by testing God's wonderful promises, ever rejoicing that "… *The eyes of the LORD run to and fro throughout the whole earth,* **to show Himself strong** *on behalf of those whose heart is loyal to Him* …" (2 Chronicles 16:9, emphasis added). What a comfort! Truly, great is God's faithfulness!

My Prayer for You:

Father in Heaven, I thank you that even when we are afflicted very much You will rescue us. You will keep us alive, and save us in our troubles. You want to rescue us, to revive us, to save us right where we are so we can test Your promises. We face different things in our lives, but when we feel like we are drowning, when we feel like a wave is coming and we haven't recovered from the last wave, that's when You want us to hear Your still small voice through Your Word and test Your promises as we hear Your voice and say, "Are you really there, God? Are you really who You have always said? Can I really trust my life to You?" And You will prove You are there by rescuing us in the midst of our problems. You don't necessarily take

18

> I know, O LORD, that Your judgments are right, and that in faithfulness You have afflicted me. …Consider my affliction and deliver me, for I do not forget Your law.
> —**Psalm 119:75, 153**

Suffering Affliction:
Focusing on Our Master Teacher

"In Italy, for thirty years under the Borgias, they had warfare, terror, murder, bloodshed—but they produced Michelangelo, Leonardo da Vinci, and the Renaissance.[83] In Switzerland, they have brotherly love, five hundred years of democracy and peace, and what did that produce? The cuckoo clock."[84] Though that statement is a bit humorous, it makes a valid point. Trials refine us, pain opens our eyes to the realities of life, and sorrow tunes us into what really matters. In fact, traumatic and painful experiences help us to be more aware, and thus a part of the world around us.

When you and I choose to view afflictions as blessings and not curses, our Master Teacher can do marvelous works through His tutorial lessons in the School of Affliction. To build the best life possible—a Word filled life—He uses fiery trials to focus us on Him as we test the theory that God promises to comfort and deliver us safely through even the toughest of times. Have you ever had something delivered to your door, right when you need

83 MP3 CD Audio DYG-31:031012AM, MP3 CD Audio DYG-29:030921AM

84 Graham Greene, The Third Man, as cited in Dr. Paul Brand and Philip Yancey's Pain—The Gift Nobody Wants (City: Harper Collins, 1993), p. 298.

it? Well, along with each trial, God promises to come right to your doorstep, just when you need Him most, and deliver ... *the way of escape, that you may be able to bear it* (1 Corinthians 10:13). What a blessed reassurance!

Of the two types of afflictions Ezra experienced in Psalm 119 (emotional and physical), physical trials have perhaps the greatest potential for turning our world upside down in a millisecond. Have you ever thought about the fact that you are a heartbeat, a brainwave, or just a breath away from meeting your Master Teacher face to face? Life is so fragile that to stay alive through today the following systems must work in perfect harmony:

- Your heart must beat 103,000 times in twenty-four hours, or you will experience weakness.
- A supply of blood must travel 168,000 miles through your body to keep tissues and organs alive.
- Your lungs must breathe 23,400 times as you take twenty breaths a minute, twenty-four hours a day, to inhale the 450 cubic feet of atmosphere needed to sustain life and respiratory needs.
- You need a body frame strong enough to resist the weight of atmosphere that stretches fifty-plus miles overhead—a total atmospheric pressure equivalent to a load of fourteen tons pressing down on you.
- Survival requires a healthy organ system so every cell can be born again in your body every twenty-eight days.

This kind of precision points to a Master Designer, rather than people being mere products of chance. The many intricacies God built into the human body are amazing! If you ever want to capture someone's rapt attention, let a person think he or she is dying. Instantly, every relationship in life is examined, every activity scrutinized, and the best of the best becomes all that is cared about. That scenario was certainly true in my own life.

Years ago, I underwent several weeks of tests, pokes, and samplings. When my doctor sat in front of me to report the results, I saw great sadness in his eyes. My first reaction was to think: *Poor guy! Something must be going wrong at home* ... And then this brother in Christ whom I trusted, admired, and respected, began to talk. Very soon I realized those sad eyes were directed at me. Finally, I heard him say, "After all possible tests—and sending you everywhere I could—it appears you have cancer, liver cancer. There are very few options we have to treat that …"

My mind went into warp speed. I left the room immersed in thought—and raced home to my family. At the time, Bonnie and I had an infant daughter, two toddler sons, five other young children and teens, as well as a growing ministry. As images of my beautiful family ran through my mind, in a millisecond *my entire life changed.* Everything I owned seemed so unimportant to me, and every person I loved instantly rose to the top of my priority list.

And suddenly, like being in a dark room when a light is turned on, this thought flooded my mind: *I might see Jesus Himself soon, in a matter of just weeks or months! Everything I have ever read in God's Word, ever heard about heaven, and ever learned about eternity, is actually going to become reality in my personal experience!* That, coupled with all the fear of the unknowns, the inevitability of all the pain, the loss of all the hopes of future ministry and family joys, immediately became a personal and massive life-dominating affliction which brought the Lord Jesus Christ right to my doorstep.

In my tribulation, verses 75 and 153 of Psalm 119 became very clear to me: *I know, O LORD, that Your judgments are right, and that in faithfulness You have afflicted me [physically]. … Consider my [emotional] affliction and deliver me, for I do not forget Your law.* God miraculously heard the prayer because my health problem turned out not to be liver cancer. But during those three weeks when I believed I had terminal cancer, God brought great blessing out of the suffering!

Whether a cancer or other disease is considered as terminal, curable, or a misdiagnosis, to be blessed through it, seek the Lord's perspective on the affliction. That is why I like the words of a classic card I spotted on the night stand of a friend who was in the hospital dying of brain cancer. These are the very words I read to him at his bedside, and they ministered comfort to his heart:

Our greatest enemy is not disease, but despair.

> Cancer is so limited ...
> It cannot cripple love,
> It cannot shatter hope,
> It cannot erode faith,
> It cannot eat away peace,
> It cannot destroy confidence,
> It cannot kill friendship,
> It cannot shut out memories,
> It cannot silence courage,
> It cannot invade the soul,
> It cannot reduce eternal life,
> It cannot quench the Spirit,
> It cannot lessen the power of the resurrection.

This personal note by a fellow sufferer was included:

> "... though the outward man perishes, yet the inner man is renewed day by day...we look not at the things which are seen, but at things which are not seen: for the things which are seen are temporary, but the things which are not seen are eternal." II Cor. 4:16 & 18

> The Great Physician isn't expensive, but His work is priceless! You are so loved, Pat [85]

That card speaks truth. Our great enemy isn't really cancer or disease—it's not anything less than the despair of not crying out to God as Ezra did: "Lord, pay attention to my suffering in affliction! It's still hard; I'm still having trials; my troubles are not gone yet. Deliver me! Come to where I am with what I need to make it through for Your glory! I haven't forgotten Your Word. This affliction isn't because I'm a pagan and don't know You. And it isn't because of neglect or disinterest. I've done my part, Lord, and now I need You to come deliver me!" The Lord loves to hear this, and He delights in answering such prayers.

[85] Pat Bartlett, a Tulsa Bible Church member who is herself health-challenged, sent this card and note to her friend Bill Robinson who had just been diagnosed with brain cancer, and went home to be with the Lord a few weeks later.

When Life Hurts

Few things hurt as much as watching those nearest and dearest to us suffer. When afflictions hit our family and close friends, it is almost more painful than experiencing our own problems and heartaches. The majority of people invest heavily in those relationships, which are life's most treasured blessings. So when we go through the affliction of suffering with those precious to us, God wants to teach us these are the times to test His promises—the times to keep focused on our Master Teacher.

What happens when we lose a loved one? What happens when a child is swept tragically away, a marriage ends horribly, a wife is taken unexpectedly, a husband is gone without any warning, or dear friends are ripped away from us and we sometimes don't know why? Those are the times of our deepest woes—times when afflictions can overwhelm like a flood. Sorrows can make the world crash all around us, and plague us so we feel like we cannot make it through another wave of affliction. What is the secret to being able to "keep on keeping on" during such painful times?

While David and his men were away, the Amalekites raided the city where their wives and children were, and burned it to the ground. When David and his men came up over the hilltop on their way home, they saw the smoke and ruins of Ziklag. Their first thought was: *Is everyone dead? Is my wife dead? Are my children dead? I can already tell I have lost everything on this planet, but are they dead?* They didn't know that the Amalekites … had taken captive the women and those who were there, from small to great; they did not kill anyone, but carried them away and went their way (v. 2). Look at how David and his men reacted when they arrived in Ziklag:

> *Then David and the people who were with him lifted up their voices and wept, until they had no more power to weep* [literally, the Hebrew says "no more tears"; they cried out everything they had]. … *Now David was greatly distressed, for the people spoke of stoning him, because the soul of all the people was grieved, every man for his sons and his daughters* … (vv. 4, 6).

Learn to Allow God to Strengthen You!

How did David respond to this highly painful affliction—the supposed loss of his family, as well as his men turning against him? In the midst of his deepest woe and grief ... *David strengthened himself in the LORD his God* (v. 6). David chose to focus on his Master Teacher instead of his problems; he immediately sought counsel of the Lord: ... *"Shall I pursue this troop? Shall I overtake them?"* God, who wanted to comfort and deliver David in his affliction, answered: *"Pursue, for you shall surely overtake them and without fail recover all"* (v. 8).

The fact ... *David strengthened himself in the LORD his God* (v. 6) is key to God's recovery program for those who are hurting. The question we need to ask is this: How did David do that? What is the answer to finding help when we struggle? Consider what Matthew Henry says about David's affliction in 1 Samuel 30:

> This was a sore trial to the man after God's own heart, and could not but go very near him. Saul had driven him from his country, the Philistines had driven him from their camp, the Amalekites had plundered his city, his wives were taken prisoners, and now, to complete his woe, his own familiar friends, in whom he trusted, whom he had sheltered, and who did eat of his bread, instead of sympathizing with him and offering him any relief, lifted up the heel against him and threatened to stone him.
>
> It is the duty and interest of all good people, whatever happens, to encourage themselves in God as their Lord and their God, assuring themselves that he can and will bring light out of darkness, peace out of trouble, and good out of evil, to all that love him and are the called according to his purpose, Rom. 8:28. It was David's practice, and he had the comfort of it, What time I am afraid I will trust in thee. When he was at his wits' end he was not at his faith's end.[86]

That great preacher, J. Vernon McGee, has also commented on David's afflictions: "Friend, there are times in our lives when the cir-

---

[86] Matthew Henry, *Matthew Henry's Commentary on the Bible* (Peabody, MA: Hendrickson Publishers, 1997).

cumstances will not produce any joy or happiness. There are times when we find ourselves in dark places, like David. We look about and the situation looks hopeless. What should we do? Be discouraged? Give up? Say we are through? Friend, if we are children of God, we will encourage ourselves in the Lord, and turn to Him at times like this. Sometimes the Lord puts us in such a spot so we will turn to Him. He wants to make Himself real to us. It was during times like these David wrote some of his most helpful psalms. When troubles come, thumb through the Psalms and find where David encourages himself in the Lord. Several times he says, 'The LORD is good ... Let the redeemed of the LORD say so.' David found this to be true."[87]

[87] J. Vernon McGee, Thru the Bible with J. Vernon McGee (Nashville: Thomas Nelson Publishers, 2000, © 1981).

Laying Hold on God

In affliction, focus on the God who promised: "I will never leave you or forsake you! I am the God who is enough—I am more than all you will ever need!" If you reach out in faith to Him, you will find, like David, God is faithful and true. The whole idea is when you are going through affliction, you are to grab onto the Lord and "hold on for dear life." That is exactly the way this word "strengthened" (Strong's #2388) is used in the Old Testament. Here are some other places where the usage of this word is very graphic: (Emphasis added in the verses below.)

- **Adonijah held on for dear life:** ... *Adonijah was afraid of Solomon; so he arose, and went and* **took hold of** *the horns of the altar (1 Kings 1:50).*

Adonijah was one of the older sons of King David, but Solomon was the son of promise to whom God had instructed David to give the throne. Because the older brother was afraid of the younger brother who became king, he ran into the Tent of the Tabernacle and "took hold of" (Strong's #2388) the horns of the altar and "held on for dear life," begging not to be killed for his capital offense. When David was at the bottom of his grief and he strengthened himself in the Lord, he literally "laid hold of" the Lord—HE

GRABBED ON TO Him. Now do you see a picture of what David did when he was struggling?

- **Joab held on for dear life:** *... News came to Joab, for Joab had defected to Adonijah, though he had not defected to Absalom. So Joab fled to the tabernacle of the Lord, and* **took hold of** *the horns of the altar (1 Kings 2:28).*

Whenever you read in the Bible about someone "laying hold of" the horns of the altar, it's the idea of grasping and "holding on for dear life." The Lord says, "You will seek Me and you will find Me when you seek for Me with all your heart." While David was in the midst of the smoke of everything dear to him rising around him at Ziklag, and his army was ready to kill him, why was he able to look up and strengthen himself in the Lord? Because David reached out and "took hold of" the Lord by seeking Him with all his heart, and that is what the Lord says is the secret to finding comfort from Him.

- **Pleading for the life of a child (like the Shunamite woman):** *Now when she came to the man of God [Elisha] at the hill,* **she caught** *him by the feet, but Gehazi came near to push her away. But the man of God said, "Let her alone; for her soul is in deep distress, and the LORD has hidden it from me, and has not told me" (2 Kings 4:27).*

This is the Shunnamite woman who built a room in her house to give Elisha a place to stay. While he was there, he asked, "How can I help you?" She responded, "My husband and I have never been able to have children, would you pray for us?" So he prayed, and God blessed them with a son. Can you imagine how special that little boy was? He was their son of promise, their blessing from the Lord. This little boy was the center of their lives, but one day he was out in the field watching his dad and all of a sudden he got sick, fainted, and died.

Since this woman believed there was only one person who could rescue her son from death, she ran to Elisha and "she caught" him by the feet. That is the same word as when Adonijah and Joab "took hold of" the horns of the altar. By her action, she was pleading for the life of her son—a beautiful picture of seeking the Lord. God honored her faith and raised the boy from the dead. Can't you just feel the intensity of emotion this woman had as she sought out Elisha and finally found him? And when she did, she would settle for nothing less than his personal intervention. She was telling him, "I won't let go of you until you help me!" That is the type of seeking God wants from us when we are undergoing afflictions.

> • **Building a wall (like Nehemiah):** *And next to them Meremoth the son of Urijah, the son of Koz,* **made repairs***. Next to them Meshullam the son of Berechiah, the son of Meshezabel,* **made repairs***. Next to them Zadok the son of Baana* **made repairs** *(Nehemiah 3:4).*

This word (Strong's #2388) appears thirty-four times in Nehemiah; it is used in chapter 3 for the repairs of the walls, and for the holding of weapons as they worked in chapter 4.

At this point, the children of Israel had returned to the land and were living in Jerusalem, surrounded by all God's enemies. The situation was very insecure, and they feared for their lives. When Nehemiah told them, "God sent me to help you to build this wall," they were comforted, and, with their whole hearts, started to put up a wall to protect them from outside enemies. What does this mean today? You can't build a wall of protection in afflictions by just saying, "I hope the wall gets built, but I wonder who will do it?" You have to work on it yourself. Those people had to sweat and push and pick up those giant rocks to find security. They got serious about what they were doing, and built with fervor. God wants to see the same attitude in us by earnestly seeking His solutions in fiery trials.

> • **Holding a weapon when endangered:** *So it was, from that time on, half of my servants worked at construction, while the other half* **held** *the spears, the shields, the bows, and wore armor; and the leaders were behind all the house of Judah. Those who built on the wall, and those who carried burdens, loaded themselves so that with one hand they worked at construction, and with the other* **held** *a weapon (Nehemiah 4:16-17).*

If your enemies were out there ready to attack you, would you just lean your weapon up against the wall and drink coffee? No, you would hold your weapon and watch, trying to protect the workers. That's the idea of being totally engaged with whole-heartedness, what you need if you are going to "hold on for dear life" to an altar. What is our greatest weapon? It is ... *the sword of the Spirit, which is the word of God* (Ephesians 6:17); as we wield the promises of God we can ... *quench all the fiery darts of the wicked one* (Ephesians 6:16).

Affliction Is the Acid Test of Our Faith

Let's now go back in our thoughts to 1 Samuel 30:6 where ... *David strengthened himself in the LORD his God.* If we are drowned by sorrow, and overwhelmed by grief, it's time to grab the Lord and "hang on for dear life." David, with his whole heart, was saying, "God, You are the only One who can help me. You are the only One, so I am going to test Your promises. You said if we seek You we would find You, so I am seeking. You said You would be our Refuge, and I want refuge. You said You would help us, so I want Your help!"

Do you see how praying God's scriptural promises back to Him is the power behind a Word filled life? The prayer of faith—seeking Him with your whole heart—glorifies God! He loves to honor such prayers! Whenever you feel drowned by sorrow and overwhelmed by grief, always remember you are on sacred ground as a believer; at a place where God's voice is heard most clearly, where God's presence is felt most closely, and where God's guidance is most powerfully given! Hallelujah!

David Never Stopped Testing God's Promises

David tested God's promises to the very end of his life and always found Him to be faithful. Psalm 71 is a testimony of how he learned to be revived, to make it through his problems, and stay focused while waiting for Him to come to his rescue.

Psalm 71:1—David fled to the Lord instead of living in confusion: *In thee, O LORD, do I put my trust: let me never be put to confusion (KJV).*

A lot of people go through life not understanding what is going on in their lives. They think: *I just don't know why this is happening to me ... Why isn't this working? Why isn't my life like I planned it to be? Why can't I live like other people?* Such thinking only leads to confusion as they try to sort it all out, and their focus stays on earthly rather than heavenly things. But David said, "That's not the way to do it. Put your trust in the Lord instead. When I didn't understand, I always looked up to my Master Teacher to find answers."

Psalm 71:2—David cried out to the Lord to avoid giving up to troubles: *Deliver me in Your righteousness, and cause me to escape; incline Your ear to me, and save me.*

When troubles were upon him, David had feelings we've all experienced—he wanted to escape the pain. This reminds me of Peter walking on the Sea of Galilee; he thought he could make it on his own, so he took his eyes off the Lord. At that moment, he started sinking, but when he cried out to the Lord, Jesus saved him. It's a parallel concept here in the second verse: David said, "Lord, save me!" He had learned to cry out to the Lord before he drowned in his troubles. So he said, "Lord, I am facing trouble; deliver me, incline Your ear, and save me!"

Many drown in their troubles because they don't cry out to the Lord. They either forgot or ignored this Truth: ... *You do not have because you do not ask* (James 4:2). Until we ask God to deliver us, our troubles will just keep multiplying. Jesus wants us to acknowledge Him in all our ways, and then He promises to direct our paths (Proverbs 3:5-6). We can acknowledge He is there by saying, "Lord, I am not sure how to do this; I am not sure how to stay on the right path. In fact, I'm not even sure how I am going to make it through life. What can I do, Lord? Help me!" Oh, how faithful He is to hear the cries of His children!

Psalm 71:3—David resisted fear by running into God's Refuge: *Be my strong refuge, to which I may resort continually; You have given the commandment to save me, for You are my rock and my fortress.*

Through "the discipline of suffering affliction," David had learned to trust God's Word more than his fears. He lived in a connector point between Europe, Asia, and Africa—a route trodden by all nations on their conquests. Israel has always been very vulnerable because it is hard to defend yourself when your enemies can come from any direction. But their location has been by perfect design. You see, God wanted them to be right in the middle of everybody trampling through so they would experience the kinds of problems that would cause them to continually run to Him for safety. They would then know the commandments to save them were to find Him as their Rock and their Fortress.

The Lord says to us also: "I want to be wherever you are in life. It doesn't matter whether you are at home, at school, on a business or mission trip, or maybe at the other end of life where you are stuck somewhere and feel fearful at what's to come. I want you to resist fear and flee to Me as your eternal Refuge! Trust My Word more than your fears!"

Psalm 71:4—David asked for God's help to avoid becoming bitter. *Deliver me, O my God, out of the hand of the wicked, out of the hand of the unrighteous and cruel man.*

Metaphorically, in verse 4 David could be talking about all his enemies in Israel, but also be referring specifically to the cruel and wicked men he continually confronted on the battlefield—the enemies of God. They were so vicious they literally skinned people alive and stacked their skulls up like bowling balls in front of the city gates. What did David say about such carnage? He said, "I am going to ask God to deliver me out of their hand!"

In the United States, we don't presently have soldiers coming against us, but we do have adversaries who mean us harm. What can we do? Choose between two options: (1) give in to bitterness, allowing anger to smolder and defile us as we continually mull over why our adversaries attack, or (2) like David, quickly turn to the Lord and say, "Adversaries are coming my way! Deliver me so I don't allow bitterness to takeover and ruin my life!" It's obvious which choice glorifies the Lord.

Psalm 71:5—David kept remembering the faithfulness of God: ... *You are my hope, O LORD God; You are my trust from my youth.*

David told God, "You are the One I am counting on because I keep remembering how faithful You've been from my youth!" In this verse, David looked back over his life and remembered the promises of God. He probably was thinking about his younger years when he went up with his family to worship God and participate in all the celebrations at the Tent. As he recalled all that, he said, "Lord, from my youth You are my hope; You are my trust." It's just as important for us to affirm we trust in Him, and say to those we love—our family and friends: "I believe, love, and trust in the God who is always faithful!"

Psalm 71:6—David remembered to praise God that He had a plan for his life: *By You I have been upheld from birth; You are He who took me out of my mother's womb. My praise shall be continually of You.*

David said, "I have learned to remember to praise You, oh God. Before my conscious existence, You have been involved in my life. You are the only One with me from the very beginning—and the only One who will be with me to the very end. And I praise Your perfect plan for my whole journey!" So, what is a good way to have a life that grows in experiencing God—one focused on the Master Teacher? It is remembering there is One Person who has guided us from the womb, and will guide us to the grave, and He wants us to focus on Him by saying, "You have been guiding this plan for my life, and I want to follow it. I want to submit, to walk, to yield to Your plan because I know that You do all things well!"

Psalm 71:7—David let his life be a testimony for the Lord: *I have become as a wonder to many, but You are my strong refuge.*

The word "wonder" means "a picture, a sign"; it's a beautiful word. David learned to let his life be a "picture, a sign"—a wonderful testimony to others. If you and I let the Lord be our Teacher, we can become a wonder to many as well. We can have a life testimony like a sign that points others to Jesus as their Refuge.

You never know who might be watching you. For example, while getting a haircut at a barbershop, I had a very interesting conversation with the girl cutting my hair. Out of the blue she announced, "I got thrown out of my church …" Then she continued sharing what happened. As the story unfolded, it was obvious she was an unbeliever who'd done something her little country church didn't like, so they kicked her out. I then asked her, "Did anyone at the church speak to you about being born again?" "No," she replied, "what's that?" I talked to her about the Franklin Graham Crusade and the gospel. When I could put my glasses back on, I got out a gospel tract and explained, "Everything they didn't tell you at your church is written down right here." After earnestly witnessing further about Jesus, it was time for me to pay my bill. As I did, one of the elders from a nearby local church said to me, "I was watching all that." He was so moved I would care enough to take the time to witness to the girl he just stood there listening so he could learn how to witness better himself. And I thought: *Like verse 7 in Psalm 71, I have become as a wonder to many ….* And you can, too, if you keep focused on the Lord and make yourself available at every opportunity He has for you to share Christ. In God's providential plan, you never know who might be watching your life!

Psalm 71:8—David praised God so much there was no time left to complain: *Let my mouth be filled with Your praise and with Your glory all the day.*

Keeping your mouth full of praise for the Lord is a powerful habit. That's why David, to the end of his life, was a blessing to people. Though he did not have a life of ease, he chose to continually praise God. In his old age, he could have gone around complaining, "Man, I've lost children! They have murdered and raped, and one tried to kill me. And even my best friends turned against me." On and on he could have listed afflictions God allowed in his life. But he refused to fill his declining years with bitterness. Instead, he chose to fill his mouth with praise for the Lord. In fact, he praised Him so much he didn't have any time left for complaining. David said, "I see you, God. I see all Your glory, and acknowledge who You really are. I see the big picture—I am only here for a little while; my life is like a vapor which is just barely here for a moment. But Your glory is over all, so I want to focus on that instead of on my problems." What a great habit!

Psalm 71:9—David trusted God to the end of life: *Do not cast me off in the time of old age; do not forsake me when my strength fails.*

By verse 9, David was already old. That verse reminds me of my dad who was born in 1914, and is presently 93 years old. I talk to him every Sunday night and almost every time he tells me: "I am going down to the supermarket to witness to the older people." The people he has been witnessing to are in their 60s and 70s, but he calls them older because my dad has the joy of the Lord as his strength. He is so gnarled with arthritis he can barely turn the pages of his Bible, but in those hands, that don't quite shut anymore, he takes gospel tracts to places offering free coffee to the elderly. And when I hear Dad's testimony, I think: Wow! Dad is saying what we should all be saying—what David learned: "Don't cast me off in the time of old age. Don't forsake me when my strength fails. I am going to trust You are going to go with me to the end of my life!"

Psalm 71:10-12—David took his fears to God in prayer: *For my enemies speak against me; and those who lie in wait for my life take counsel together, saying, "God has forsaken him; pursue and take him, for there is none to deliver him." O God, do not be far from me; O my God, make haste to help me!*

This verse makes me think of these well known lyrics: "Do thy friends despise, forsake thee? Take it to the Lord in prayer. In His arms He'll tend and shield thee—thou shalt find a solace there!" At one place Bonnie and I lived, we went to a community meeting attended by all older people. They talked about nothing but the desire to have a closer emergency station. After timing how long it would take an ambulance to reach them if they had a heart attack, they concluded they'd be dead by then. So they lived in fear help wouldn't arrive in time. That reminded me of David saying, "Oh God, don't be far from me. You promised to be with me even to the end of the age. So make haste to help me. Come with the sirens on!"

In a modern sense, David trusted God as much as we trust 9-1-1. A lesson he learned as an old man was he could trust God at the end of life, praise Him so much he wouldn't complain, be a testimony to others, and have faith in God's plan for his entire life. David continually talked about God's faithfulness, and escaped bitterness by continually asking Him for help. When it got dark, and he heard frightening sounds, he fled home to His safe Refuge, to God. That's why at the end of his life David could say, "I have had a lifelong relationship with the Lord, and I have been experiencing Him." In contrast, David's son, Solomon, didn't learn from his dad's example. So when troubles came, he didn't look up and focus on his Master Teacher. Instead, in spite of being the wisest man who ever lived, Solomon tried to figure everything out by himself. Thus, as he testified in Ecclesiastes, life for him was empty and vain. What a tragedy—to be so smart, and yet so foolish!

> **Psalm 71:13-14—David tested God's promises by never giving up:** *Let them be confounded and consumed who are adversaries of my life; let them be covered with reproach and dishonor who seek my hurt. But I will hope continually, and will praise You yet more and more.*

Isn't this a beautiful passage? In twenty-first century language, one might say, "I am going to never give up! Even when I am alone, neglected, sick, ignored, rejected, maligned, and forgotten by everybody in the world, I am going to remember You, oh Lord, because You've never forgotten me!" Because you and God make a majority, you don't have to have anybody else. That's the concept of testing the promises of God.

> **Psalm 71:15—David tested God's promises by finding ways to bring Him into the conversation:** *My mouth shall tell of Your righteousness and Your salvation all the day, for I do not know their limits.*

David said, "My mouth will continually talk of Your salvation!" You and I are supposed to do the same. Here's a simple illustration of how to talk about the Lord—

A while back, my whole family was at an East Coast dock where fishing boats unloaded tuna from 112 miles out in the Atlantic. The fishermen showed us the big tuna tails they chopped off, to keep record of the catch. It was captivating listening to them talk. One man said, "I have lived on the boat for thirteen years." I asked him, "Do you go to church?" He promptly stated, "No, my church is the ocean and I worship God on my boat." He was one of the three crustiest old salts I'd ever seen. I gathered my family up closer to the edge of the boat, and I looked at those men and thought in my heart: *They don't know the Lord, and Psalm 71:15 says my mouth should bring up the Lord.*

So I asked them, "Have you ever heard of the perfect storm? Have you ever thought about being 112 miles out in the ocean in a boat during such a fierce storm? Are you ready to meet the Lord?" At that moment, it was so precious, my buddies, the little guys, wanted to give them tracts. So I opened my wallet and pulled out three tracts—and one by one those boys walked up to each crusty fisherman and handed him a gospel tract. Daddy then stood and explained the gospel to them. I thought about that later: *We could have talked about the ocean, the boat, and how much their tuna was, and what life was like on the boat, but look what verse 15 says—God says we test His promises by finding a way to bring God into the conversation.* Why did I share that? Because, if you aren't already doing so, form the habit of naturally talking about the Lord to others.

If you do not feel comfortable with witnessing, you could at least talk about the Lord by telling someone the latest thing you've learned from the Bible. When I was a youth pastor, I used to make my high school students take turns standing to tell what they'd learned that week in the Bible. Talk about glassy-eyed teenagers! After about the fifth time of my springing the exercise on them, they finally started to look for stuff to share, and even got excited to talk about it. Did you know there are men who are supposed to be leading families but never stand up and bring God into the conversation? They never say, "I read the Bible, and this is what God teaches me …" The Lord wants us to continually bring Him into the conversation.

Psalm 71:16—David tested God's promises by humbly depending on the Lord: *I will go in the strength of the LORD God; I will make mention of Your righteousness, of Yours only.*

Apart from the Lord's strength, we do not have hope. We do not have any peace while going through physical problems, and we don't have comfort when everything is lost. As a result, we can't easily bring Him into conversations. Verse 16 tells us we need to humbly depend on the Lord: "I go in His strength; I make mention of His righteousness." If you ask, saying, "Lord, I want to speak for You," He will bring you opportunities. It's what He left us here to do. So what did David say? He reported, "One day I came home and everything dear to me on earth was burning. My wife was gone, my children were gone, my home destroyed, my friends turning against me, and I was at the bottom of life. But I reached out and clung to the Lord for dear life, like the Shunnamite woman held to Elisha's feet, and I said, 'Lord, You are the One who promised to help me. I'm depending upon You, and You alone!' "

Making Some Resolves for Your Own Life

One of the great treasures Jonathan Edwards left to us as believers was his list of personal resolves, which are now both famous and very challenging. But making some spiritual resolves of your own would be even better than knowing his. A good place to start would be by echoing David's resolves as listed in Psalm 71:17-24 below. For David understood the blessing of affliction—testing God's promises in His Word and then "holding on for dear life" until He delivers you in your affliction. I therefore encourage you to embrace these personally for your own life as well!

• **Psalm 71:17—Make a lifelong commitment to the Lord:** *O God, You have taught me from my youth; and to this day I declare Your wondrous works.*

- **Psalm 71:18—Serve God even when you get out of season, past your prime, and are old and gray:** *Now also when I am old and grayheaded, O God, do not forsake me, until I declare Your strength to this generation, Your power to everyone who is to come.*

- **Psalm 71:19—Seek to never stop experiencing God daily:** *Also Your righteousness, O God, is very high, You who have done great things; O God, who is like You?*

- **Psalm 71:20—See affliction as a blessing:** *You, who have shown me great and severe troubles, shall revive me again, and bring me up again from the depths of the earth.* (Just like Ezra, Job, Joni Eareckson Tada, Philip Yancey, and many other sweet saints who have gone through or are still suffering today!)

- **Psalm 71:21—Allow the Lord to be in charge of your life:** *You shall increase my greatness, and comfort me on every side.*

- **Psalm 71:22—Stay involved in personal worship**: *… With the lute I will praise You—and Your faithfulness, O my God! To You I will sing with the harp, O Holy One of Israel.*

- **Psalm 71:23—Stay enthusiastic for the Lord:** *My lips shall greatly rejoice when I sing to You, and my soul, which You have redeemed.*

- **Psalm 71:24—Allow God to invade all of your life**: *My tongue also shall talk [hagah = meditate] of Your righteousness all the day long; for they are confounded, for they are brought to shame who seek my hurt.*

Through lessons designed specifically for what you need most, God will lead and reorder your life back to His priorities. And if you respond to afflictions by viewing them as blessings, and not curses, you will be a wonder to those whom God has ordained to be watching your life. Like the Apostle Paul, you can wholeheartedly say: *Blessed be the God and Father of our Lord Jesus Christ, the Father of mercies and God of all comfort, who comforts us in all our tribulation, that we may be able to comfort those who are in any trouble, with the comfort with which we ourselves are comforted by God* (2 Corinthians 1:3-4). What a wonderful ministry!

In closing, exercising "the discipline of suffering affliction" can be a great blessing if it causes you to more clearly focus on your Master Teacher and rejoice in: His Word (Psalm 119:50), His path (Psalm 119:67); His plan for your life (Psalm 119:71); His pruning of your life (Psalm 119:75); His source of hope (Psalm 119:92); His offer of personal revival (Psalm 119:107), and His ability to rescue you (Psalm 119:153)! If you continually keep your eyes on God, He promises to keep you in perfect peace because your mind is focused on Him, and you are trusting in the Lord (Isaiah 26:3). If you do this daily, you will, like David, end well!

My Prayer for You:

Father in Heaven, teach us more than in a mental way, more than just another fact, more than another truth we simply tuck away in the pages of our Bible. Write upon our hearts the reality that afflictions produce blessings. And those blessings let us test Your promises, lay hold on You, hear Your Divine voice, feel Your presence, and know Your guiding hand more clearly than at any other time in our life. I pray we would learn lessons from David, this man after Your own heart, who strengthened and encouraged and found what he needed from You and You alone. For You are the only true comforter—the God of All Comfort—who can teach us how to grab hold of that truth and hang on for dear life! In the name of Jesus I pray. Amen.

19

Be sober, be vigilant; because your adversary the devil walks about like a roaring lion, seeking whom he may devour. Resist him, steadfast in the faith, knowing that the same sufferings are experienced by your brotherhood in the world. But may the God of all grace, who called us to His eternal glory by Christ Jesus, after you have suffered a while, perfect, establish, strengthen, and settle you.

—**1 Peter 5:8-10**

Suffering Affliction:
Conquering Our Unseen But Dangerous Enemy

EVERY YEAR AMERICANS BUY MILLIONS of gallons of anti-bacterial substances—*because we fear unseen, but dangerous germs.*[88] At the same time many of those Americans take no precautions at all against Satan and his soul-threatening, spiritual demons that are also known as **unseen, but dangerous.**

88 MP3 CD Audio DYG-38:070401AM

Rather than protect their lives from deadly spiritual infections, viruses, and contaminants—many deliberately infect themselves with agents causing spiritual sickness. These deadly influences, through unseen, but dangerous beings, should be avoided at all cost—yet people read them, listen to them, buy, hoard, and collect them, and meditate upon them regularly.

Are you aware Satan, the incredibly powerful, **unseen, but dangerous** god of this world wants to poison your thoughts and emotions away from the purity of God's Truth? This super-powerful, fallen angelic crown prince against who not even Michael the archangel dared to face off, focuses his attacks upon us in two areas: our thoughts and our emotions.

If we stay unaware of Satan's ***unseen, but dangerous*** plan, he starts using the unguarded pieces of our life. Each little area we fail to guard, Satan grabs, reconfigures for evil against us, and makes another base to attack.

There Is a War Swirling Within Us

In C. S. Lewis' ***The Screwtape Letters,*** Uncle Screwtape offers his nephew a little advice on the goal and strategy of Satan's attacks.

> You will say that these are very small sins; and doubtless, like all young tempters, you are anxious to be able to report spectacular wickedness. But do remember the only thing that matters is the extent to which you separate the man from the Enemy. It does not matter how small the sins are, provided that their cumulative effect is to edge the man away from the Light and out into the Nothing. Murder is no better than cards if cards can do the trick. Indeed, the safest road to Hell is the gradual one—the gentle slope, soft underfoot, without sudden turnings, without milestones, without signposts.[89]

[89] C. S. Lewis, The Screwtape Letters

How true. Don't yield ground to the devil. Nothing in life is neutral or harmless. Everything is either for God or against Him. Everything is either promoting God's glory or opposing it.

Every true believer is part of this cosmic conflict C. S. Lewis aptly described. If you are a born-again Christian, you can count on being a target in this ongoing "battle of the heavenlies." Satan is a treacherous adversary who never sleeps. He and his forces never stop stalking God's children, so never take lightly his hatred of you and God (see 1 Peter 5:8).

But, all is not doom and gloom. The Lord God Almighty has made powerful provisions for His children to be ... *more than conquerors through Him who loved us* (Romans 8:37). As the Lord fulfills His promises, afflictions actually become blessings—and the greater the trial, the more potential for blessing!

To understand how Satan operates, we'll discuss when and how this whole "battle of the heavenlies" began. I'll point out common areas Satan targets in believers' lives. Then we'll look at what God has to say about becoming a conquering warrior!

The Beginning of the Downfall of Satan

Before God ever created the heavens and earth, He fashioned for Himself His own servants—the angels. In this angelic host of the Lord God in heaven, above the archangels, the seraphim, and above the cherubim, there was one whom God chose to be the crown prince of them all. His name was Lucifer, *"the star of the morning,"* the leader of the host of heaven, the guardian of the throne of God.

God committed all He had made into Lucifer's hands. For Lucifer was the most beautiful of angels; he was perfect. But in his beauty, perfection, and pride, he declared he would be like the Most High God.

The Bible does not explain how Lucifer could fall into sin as a perfect being in a perfect environment; God's Word just declares he did. However, Ezekiel has given us a description of what took place in his heart: *"Your heart was lifted up because of your beauty; you corrupted your wisdom for the sake of your splendor ..."* (Ezekiel 28:17). In other words, Lucifer became enamored with his beauty instead of God's, his splendor not God's, and that produced in him the sin of pride, which led to his rebellion.

Lucifer's rebellion occurred sometime after the sixth day of the creation of man in the Garden of Eden. His extraordinarily high rank led to his proud thoughts recorded in the five "I will's" of Isaiah 14:13-14: (Emphasis added to the verses below.)

- *I WILL ASCEND* **[self-assertion]** *into heaven,*
- *I WILL EXALT* **[self-promotion]** *my throne above the stars of God;*
- *I WILL ... SIT* **[self-centeredness]** *on the mount of the congregation on the farthest sides of the north;*
- *I WILL ASCEND* **[self-exaltation]** *above the heights of the clouds,*
- *I WILL BE LIKE* **[self-deception]** *the Most High. Yet you shall be brought down to Sheol [hell], to the lowest depths of the Pit.*

Each of those acts always leads to pride. Pride made Lucifer act independently of God, and that sin had horrible consequences. When he fell from his position of being the *"anointed cherub who covers,"* the highest ranking angelic being, concerned particularly with the glory of God, he was cast out from being "on the holy mountain of God," and was no longer permitted to *"walk back and forth in the midst of fiery stones of fire"* as he dwelled in the immediate presence of God (Ezekiel 28:14).

Because of his sin, Lucifer was cast from his station among the other holy ones who serve in God's presence (Ezekiel 28:16). After his fall, Lucifer became known as the *Serpent of old; Satan, the adversary; Apollyon, the destroyer; the Devil, the slanderer; the Roaring Lion stalking believers; and the Accuser of the saints* (1 Peter 5:8; Revelation 12:9-11). He has waged a vicious war against God and His children ever since.

Satan is the author of sin. He introduced sin into the universe when he incited Adam and Eve to follow his rebellion against God: *And the LORD God said to the woman, "What is this you have done?" The woman said, "The serpent deceived me, and I ate"* (Genesis 3:13).

> "Sin was not a creation but an origination. It came into existence by the aid of that which had prior existence, namely, personality and the power of free choice. God created this being not as the devil, but as a holy angel, who originated sin through disobedience and transformed himself into the wicked Devil which he is today".[90]

Satan is the author of suffering. "In the final analysis, Satan is the ultimate source of all suffering, because he is the ultimate source of all sin, its primal cause. He is also immediately responsible for many individual cases of sickness and disease; of which examples are furnished us in the New Testament."

Acts 10:38 records Jesus healed sickness and disease directly related to the devil's work: *"... God anointed Jesus of Nazareth with the Holy Spirit and with power, who went about doing good and healing all who were oppressed by the devil ...."* And in Luke 13:16 Jesus reported healing a woman *"... whom Satan ... bound for eighteen years ...."*

---

[90] These three quotations are from Emery H. Bancroft, Elemental Theology: Doctrinal and Conservative (Hayward, CA: J. F. May Press, 1948), pp. 263-264.

Satan is the author of temptation. "Satan incites men to sin. He so arranges times and controls events and circumstances to make the greatest possible appeal to the sinful tendencies of man. He is the tempter." As the tempter, Satan tests and tries believers so they end up as failures.

Above all, Satan wanted Jesus to fail. At the very beginning of Christ's ministry ... Jesus was led up by the Spirit into the wilderness to be tempted by the devil (Matthew 4:1). During forty days and forty nights, He was tested in three levels: ... the lust of the flesh, the lust of the eyes, and the pride of life ... (1 John 2:16; see also Matthew 4:2-3, 5-6, 8-9). Had Jesus succumbed to any of these temptations, no one could hope of eternal life. But, praise God, we now have a High Priest who can sympathize with our own temptations because He ... was in all points tempted as we are, yet without sin (Hebrews 4:15).

Satan is the author of death. Paul reported: *Inasmuch then as the children have partaken of flesh and blood, He Himself likewise shared in the same, that through death He might destroy him who had the power of death, that is, the devil ...* (Hebrews 2:14).

In Colossians 2:15, Paul says Jesus has already triumphed over death at the cross. However, under special permission Satan seems to have the right to use the mighty weapon of death.

As the author of sin, suffering, temptation, and death, Satan's power must never be underestimated. But he is under a perpetual curse. His conquest was secured at the cross, and he is destined to be cast out of the heavenlies (Revelation 12:9)—confined to the abyss for a thousand years (Revelation 20:1-3), released for a little while (Revelation 20:3), and then finally thrown into the Lake of Fire where he and his demonic hoards ... *will be tormented day and night forever and ever* (Revelation 20:10).[91]

In the meantime, you and I must stay alert to his wiles so we aren't taken captive!

[91] For a very detailed analysis of Satan's future, see my devotional on the book of Revelation entitled Living Hope for the End of Days. The book is available through www.discoverthebook.org.

How Satan Targets Believers

The Apostle Paul has provided some very clear insights into the nature of the battle we face:

> ... Though we walk in the flesh, we do not war according to the flesh. For the weapons of our warfare are not carnal but mighty in God for pulling down strongholds, casting down arguments and every high thing that exalts itself against the knowledge of God, bringing every thought into captivity to the obedience of Christ ... (2 Corinthians 10:3-5).

To tear down satanic strongholds, we need to be ... bringing every thought into captivity to the obedience of Christ .... Only God and His Word have the power to counter "the father of lies" and his hosts of wickedness. And to effectively do battle, our eyes need to be opened to how Satan and his evil forces commonly target believers' lives.

Satan can fill believers' hearts with a desire to misrepresent their devotion to God:
> ... Peter said, "Ananias, why has Satan filled your heart to lie to the Holy Spirit and keep back part of the price of the land for yourself?" (Acts 5:3).

Warren Wiersbe's comments are quite insightful regarding the cause and the root sin which led to the death of Ananias and Sapphira:

> The sin of Ananias and Sapphira was *energized by Satan* (Acts 5:3); and he knows how to lie to the minds and hearts of church members, even genuine Christians, and get them to follow his orders. Always remember that the spiritual armor (Eph. 6:10–18) was given to believers, not to unbelievers; and it is believers who are in danger of being used by Satan to accomplish his evil purposes.

> Their sin was *motivated by pride,* and pride is a sin that God especially hates and judges (Prov. 8:13). While the church was praising God for the generous offering of Barnabas, Satan whispered to the couple, "You can also bask in this kind of glory and make others think you are as spiritual as Barnabas!" Instead of resisting Satan's approaches, they yielded to him and planned their strategy.

It is easy for us to condemn Ananias and Sapphira for their dishonesty, but we need to examine our own lives to see if our profession is backed up by our practice. Do we really mean everything we pray about in public? Do we sing the hymns and Gospel songs sincerely or routinely? "These people honor Me with their lips, but their hearts are far from Me" (Matt. 15:8, NIV). If God killed "religious deceivers" today, how many church members would be left?

We must keep in mind that their sin was not in robbing God of money but in robbing Him of glory. God didn't demand they sell the property; and, having sold it, God didn't demand they give any of the money to the church (Acts 5:4). Their lust for recognition conceived sin in their hearts (Acts 5:4, 9), and that sin led to death (James 1:15)."[92]

92 Warren W. Wiersbe, The Bible Exposition Commentary (Wheaton, IL: Victor Books, 1997), p. ?.

Don't allow Satan to make you proudly affirm a deeper spiritual sacrifice and devotion than what God knows is real in your heart. Repent of all half-hearted devotion and surrender completely to Jesus Christ.

Satan can cause bodily harm as well as lead us into destructive behavior:
And the LORD said to Satan, "Behold,
he is in your hand, but spare his life" (Job 2:6).

When God bragged on His servant Job to Satan, the devil countered with an accusation that led to his being given permission to try Job—except for his body. In just one day, Job's livestock was removed and his servants and children were killed; only four messengers escaped. But Job ... *fell to the ground and worshiped. ... In all this Job did not sin nor charge God with wrong* (Job 1:20, 22).

Satan was furious, so he challenged the Lord to *"touch his bone and his flesh"* (Job 2:5) for surely then Job would curse God. After Satan had struck Job with painful boils all over his body, Job honored the Lord by how he responded to his less-than-supportive wife: *"... Shall we indeed accept good from God, and shall we not accept adversity?" In all this Job did not sin with his lips* (Job 2:10).

Turning Job over to Satan, allowing an attack on his health had its limitations, and was intended both for Job's good and God's glory. But in this next verse, we see that our dangerous adversary can also lead someone into destructive behavior that has severe consequences.

> … Deliver such a one to Satan for the destruction of the flesh, that his spirit may be saved in the day of the Lord Jesus
> (1 Corinthians 5:5).

The man in the above verse had been judged guilty of gross sexual immorality. He was therefore put out of the church, and no longer allowed to fellowship with the other saints because … a little leaven leavens the whole lump (v. 6). Thus, whatever pain he went through as a result of God's judgment would not affect the other church members, but it was hoped his suffering would be sufficient to lead to genuine repentance.

That is a heartbreaking example of the consequence engine in action. For God is not mocked; we always reap what we have sown (Galatians 6:7). If you have also been guilty of immorality, I urge you to stop now—before God's chastening begins. Give your body back to God as *"a living sacrifice"* (Romans 12:1-2)!

Satan uses temptations to inflame our lusts on three levels: lust of the flesh, lust of the eyes, and the pride of life:

> Do not deprive one another except with consent for a time …
> so that Satan does not tempt you because of your
> lack of self-control (1 Corinthians 7:5).

Satan works as a co-conspirator with your flesh and mine. He has power to cause our flesh to be tempted. Temptation is our flesh longing to be satisfied—either by the cravings of our **bodies chasing pleasures** (lusts of flesh), or the longing of our **eyes chasing possessions** (lust of the eyes), or by the boastings of our **hearts and mouths chasing status** (pride of life). (See 1 John 2:15-17.)

Don't play around with temptation lest Satan catch you in his trap—especially in the sexual realm, as 1 Corinthians 7:5 above states. If you have succumbed to any of the three levels of temptation, I encourage you to repent now; ask Jesus to deliver you from all evil in your life, and take the escape He makes as you cry for help.

Satan uses his mind to overpower ours
if our minds are not protected by captivity to Christ:
> … *lest Satan should take advantage of us;*
> *for we are not ignorant of his devices* (2 Corinthians 2:11).

"This and similar passages of the Word of God teach that Satan is a personal being; that he exerts great influence over people's minds; that although he is finite (and therefore not everywhere present), he nevertheless works on people's minds generally and not merely on those in any one place. His powers of intelligence and agency must, therefore, be unimaginable. No individual and no community can ever be sure that he is not plotting their destruction."[93]

This dangerous enemy steals God's Word from hearts and minds (Mark 14:15). He can also invade the minds of the lost (John 13:2), the disobedient (Acts 5:3), and the unguarded (Ephesians 4:27).

> Satan seems to have the power of mental suggestion, which in the individual becomes auto-suggestion, and which unless halted and hindered by the Word and Spirit of God will also in him be expressed by word and action.[94]

Because Satan accuses believers constantly (Revelation 12:9-10), his continual accusations can make believers who have sinned feel their case is hopeless. How can you tell the difference between conviction and accusation? The Holy Spirit convicts us of sin so we will confess it and turn to Christ for cleansing; Satan accuses us of sin so we will despair and give up. If you have been feeling defeated, I exhort you to thank Jesus right now for purchasing your salvation by becoming sin for you, and thus bearing your sin away forever.

Satan can trick believers who listen to his lies
into losing their focus upon Christ:
> … *As the serpent deceived Eve by his craftiness, so your minds may be corrupted from the simplicity that is in Christ* (2 Corinthians 11:3).

"Satan's focus is on the mind; he is a liar and tries to get us to listen to his lies, ponder them, and then believe them. Remember what he did with Eve in Genesis 3:1-5. First, he *questioned* God's word ('Yea,

---

[93] Charles Hodge, 2 Corinthians: The Crossway Classic Commentaries (Wheaton: Crossway Books, 1997), p. ?

[94] Emery H. Bancroft, Elemental Theology: Doctrinal and Conservative (Hayward, CA: J. F. May Press, 1948), p.264.

hath God said?'), then he denied God's word ('Ye shall not surely die!'), and he *substituted his own lie* ('Ye shall be as gods')."[95]

Satan loves to play "mind wars"—especially when he can blind unregenerate minds to the gospel (2 Corinthians 4:4).

> Unbelief of the truth seems to be the same as a special invitation to Satan to bring in the darkness of error and falsehood. He blinds the minds of unbelieving men to prevent them from receiving the light of the gospel.[96]

In contrast to Satan's quest to corrupt and blind minds, Jesus wants to captivate and guard (see 2 Corinthians 10:5 and Philippians 4:7). If a believer's mind is not single-minded for Christ it is considered corrupted. Satan is able to mess with our thinking because his mind is super-powerful, and ours, apart from Christ, is no match. If you are prone to live one way here and another way there, you need to repent. Such double-mindedness invites Satan's corruption. Instead, pray for Christ's "simplicity," which means "single-mindedness."

Satan can appear to be a messenger from God (angel of light) when he and his servants masquerade themselves:

> … *Satan himself transforms himself into an angel of light. Therefore it is no great thing if his ministers also transform themselves into ministers of righteousness* … (2 Corinthians 11:14-15).

Satan has a counterfeit gospel (Gal. 1:6–12) that involves a different savior and a different spirit. The *preachers* of this false gospel (and they are with us yet today) are described in 2 Corinthians 11:13–15. Instead of being empowered by the Spirit, these ministers are energized by Satan. Three times, Paul used the word *transform* in referring to their work (see 2 Cor. 11:13–15). This Greek word simply means "to disguise, to masquerade." There is a change on the outside, but there is no change on the inside. Satan's workers, like Satan himself, never appear in their true character; they always wear a disguise and hide behind a mask.[97]

Don't get taken captive by false teachers claiming to present the

Truth! God warns: *... Do not believe every spirit, but test the spirits, whether they are of God; because many false prophets have gone out into the world* (1 John 4:1). Like the people of Berea, search the Scriptures daily to discern Truth from falsehood (Acts 17:11).

Satan can buffet God's servants:

> *... There was given me a thorn in the flesh, a messenger of Satan to buffet me—to keep me from exalting myself!* (2 Corinthians 12:7).

"In the Bible the idea is often presented that bodily diseases are at times produced by the direct agency of Satan, so that they may be regarded as his messengers, sent by him."[98] Paul's *"thorn in the flesh"* literally means "a stake for the flesh." His *"... language indicates it was physical, painful, humiliating. It was also the effect of divinely permitted Satanic antagonism. The verbs are in the present tense, signifying recurrent action, indicating a constantly repeated attack. What is stressed is not the metaphorical size, but the acuteness of the suffering and its effects."*[99]

[98] Hodge, The Crossway Classic Commentaries.

[99] Strong's #4647, p. 229.

The angel in 2 Corinthians 12:7 was from Satan, and may even have been a demon afflicting Paul. The apostle's suffering was so intense that he *... pleaded with the Lord three times that it might depart ... from him, but the Lord answered, ... "My grace is sufficient for you, for My strength is made perfect in weakness"* (2 Corinthians 12:8-9). Paul honored the Lord by responding: *... Most gladly I will rather boast in my infirmities, that the power of Christ may rest upon me* (2 Corinthians 12:9).

Don't allow Satan's buffeting lead to you giving in to despair. Remember his goal is to overthrow the faith of God's servants (Luke 22:31). Although Satan can buffet, resist, and hinder in every possible way, God's grace is always sufficient to give victory.

Satan looks for and uses landing places like anger to control the believer:

> *... nor give place to the devil (Ephesians 4:27).*

Anger gives Satan great power over us. It furnishes a motive to yield to his evil suggestions. When anger begins to control, rather than the believer being under Christ's control, the devil gets an opportunity for leading that Christian into further sin.

According to Jesus, anger is the first step toward murder (Matthew 5:21–26), because anger gives the devil a place in our lives, and Satan is a murderer (John 8:44). Satan hates God and God's people. When he finds a believer with the sparks of anger in his heart, he fans those sparks, and adds fuel to the fire.

Feelings like being annoyed, irritated, antagonistic, or resentful are all "sparks of anger" that, if not put out immediately, can smolder and be used by Satan to turn into wrath. God's way is to ... *be swift to hear, slow to speak, slow to wrath; for the wrath of man does not produce the righteousness of God* (James 1:19-20). If you have a problem with anger, ask the Lord to help you break free from this sin—the devil's bondage.

Satan uses a variety of hindrances to disrupt our ministry for God:

... *We wanted to come to you—even I, Paul, time and again— but Satan hindered us* (1 Thessalonians 2:18).

In the Greek, the literal meaning for "hindered" is "breaking up the road and putting up obstacles"—like one army hindering the advance of their enemies. Satan is always at work seeking to tear down the church Christ promised to build (cf. Matthew 16:18). Throughout the Scriptures we find Satan present at the churches of Jerusalem (Acts 5:1–10), Smyrna (Revelation 2:9-10), Pergamum (Revelation 2:13), Thyatira (Revelation 2:24), Philadelphia (Revelation 3:9), Ephesus (1 Timothy 3:6-7), and Corinth (2 Corinthians 2:1–11). Be assured he and his evil influences are presently arrayed against each of us in Christ's church today.

When your dedicated efforts in Christ's ministry seem thwarted from every angle, first ask the Holy Spirit to show you any sin you haven't yet confessed, then repent and get back on track. However, if He does not bring conviction, seek His empowerment to break free from Satan's clutches, and press on in your ministry for God's glory.

**Satan is a master hunter
who is very skilled at using snares:**
> ... *that they may come to their senses and escape the snare of the devil, having been taken captive by him to do his will*
> (2 Timothy 2:26).

The word translated *"come to their senses"* describes someone ensnared by Satan who must come out of a drunken-like stupor. The devil first traps people by getting them drunk with his lies so, without the restraint of God's Truth, they disobey the Lord. Using the Bible to "sober them up" is the only way anyone can be rescued from such captivity.

In 1 Timothy 3:7 Paul offers another example of snares: any man desiring to become a bishop, or overseer, of Christ's church ... *must have a good reputation with those outside the church, so that he may not fall into reproach and the snare of the devil.* Should Satan successfully entice a man to let down his guard "just this once," Satan can slam the door shut so tightly this future leader loses his testimony not only in the church but also in the local community—and may even lose his own family. Such sin also brings public reproach to God.

Here is yet a third example: ... *Those who desire to be rich fall into temptation and a snare .... For the love of money is a root of all kinds of evil ...* (1 Timothy 6:9-10). Money itself is not evil, for God gives *"power to get wealth"* (Deuteronomy 8:18). Evil comes in when a man or woman becomes obsessed with *"the love of money"* and will do anything to get it—even neglecting family, church, and spiritual life. Once a believer is ensnared, Satan darkens the person with discouragement so he or she is never satisfied, and always wants more and more.

Know this: the devil will set a trap for you in any area he thinks will cause you to fall for his crafty deceptions. Don't believe his lies! Stay alert by filling your mind with God's Word. Always protect your reputation by being staying above board in all you do, and never let *"the love of money"* or *"possession obsession"* gain a foothold.

Have You Been Taken Captive?

Having considered common ways Satan targets believers, let's now get even more personal. As you read through the following questions, I encourage you to ask the Holy Spirit to open your eyes to ways you may have been taken captive—and not yet know it.

• **Satan wants to *twist* your thinking.** He is the one who uses things like ungodly music to put sinful ideas into your mind. Would the pure and holy God of the Universe ever own, listen to, or memorize that music? Are you slowly becoming less and less offended by the suggestions, blatant sins, and foul language heard in the background? Satan, the fallen, warped one (Isaiah 14:12), is twisting your thinking.

• **Satan wants to get you to *crave* material possessions.** Is there an endless list of things others have that you desire? Are you willing to sacrifice to get those things? Do you ever sacrifice time with God, time with the saints gathered at church, time in His Word, or time in prayer in order to get those things? Do the desires for those things sometimes push God right out of your thoughts? Satan, the original idolater and covetous one (Isaiah 14:13-14), is enticing you to crave something other than God.

• **Satan wants to *little-by-little* cause you to think sin is not so bad.** Do entertainment activities you select make it seem, bit-by-bit, that sin is really not so bad after all? Satan, the evil one (James 6:13), is tampering with your thinking.

• **Satan wants to entice you to *slowly* learn to laugh at sin.** Do you ever laugh at comments where there is sexual innuendo? Or when God's absolute holiness and righteous standards are mocked? Satan, the wicked, unholy one (1 John 2:13), is teaching you to laugh at sin.

• **Satan wants to gradually *destroy* your conscience.** Do offensive words no longer offend you? Do images you used to recognize as displeasing to God no longer trouble your conscience? Do places you once felt dishonored the Lord no longer seem so bad? Do immoral, godless activities no longer raise righteous indignation? Are you, like Lot, sitting in the gates of Sodom with evil being played out in front of you—without your righteous soul being vexed? Satan, the deceiver (2 Corinthians 11:3), is destroying your conscience.

- **Satan wants to tempt you to become *obsessed* with entertainment.** Are your favorite entertainers all godless? Have any become your heroes or heroines? God says: *Do not be deceived: "Evil company corrupts good habits"* (1 Corinthians 15:33). Satan, the tempter (1 Thessalonians 3:5), is enticing you with temptations that grieve God!

- **Satan wants to *addict* you to violence.** Do you love action-packed movies and video games where people are blown up and blasted away—as well as grisly, bloodied action heroes who get beaten, tortured, and end up taking out whole armies? God specifically says we must not enjoy looking upon gratuitous violence (Isaiah 33:15-16). Have you become addicted to violence? Satan, the murderer from the beginning (John 8:44), is trying to destroy you (John 10:10).

- **Satan wants to *fill* your mind with doubts, lies, immorality, and false doctrine.** On any given day do you feel unable to stop thinking, imagining, and replaying thoughts that displease God? Does God feel distant as His Spirit is grieved by doubts about His Word and expectations of your behavior as His child? Is God's grace enabling you to say no to sin? Or have you been deceived into thinking grace gives you a "pass" to continue in some besetting, habitual, secret sin? Satan, the one who shoots flaming darts (Ephesians 6:16), is attacking you.

- **Satan wants to *debilitate* your will.** Does the crowd you run with slowly lead you further and further away from God? Do the places you find yourself with your friends slowly make you participate in more displeasing things? Is it getting harder to say no to sin? Satan, the devouring lion (1 Peter 5:8), is debilitating your will to obey God.

- **Satan wants to *snatch* the truth of God's Word from your mind.** Do your pursuits and activities help Satan snatch God's Word from your mind? Do you seem to never get anything out of the Bible or church anymore? Satan, the father of lies (John 8:44), is snatching God's Word from your mind.

- **Satan wants to *confuse* your emotions by corrupting your desires and drawing your affections to the wrong things.** Whenever we love something, we gradually begin to look like whoever or whatever it is. If we believe God's Word is the ultimate Truth, we are guided closer each day toward what God loves; if we are strangers to His Truth, we are drawn further from what pleases and glorifies Him. There are only two sources of wisdom—above and below (James 3). If you are not being filled by God through His Word with His Truth, then you are being filled with counterfeit truth, which is not from God, nor is it pleasing to Him. Loving the world (anything displeasing to God) is the sure road to confusion, corruption, and emptiness. Satan, the counterfeiter of Truth (2 Corinthians 11:14), is confusing your emotions, desires, and affections.

- **Satan wants to *drown* you in a sea of sin.** Are you slowly accepting defeat in some areas of life because it is just too hard to obey the Lord? Are the thresholds of what is not to be tolerated in your life slowly diminishing, and small questionable areas in your life increasing? Satan, the adversary of God (Revelation 12:9), is drowning you!

How Then Can We Conquer Our Unseen But Dangerous Enemy?

James very clearly tells us how to conquer Satan: ... *Resist the devil, and he will flee from you* (James 4:7). Paul tells us to resist Satan ... *steadfast in the faith* ... (1 Peter 5:9). "Resist" is a military metaphor meaning "to stand against," as in combat. This martial language suggests the parallel language of Ephesians 6, telling the preparation for resisting the devil. The primary element is an understanding of the enemy, which Paul memorably gives in these verses:

Put on the whole armor of God, that you may be able to stand against the wiles [schemings] of the devil. For we do not wrestle against flesh and blood, but against principalities, against powers, against the rulers of the darkness of this age, against spiritual hosts of wickedness in the heavenly places (vv. 11-12).

From this we learn the struggle is supernatural—supra-flesh and blood. We also learn it is *personal*, because the word for *"wrestle"* suggests hand-to-hand combat—*swaying* back and forth in sweaty battle. Finally, it is futile if fought with conventional weapons because we are fighting against serried ranks of evil angels led by fallen angelic princes.

To counter Satan's attacks, the Lord tells us we need to dress for war. In His word He has described just what will insure both momentary and continued victory.

... Take up the whole armor of God, that you may be able to withstand in the evil day, and having done all, to stand. Stand therefore, having girded your waist with truth, having put on the breastplate of righteousness, and having shod your feet with the preparation of the gospel of peace; above all, taking the shield of faith with which you will be able to quench all the fiery darts of the wicked one. And take the helmet of salvation, and the sword of the Spirit, which is the word of God; praying always with all prayer and supplication in the Spirit, being watchful to this end with all perseverance and supplication for all the saints— (vv. 13-18).

I can just picture the old warrior Paul wearing his own spiritual armor, his worn war belt is sweat-through, salt-stained and comfortable—like an old horse's bridle that holds everything perfectly in place. The *"belt of truth,"* God's Truth, has girded him so tightly through years it permeates his life, and Truth reigns within. Because he is armed with the clear eyes of a clear conscience, he can face anything.

Paul's torso is sheathed with a battle-tarnished breastplate. It is criss-crossed with great lateral grooves from slicing sword blows and dents from enemy artillery. The *"breastplate of righteousness"* has preserved his vitals; his holy life has rendered his heart impervious to Satan's spiritual assaults.

As a mature warrior, his gnarled legs are comfortable in his ancient war boots. The apostle has stood his ground on several continents. The boots are the "gospel of peace," coming through faith in Him, and the resultant peace of God—the sense of well-being in wholeness. Paul stands in peace, is rooted in peace, and he cannot be moved.

His great shield terrifies the eyes, for the broken shafts and many charred holes reveal him the victor of numerous fierce battles. He has held the *"shield of faith"* as he repeatedly believed God's Word and thus extinguished every fiery dart of doubt and sensuality and materialism. None have touched him.

On his old gray head, his helmet has seen better days. Great dents mar its symmetry, reminders of furtive blows dealt him by the enemy. The *"helmet of salvation"*—the confidence of knowing he is saved and will be saved—has allowed him to stand tall against vicious assaults. His imperial confidence gives him a regal bearing.

Paul's sword is equal to a hundred soldiers. The *"sword of the Spirit, which is the word of God,"* the ultimate offensive weapon, cuts through everything—armor, flesh, glistening bone, and running marrow—even the soul (cf. Hebrews 4:12).

This is the armament God has provided for victory in our spiritual warfare: *truth, righteousness, peace, faith, salvation, the Word of God.* Any believer who resists with these will put the devil and his armies to flight. You and I can withstand the devil if we wear the armor God provides.

Resist the devil—
and he will flee from you!

> ... "God resists the proud, but gives grace to the humble." Therefore submit to God. Resist the devil and he will flee from you. Draw near to God and He will draw near to you ... (James 4:6-8).

Wearing the whole armor of God in *humility* is key to being a conqueror in any spiritual battle. Dr. Donald Grey Barnhouse understood this truth. At a convention years ago, he addressed the vast throng by dramatically saying, "Up is down!" And then, after a lengthy pause, he declared, "Down is up!" In doing so, he was intoning an unbreakable spiritual law: God exalts the humble and debases the proud.

God wants His people to understand His law will never be broken, ever! When the stars turn to ashes, it will still be intact. Everyone who has ever lived, including every angel and spirit, will be subject to this irrefragable law.

The gravity of grace will always channel the rivers of divine favor to the lowly—to those who submit to God, whose soul's momentum is away from the devil and toward God, who purify their inner and outer lives, who mourn over their sins, and who obey the final summary command: *Humble yourselves in the sight of the Lord, and He will lift you up* (James 4:10).

> We are not to wait passively for this to somehow happen. We are not to wait for someone else to humble us, nor should we wait for the vicissitudes of life to do it. Rather, self-humbling is *our* Christian duty. We must take inventory of our sinfulness and weakness, then bow in total submission to God, yielding our total being, our dreams, our future, our everything to him. It is then that he will pour on the grace—grace upon grace—grace upon grace—"and he will lift you up."[100]

[100] R. Kent Hughes, Preaching the Word: James—Faith That works (Wheaton: Crossway Books, 1997), electronic edition, in. loc.

Humbling ourselves so we may be filled with God's grace is especially vital if we are to achieve victory when we're being bombarded with Satan's *"fiery darts"*! At such times, we need to "hold on for dear life" until God delivers us as we resist the devil and his demonic hosts through faith in this promise:

> "Behold, **I give you** the **authority** to trample on serpents and scorpions, [demonic powers] and **over all** the power of the enemy, and **nothing shall by any means hurt you**" (Luke 10:19, emphasis added).

Just as a policeman does not have the power to stop traffic, he does have the authority "in the name of the government." We, ourselves, do not have the power to stop Satan, but "in the name of Jesus" we have the authority to stop him and his demonic forces. Instead of being whipped around by the devil, when we boldly take authority and stand our ground, things turn around: *"... They overcame him by the blood of the Lamb and by the **word of their testimony** ..."* (Revelation 12:11, emphasis added).

The way to resist the devil, however, is not to merely or solely depend on words directed at him and his demons, but to rely wholly upon God's Word as we pray and resist and rebuke by faith in Him who has already conquered, defeated, and destroyed the power of the devil and his armies. By using the Truth of God's Word, we can defeat his lies in our mind. When believers know sound doctrine and obey God's truth, Satan can be withstood by the sword of God's Word!

Just as Jesus responded with Scripture to each of the devil's temptations in the wilderness (see Matthew 4:1-11), so must we. And to do that, you and I must first hide God's Word in our hearts so we don't sin against Him (Psalm 119:11). Storing up an arsenal of verses provides the necessary offensive weaponry for the moment Satan shoots his *"fiery darts."*

Whenever Satan tempts you to succumb to ... *the lust of the flesh* [bodies chasing pleasures], *the lust of the eyes* [eyes chasing possessions], *and the pride of life* [hearts and mouths chasing status] ... (1 John 2:16), stand against him through the Word and prayer. Ask the Holy Spirit to bring appropriate verses to mind that enable you to *"fight the good fight of faith."*

If you haven't yet developed a strong arsenal of memorized verses, keep a small notebook handy, and as you read the Scriptures record verses that apply to your most vulnerable areas. Meditate and then memorize those verses. Whenever you're under attack, and Satan tries to snatch them from your mind, grab the notebook and pray the appropriate Scriptures. You might also want to purchase a book of categorized promises of God for an instant reference.[101] The more you practice this discipline, the more effectively you will combat Satan's attacks. Immersion in God's Word is the best defense and offense!

---

101 Note: If you have access to the Internet, you may wish to go to a site like www.amazon.com and google in "promises of God"; that will link you to books that contain numerous verses listed in categories.

Draw near to God
and He will draw near to you.

Now let's look at the second half of … Resist the devil, and he will flee from you (James 4:7). In verse 8, James went on to tell us: *Draw near to God and He will draw near to you.* By combining verses 7-8, we can conclude that every Christian should cultivate to the uttermost these two views: *"the devil's back"* and *"the face of God."*

The soul-tingling truth here is this: **If you go after God, He will go after you!** That was the prodigal son's experience when he neared his home: *"… When he was still a great way off, his father saw him and had compassion, and ran and fell on his neck and kissed him"* (Luke 15:20). Your heavenly Father's heart is the same toward you!

Inch toward God, and He will step toward you.
Step toward God, and He will sprint toward you.
Sprint toward God, and He will fly to you!

What is James's overall point in this positive call to draw near to Him? In a word—prayer. The essence of prayer is the heart drawing near to God. Prayer is the soul's desire to come to Him, to receive His love, to feel His power as we conform to His will, and is exactly what Paul's soldier in spiritual armor does. Every piece is in place. As the spiritual forces of wickedness approach, there will be a lethal battle. But first the soldier falls to his knees and prays in the Spirit (cf. Ephesians 6:18). This warrior knows … *that if we ask anything according to His will, He hears us. And … whatever we ask, we know that we have the petitions that we have asked of Him* (1 John 5:14-15)!

There is only one view more welcome than the backside of the devil—the face of God! As His children, and in His Son, we are near: *… In Christ Jesus you who once were far off have been brought near by the blood of Christ* (Ephesians 2:13). But there is an even nearer nearness available to all: *Draw near to God and He will draw near to you.* Just take a step, and a new nearness to God will be yours, with buoying tides of His grace upon grace!

In closing, God desires warriors who will make the most of time here on Earth, viewing the world as a spiritual battleground—not a playground. With that perspective, you and I can triumph through suffering afflictions as *"more than conquerors through Him who loved us* (Romans 8:37; see also vv. 31-39). For the phrase *"more than conquerors"* in the Greek means " *'to gain a surpassing victory,'* ... lit., 'we are hyper-conquerors,' i.e., we are pre-eminently victorious.' "[102] What a magnificent promise!

My Prayer for You:

Father in heaven, You who searches us and knows us. You know about us and our words before we speak. Because you know us so well, and how weak we are, You have said we must consciously give ourselves into Your captivity. Our mind will be captivated by something. If not captivated by You, if captivated by anything except You, Your Word and Your Spirit, then our actions are of the world and displeasing to You. Anything of this world is counterproductive, and will to lead us away from You. We want to consciously bring our minds into Your captivity, Christ Jesus, and have our bodies follow those minds toward being a living daily sacrifice for You. I pray we would be brought into the captivity of You, oh Christ, and resist and guard against our unseen but dangerous adversary, the devil. Father, Your Word says if anyone will cry out and ask for Your mercy, believe the Lord Jesus died in our places and ask for Your forgiveness and cleansing, that whosoever shall call upon the name of the Lord shall be saved. Thank You, Lord Jesus. Guard us. In the name of Jesus we pray, Amen.

---

[102] Strong's #5245

20

... If anyone is in Christ, he is a new creation; old things have passed away; behold, all things have become new.

—**2 Corinthians 5:17**

The Word Filled Life—
A Victorious Life Full of New Beginnings

GOD'S WORD OFFERS US A life of new beginnings. The ultimate new beginning is called the new birth —being born again.

Being born again is by God's Word:

Since you have purified your souls in obeying the truth through the Spirit in sincere love of the brethren, love one another fervently with a pure heart, having been born again, not of corruptible seed but incorruptible, through the word of God which lives and abides forever, because

"All flesh is as grass,
and all the glory of man as the flower of the grass.
The grass withers,
and its flower falls away,
but the word of the LORD endures forever."

Now this is the word which by the gospel was preached to you (1 Peter 1:22-25).

God's Perfect Battle Plan[103]

[103] MP3 CD Audio DYG-23:030803AM

By now, it should be clear Satan and his evil forces "... are always active, looking for opportunities to overwhelm the believer with temptation, persecution, and discouragement (cf. Pss. 22:13; 104:21; Ezek. 22:25). Satan sows discord, accuses God to men, men to God, and men to men. He will do what he can to drag the Christian out of fellowship with Christ and out of Christian service (cf. Job 1; Luke 22:3; John 13:27; 2 Cor. 4:3,4; Rev. 12)."[104]

[104] The MacArthur Study Bible, p. 1949.

This certainly explains why so many Christians are living defeated lives, taken captive by Satan's craftiness. And even worse, our unseen but dangerous enemy convinces disheartened saints that because of their failures they have no hope of future service for God!

Have you also fallen prey to Satan's wiles? Are you struggling with "defeatism" when suffering afflictions? If so, I need you to counter the *devil's lies by focusing your thoughts on this incredible truth: Every believer's entire Christian life is simply a series of new beginnings.* That is what the new birth, or being born again is—an adventure in faith of continually being filled by Christ with a new hope, a new peace, a new joy, and a new power to live!

Joni Eareckson Tada, a popular author and speaker who promotes Christian ministry among people with disabilities, is an extraordinary example of how to triumph through suffering afflictions and bring glory to God. Having become a quadriplegic in her teens as a result of a tragic swimming accident, she learned to fight *"the good fight of faith"* (1 Timothy 6:11-12) through what God taught her about living a victorious life full of new beginnings.

Joni, a seasoned veteran for Christ, understands the importance of daily disciplining yourself ... *Put on the whole armor of God* ... (see Ephesians 6:10-18). She writes:

> I love adventure stories ... It's one reason why I love the Bible!
> It's the fascinating account of how the evil villain, Satan, enslaved the citizens of the kingdom of Earth through treachery and

deceit—how he usurped the authority of the rightful Ruler and set up his own rival government. Furthermore, it's the story of how the good Ruler sent His only Son to invade Satan's territory in order to free the captives and retake the kingdom under the family banner. But what is most poignant is that the Son defeated the enemy using "inferior" tactics—servanthood and then death on the cross. It is this that proves Him mightier still. For just when the Son was pinned against the wall, just when it seemed He had lost all chance of winning, He overcame in spite of the odds. And the Prince of Peace ends up twice the hero! And He asks us, His subjects, to follow Him in His battle plan. That's the way God brings maximum glory to Himself. We are not a jewel-encrusted sword in God's hand. You and I in all of our weakness, in all of our inabilities, are … doing—by the grace of God—a sword's job. As we persevere and obey, as we put on the armor of God and fight with spiritual weapons, not carnal, we overcome in spite of the odds and end up giving twice the glory to the King.[105]

[105] Tada, Joni Eareckson, et al., "At the Heart of the Hymn," When Morning Gilds the Skies (Wheaton: Crossway Books, 2002), pp. 16-17.

Remember, no matter who you are, what age you are right now, where you are in life, or how you may have failed the Lord, our God of New Beginnings has a perfect battle plan for offering a victorious life full of wonderful new beginnings.

To help you better grasp what this idea of "new beginnings" is about, look now at some of the most beautiful verses in Psalm 119 which reveal how Ezra responded when suffering afflictions. I pray his whole life's testimony has been, and will continue to be, an encouragement to your heart!

God offers
a new beginning in obedience:

Deal bountifully with Your servant,
that I may live and keep Your word (119:17).

The expression *"that I may live"* is a Hebrew word, *chayah*, which means "revive me." It is the word for "imparting life," to be renewed or energized. In the King James Version, the word is "quickened"; in the New King James it is "revived." The New International Version says "preserve." What does "preserve" mean? It means "trying to keep something fresh, alive, and new." In verse 17 God was saying, "When you are full of doubt and discouragement, I will give you a new beginning. I will quicken and refresh you, restore you to life, and revive you in obedience."

The devil's two-edged sword—doubt and discouragement—slashes any hopes of a new beginning so you become disheartened and convinced God can never use you again. But Ezra refused to succumb to Satan's evil scheme. Instead, he went to God for strength, saying, "I want a new beginning in obedience. I want to keep Your Word. I want You to give me a new heart and new desire." This is possible because God's promise is not just "for as long as I can hold on." Thus, in verse 17, Ezra could rightfully invoke the power of God in his life, what a new beginning is about. It doesn't just affect your obedience; it also affects the very fiber of your emotional make up. Look at the next verse, and you will see this.

God offers
a new beginning in the only lasting help:
My soul clings to the dust;
revive me according to Your word (119:25).

In verse 25, Ezra revealed he was often discouraged as he struggled through numerous problems: sleepless nights, attacks on his character, threats on his life, and so forth. Whenever he felt discouraged, he asked God to revive him—to quicken him, to give him life, to bring back the freshness and reality of life. Ezra was saying to God, "I want a new beginning in the only lasting help I have in life—You." The word *"revive"* means "I slipped away from that." Therefore, when you are in need of reviving, I encourage you to pray: "I come to You, Lord, to re-offer myself anew and afresh to You. I come to You acknowledging I have sinned." Since God has already completely forgiven you in Christ, what He will do "on the spot" is to cleanse you (1 John 1:9). Ezra asks for this in verse 25: "Lord, I want the benefit of Your cleansing. Please revive me according to Your Word. I want to know You are my source of hope and help!"

God offers
a new beginning in what is worth living for:
Turn away my eyes from looking at worthless things,

and revive me in Your way (119:37).

Not only are there twenty-two stanzas that match the number of books of the Old Testament, but each stanza parallels a book of the Hebrew Old Testament. Amazing! Even more, as you saw in chapter 2, Ezra used ten different descriptions or synonyms for God's Word. Why did he use ten synonyms for the Bible? In the Hebrew mind, what we call the Ten Commandments, the four on one side of the stone tablet and six on the other, Hebrews call the Decalogue, or the Ten Words. Because they have ten words, Ezra used ten different synonyms for the Bible. Verse 37 contains one of them: *Turn away my eyes from looking at worthless things, and revive me* **in Your way** (emphasis added). That is also the word used in Psalm 119:1, a synonym which covers all ten. Ezra was saying this Christian life, this walk with the Lord, is a *"way."* The same term is used in Acts (See Acts 19:9, 23; 22:4; 24:14, 22 and John 14:6). The *"way"* applies to following God's law, truth and precepts. In verse 37, Ezra was actually saying to God: "I want a new beginning in what is really worth living for."

Do you know what commonly happens? If you start to look longingly at everything that captivates the pleasure-seeking world, you are likely to begin thinking: *Oh, it would be so nice, and comfortable, and secure if I could have … I'd love to get to do … I really want to pursue ….* The more you entertain such thoughts, the more likely your focus can be drawn away from the eternal to what won't last beyond a lifetime. It doesn't mean those things are necessarily wrong, but God has said, *Turn away* [your] *eyes from looking at worthless things.* Ezra viewed his life as a constant new beginning in God's "way." He continually focused back to the forever important. And I'm so glad he did because we still have his testimony—the Old Testament Jesus taught. Because Ezra lived by what he preached, you and I reap many benefits today. Now look at the next verse for another use for this word "revive" or "quicken."

God offers
a new beginning in hope:
This is my comfort in my affliction,

for Your word has given me life (119:50).

The words *"given me life"* mean "to be revived, renewed, quickened, preserved, start over again." Unlike those who are lost and have no hope, when you suffer afflictions, you can have a new beginning every day.

I once read an article about a lady in Italy who lives in a community dying out due to low birth rate. This lady was in the group of elderly interviewed to learn what it was like to be dying out, knowing their village wouldn't exist in ten years. Most citizens were over seventy, and experiencing a variety of complaints common to the aged (the loss of good health, sight, hearing, and appetite). To make a long story short, the article ended with everyone raising a glass and downing a little more alcohol to ease their troubles.

That may be the world's solution to troubles, but God offers new hope. As you and I grow older and face ongoing adversities, God's Word will be a true comfort because we can say, "I know how I got here (my origin); I know why I am here (my purpose); and I know where I am going (my destiny)." That is very reassuring! I would hate to live in some Italian village and just be drinking alcohol while I wondered these things. God says this is the ultimate answer to the perplexities of life: "Find a new beginning of hope in Me, even when you are suffering affliction!"

**God offers
a new beginning in His assurance:**
*Let Your tender mercies come to me,
that I may live; for Your law is my delight (119:77).*

The words *"tender mercies"* remind that none of us get what we deserve, which is what mercy is about. Grace is getting the undeserved favor of God; mercy is not getting the rightly deserved punishment of God. When God is merciful, He withholds what you and I deserve. Ezra was saying in this verse, "You are tenderly withholding Your wrath on my sin, and will cause me to be revived so I may live." It is the same word: chayah. *"For Your law is my delight"* translates into "As I read Your Book I realize You have made provision for my sins."

The great news of salvation is the only thing you and I have to give to God is our sins. In and of ourselves, we don't have anything good enough to give to Him. So He says to us, "Do you know you are a guilty sinner? Then give Me your sins, and let Me put them upon Christ!" He became sin for us, and is what Ezra was thinking about when he said, "I have a new beginning in my assurance of You. Because of Your tender mercies, You are withholding Your wrath from me. That has revived me so I may live, for Your law is my delight!"

Have you ever struggled because you lack assurance of your salvation? This is one of the greatest pains many believers go through—doubting they are really saved. The solution? Simply this: your faith came by hearing the Word of God. Having received the Lord in faith through the power of God's Word, continue your Christian walk in the same manner. A lot of people don't feel saved because they are anorexic or bulimic in their spiritual life. They go to church on Sunday, gorge themselves on the Bible, and then lose it all on the way home. Conversely, anorexic Christians don't even eat in between Sundays. They aren't in the Word as newborn babes, desiring the sincere milk of God's Word. But Ezra was; he had a new beginning in his assurance of God, knowing His tender mercies were revealed in the Word—a new hope for his troubles!

God offers
a new beginning in trusting the Lord:
Revive me according to Your lovingkindness,
so that I may keep the testimony of Your mouth (119:88).

Thomas was one of the most notorious doubters in God's Word, and clearly declared doubts about the Risen Christ. Consider what James Boice has to say about Thomas:

> Thomas is our pattern. Thomas had not been present on that first occasion when Jesus appeared to his disciples. The others told Thomas about it afterward, but Thomas replied, "Unless I see the nail marks in his hands and put my finger where the nails were, and put my hand into his side, I will not believe it" (John 20:25). A week later Jesus appeared again, Thomas being present, and offered to fulfill the conditions of Thomas's test. But the mere sight was enough for Thomas. Thomas fell at Christ's feet and

worshiped, saying, "My Lord and my God" (v. 28).

Is that sight not clear enough for you also? Are Jesus' wounded hands not evidence enough for you of his love? God says that his action in Christ is perfectly clear, so much so that there is no excuse for a failure to believe it. In fact, he says that the way of salvation in Christ has been "made known" (Rom. 3:21). The way of salvation has been made as clear as a striking hand or a blow to the face.

Today it is the hand of a gracious God who holds out the way of salvation to you. If you reply that you cannot see it, he asks you to look at the hand itself; for it is a wounded hand, one bearing the print of the nail received by Jesus in dying for your salvation.

By faith you may put out your hand and touch that wound. You may know that it is evidence, irrefutable evidence, of God's great love for you. That hand was struck for you.

The one extending that hand died for you. Allow him to enclose your hand, to enclose you, and to bring you into that great company of those who possess eternal life and who shall never perish.[106]

As Boice said, Jesus was not present at the time Thomas confessed his lack of trust. But just think of what Jesus can do now that He is available anywhere, anytime, and to anyone!

If you don't yet know Him personally, know this: wherever you are, Jesus is passing by right now, and offering you a new life through the free gift of salvation. Being born again by God's Word is the ultimate new beginning, because you get to completely start life over: ... *if anyone is in Christ, he is a new creation; old things have passed away; behold, all things have become new* (2 Corinthians 5:17). The phrase "all things have become new" in the Greek "indicates this newness is a continuing condition of fact. The believer's new spiritual perception of everything is a constant reality for him, and he now lives for eternity, not temporal things. James identifies this transformation as

[106] James Montgomery Boice, John Volume 3: Those Who Received Him John 9-12 (Grand Rapids: Baker Books, 1999), pp. 785ff.

the faith producing works ...."[107] And that faith, through the power of the Holy Spirit, will enable you to discipline yourself for godliness to fight *"the good fight of faith"* for the Eternal King's glory!

May God grant these verses to be true in your life:

> ... *His abundant mercy has begotten [you] again to a living hope ... to an inheritance incorruptible and undefiled and that does not fade away, reserved in heaven for you, who are kept by the power of God through faith for salvation ready to be revealed in the last time ... whom having not seen you love ... receiving the end of your faith—the salvation of your souls (1 Peter 1:3-5, 8-9).*

[107] The MacArthur Study Bible, p. 1771

God offers
a new beginning in spiritual renewal:

I will never forget Your precepts,
for by them You have given me life (119:93).

Ezra was saying to the Lord, "You have revived me, and given me a new beginning." The ultimate spiritual renewal comes from the Word. For a retreat, many feel they have to go to some special place like the mountains, lake, or seashore. I love doing that as well, but I don't have to wait for some special place to be revived in the Lord. All I have to do is find a quiet spot where I can sit and open my "Spiritual Renewal Package"—the Bible. You and I can have a new beginning for spiritual renewal simply by pausing and looking into God's Word, with an open heart, and praying, "Revive me. Quicken me. Cleanse me; put my eyes on the right thing! Encourage my soul, and assure me of Your salvation."

God offers
a new beginning in strength:

I am afflicted very much;
revive me, O LORD, according to Your word (119:107).

God promises strength for times when you are weak (2 Corinthians 12:9), but He also likes to work through your weakness (1 Corinthians 1:27). What happens when He can gain access to your life during weakness? He begins to live through you in mighty ways. Why?

Because when you can do nothing on your own (John 15:5), He gets all the credit for what He does through you. To get started in a new beginning, read prayerfully through Isaiah 40:25-31, then ask Him to strengthen you today!

God offers
a new beginning in boldness:
Uphold me according to Your word, that I may live; and do not let me be ashamed of my hope (119:116).

Perhaps you have tried to share the gospel, became embarrassed or scared, and couldn't do it. As a result, you no longer witness at all. Do you want a wonderful new beginning? Verse 116 promises God will give you a new beginning in boldness so you can unashamedly share the gospel of Jesus Christ! So ask Him to provide regular opportunities for you to tell others about Jesus—before it is too late. For ... *he who wins souls is wise* (Proverbs 11:30).

God offers
a new beginning in understanding His plan:
The righteousness of Your testimonies is everlasting; give me understanding, and I shall live (119:144).

Proverbs 3:5-6 promises: *Trust in the LORD with all your heart, and lean not on your own understanding; in all your ways acknowledge Him, and He shall direct your paths.* If you will give Him first place in your life, you can rest in the fact you can entrust all your plans to Him. If your plans are not according to His will, He will redirect your steps so that His sovereign purposes for your life are being carried out (Proverbs 16:9). What a comfort!

God offers
a new beginning in patience:
Hear my voice according to Your lovingkindness; O LORD, revive me according to Your justice (119:149).

Patience is a fruit of the Spirit as you start over again in walking in the Spirit (Galatians 5:16-18)—allowing His timing in life to be your desire. Proverbs 13:12 says: *Hope deferred makes the heart sick, but when the desire comes, it is a tree of life.* Waiting on God's perfect timing is not always easy, but in the long run, it is always the right choice. Never run ahead of the Lord to try to make something happen NOW. If you do, you may pay a high price for your impatience.

God offers
a new beginning in His Word:
Plead my cause and redeem me;
revive me according to Your word (119:154).

Psalm 119 is the greatest commentary ever written on the treasure of God's Word. May you never take His precious Word for granted, or form a habit of simply reading the Scriptures mechanically! If you feel yourself slipping in this area, prayerfully remind yourself: *This Bible is God's voice—the actual words of the Eternal God of the Universe—and now He wants to speak to me personally!*

Jesus wants to take you from wherever you are and get you back to seeing Him in all the Scriptures. Just as He opened the Word to the two travelers on the road to Emmaus (Luke 24:27), ask and He will do the same for you. As Jesus opens the Scriptures to you, He will cause you to long after Him (Luke 24:32). Finally, if you wait upon Him, by His Spirit He will increase your understanding of His Word (Luke 24:45).

God offers
a new beginning in love:
Consider how I love Your precepts;
revive me, O LORD, according to Your lovingkindness (119:159).

Perhaps you've heard someone say, "I just can't love that person anymore. I've tried, but he has failed me far too many times." Aren't you glad God doesn't treat us this way? How many times have you and I failed God? Yet, His love and His mercy are new every morning.

Romans 5:6-8 says … *when we were still without strength, in due time Christ died for the ungodly. For scarcely for a righteous man* will one die; yet perhaps for a good man someone would even dare to die. But God demonstrates His own love toward us, in that while we were still sinners, Christ died for us. He gave Himself for you when you did not yet love Him. That is what love is, and why God wants to continually renew your love for Him and others.

**God offers
a new beginning in praise:**
> Let my soul live, and it shall praise You;
> and let Your judgments help me (119:175).

"*Let my soul live*" simply means "Let my soul be quickened and revived." Do you know what God wants to do? He wants to revive you so you can praise Him. Do you want a little monitor of how well you are doing spiritually? Ask yourself: *Can I worship, magnify, and praise the Lord with all my being? If not, you need a new beginning.*

The good news is you don't have to continue feeling distant from God, and defiled in your heart. The Lord Jesus Christ says, "You don't have to live with a hardened heart. You don't have to live with a sin-stained heart or in despair with no purpose—feeling hopeless and helpless. My ever-present power can give you a new beginning!"

If you have been slipping in your praises, ask the Holy Spirit to revive you so this becomes your deepest heart's cry:

> O God, You are my God; early will I seek You; my soul thirsts for You .... Because Your lovingkindness is better than life, my lips shall praise You. Thus I will bless You while I live .... My soul shall be satisfied ..., and my mouth shall praise You with joyful lips. ... Praise the LORD! Praise the LORD, O my soul! While I live I will praise the Lord; I will sing praises to my God while I have my being (Psalm 63:1,3-5; 146:1-2).

God's Incredible Gift

The God of New Beginnings freely offers you an incredible gift—a Word filled life through which He wants to give you:

- A new beginning in obedience.
- A new beginning in the only lasting help.
- A new beginning in what is worth living for.
- A new beginning in hope.
- A new beginning in His assurance.
- A new beginning in trusting the Lord.
- A new beginning in spiritual renewal.
- A new beginning in strength.
- A new beginning in boldness.
- A new beginning in understanding His plan.
- A new beginning in patience.
- A new beginning in His Word.
- A new beginning in love.
- A new beginning in praise.

In closing, I exhort you to prayerfully consider all the Lord taught Ezra about living the Word filled life—a life of new beginnings that empowered him to live triumphantly in this sin-darkened world. The more you commit to disciplining yourself for godliness through the seven disciplines of a Word filled life, the more you, too, will (Ephesians 6:10). What a life-changing Truth to grab hold of and hang onto for dear life!

My Prayer for You:

Father in Heaven, I pray You would communicate to each of our hearts the reality of the new beginning we have through Your Word. May we truly grasp that the new birth, being born again, is to revive, renew, and quicken us so we can have a new beginning in our life. Thank You that, at the instant of our salvation, You enable us to start over brand new because You have forgiven our sins, and given us a new heart and a new spirit. Teach us to fully value the priceless gift of being born from above with Your very life so we may become Your sons and daughters. I am so thankful, Lord, to know it doesn't end there because our Christian life is but a series of new beginnings with You! As we agree with You about our sins, and desire to walk in the power of Your Spirit, You will continually cleanse us. I pray You would open our eyes to perceive the preciousness of the awesome new beginning You freely offer to us in Christ! In the name of Jesus I pray. Amen.

Appendix A
Psalm 119's Ten Synonyms for the Bible

1. WAY: Walking the Divine Path
When God's Word is filling our lives, we are walking the divine path, with the Divine Guide, down the journey of life.
v.1 "way"
Occurs 13x
Hebrew word:
Strong's # 1870

2. TESTIMONIES: Listening to the Divine Witness
When God's Word is filling our lives, we are listening to the Divine Witness testifying to the Truth that is sure and makes us wise.
•v. 2 "testimonies" "statutes" (NIV) Occurs 14x
Hebrew word:
Strong's # 5713

3. PRECEPTS: Following the Divine Directions
When God's Word is filling our lives, we are following the divine directions for life that are right, and cause great rejoicing.
v.4 "precepts" Occurs 21x
Hebrew word:
Strong's # 6490

4 COMMANDS: Obeying the Divine Orders
When God's Word is filling our lives, we are obeying the divine orders—the decrees of our heavenly Captain—that are perfectly pure and enlighten our lives.v. 6 "commands" Occurs 22x
Hebrew word:
Strong's # 4687

5. WORD (Written): Reading the Divine Word
When God's Word is filling our lives, we are reading the divine Word to obtain the will of God.v. 11 "word" Occurs 19x
Hebrew word:
Strong's # 565

6. LAW: Receiving the Divine Instructions
When God's Word is filling our lives, we are receiving the divine instructions from the Ultimate Teacher who gives perfect instructions that restore and transform. (Congo) v. 18 "law"
Occurs 25x
Hebrew word:
Strong's # 8451

7. JUDGMENTS: Building Life Upon Divine Decisions
When God's Word is filling our lives, we are building life upon the divine decisions— judgments that are always true and vindicate. (Wm. Borden)
v. 20 "judgments" "laws" (NIV) "ordinances"(NAS)
Occurs 23x
Hebrew word:
Strong's # 4941

8. FEAR: Practicing the Divine Condition
When God's Word is filling our lives, we are practicing the divine condition of fearing God that makes life clean and enduring. (Bema)
v. 38 "fear" Occurs 1x
Hebrew word:
Strong's # 3373

9. STATUTES: Using the Divine Plans
When God's Word is filling our lives, we are using the divine plans, or specifications, to build the ultimate life.v. 64 "statutes" "decrees" (NIV)
Occurs 22x
Hebrew word:
Strong's # 2706

10. WORD (Spoken): Hearing the Divine Voice
When God's Word is filling our lives, we are hearing the Divine Voice walking us all the way through life.v. 65 "word"
Occurs 24x
Hebrew word:
Strong's # 1697

BIBLIOGRAPHY

Disciplining Yourself for Godliness

Alcorn, Randy, Money, Possessions, and Eternity, <http://www.epm.org/articles/monnewma.html>.

——— The Treasure Principle (Sisters, OR: Multnomah Publishers, 2001).

Bancroft, Emery H., Elemental Theology: Doctrinal and Conservative (Hayward, CA: J. F. May Press, 1948).

Barnett, Dr. John S., The Joy of a Word Filled Family (Tulsa: Mullerhaus Publishing, 2004).

Boice, James Montgomery, John Volume 3: Those Who Received Him John 9-12 (Grand Rapids: Baker Books, 1999).

Brand, Dr. Paul and Philip Yancey, Pain—The Gift Nobody Wants (New York: Harper Collins, 1993).

Chisholm, Thomas O., "Great Is Thy Faithfulness," © Copyright 1923. Renewal 1951. Hope Publishing Company.

Christenson, Larry, The Christian Family (Minneapolis: Bethany Fellowship, Inc., 1974).

Henry, Matthew, Matthew Henry's Commentary on the Bible (Peabody, MA: Hendrickson Publishers, 1997).

<http://www.cwc.lsu.edu/cwc/other/stats/warcost.htm>.

<http://www.plymouthbrethren.org/page.php?page_id=4000>.

<http://www.space.com/scienceastronomy/solar-system/solar_storm_000713.html>.

<http://www.truthnet.org/Christianity/biography/hudsontaylor/chapter18.html>.

Hodge, Charles, 2 Corinthians: The Crossway Classic Commentaries (Wheaton, Crossway Books, 1997).

Hughes, R. Kent, Disciplines of a Godly Man (Wheaton: Crossway Books, 1991).

———, Preaching the Word: Ephesians—The Mystery of the Body of Christ (Wheaton: Crossway Books, 1997), electronic edition, in loc Ephesians 5.

———, Preaching the Word: James—Faith That Works (Wheaton: Crossway Books, 1997).

Hummel, Charles E., The Tyranny of the Urgent! (Downers Grove, IL: InterVarsity Press, 1997).

Israel my Glory, Feb/Mar 1993.

Knight, George F., Daily Study Bible: Psalms, Volume I (Louisville: Westminster John Knox Press, 2001, © 1984).

Kubler, Theodore, The Psalms Chronologically Arranged (New York: MacMillan, 1891).

Lewis, C. S., The Screwtape Letters (city: publisher, date).

MacArthur, John F., The MacArthur New Testament Commentary: I Corinthians 16 (Chicago: Moody Press, 1983).

———, The MacArthur Study Bible (Nashville: Word Publishing, 1997).

MacDonald, William, True Discipleship (Kansas City, KS: Walterick Publishers, 1975).

McGee, J. Vernon, Thru the Bible with J. Vernon McGee (Nashville: Thomas Nelson Publishers, 2000, © 1981).

Morrell, Doug, Disciples Corner e-mail letter, October 11, 2003.

Osbeck, Kenneth W., Amazing Grace—366 Inspiring Hymn Stories for Daily Devotions (Grand Rapids: Kregel Publications, 1997).

———, 101 Hymn Stories (Grand Rapids: Kregel Publications, 1997), electronic edition, in loc.

Payne, J. Barton, Encyclopedia of Biblical Prophecy (Grand Rapids: Baker, 1980).

Scroggie, W. Graham, Method in Prayer (London: Pickering, 1955).

Stanley, Charles, Relying on the Holy Spirit (Nashville: Thomas Nelson, 1996), electronic edition, in loc.

Strong, James, LL.D., S.T.D., The New Strong's Expanded Exhaustive Concordance of the Bible (Nashville: Thomas Nelson, 2001).

Studd, C. T., Cricketeer and Pioneer (Oxford: Worldwide Revival, 1935).

Swenson, Robert, The Overload Syndrome (Colorado Springs: NavPress, 1998).

Swindoll, Charles, Intimacy with the Almighty (Dallas: Word Publishing, 1996).

Tada, Joni Eareckson, et al., O Worship the King (Wheaton: Crossway Books, 2000).

———, "At the Heart of the Hymn," When Morning Gilds the Skies (Wheaton: Crossway Books, 2002).

"Technology–Club-Goers in Spain Get Implanted Chips for ID, Payment Purposes," April 14, 2004, <www.worldnetdaily.com>.

Vander Laan, Ray, 4-L 314 Faith Lessons On The Life & Ministry Of The Messiah. Leader's Guide (Grand Rapids: Zondervan, 1999).

Verwer, George, "Non-Stop Prayer," Interest Magazine, March 1991.

Wiersbe, Warren W., The Bible Exposition Commentary: Ephesians 4 (Wheaton: Victor Books, 1997), electronic edition, in loc.

———, Running with the Winners: A Study of the Champions of Hebrews 11 (Wheaton: Tyndale House, 1985).

"Worldview and the Clock," Break Point with Charles Colson, July 31, 2003.

Discover the Book
Everyday
at DTBM.ORG

You are invited to visit the online home of Discover The Book Ministries. Learn more about Dr. John Barnett and the global mission of DTB. Immerse yourself in a rich wealth of Biblical studies, ministry resources and practical daily direction for real life. From podcasts to videos, hundreds of Dr. Barnett's best sermons and teachings are offered in a variety of modern media formats—one to fit every need.

- Radio Broadcasts
- Podcasts
- Holy Land Video Tours
- Audio, Print and Video Sermons

- Multi-Lingual PDF Library
- MP3 and Book Library
- Online Shopping
- E-newsletter

Whether you choose to expand your spiritual horizons from home, while you're at work, or in quick moments spread throughout your busy day, our interactive website is here to serve you in your Christian walk.

Visit Us Today

Discover The Book Ministries
A Nonprofit 501(c)3 Bible Teaching Ministry

NOTES

NOTES

NOTES

Biography of Author

JOHN BARNETT HAS BEEN A pastor for 30 unbroken years of ministry in local churches across the United States. He has been the teaching pastor at Tulsa Bible Church in Tulsa, OK for the past 13 years and also serves as the President of Discover the Book Ministries. John is a happily married husband to Bonnie, and with her has home educated their eight wonderful children. He was a professor of Theology and Church History at the Masters Seminary, as well as an Associate Pastor to John MacArthur in Sun Valley, CA. John has written numerous books, articles and is heard daily on OnePlace.Com radio. He has also served as a missionary teacher and evangelist in over 60 countries around the world as well as on the boards of various mission agencies.